Boxed In

Boxed In

Making Identities Safe for Democracy

DERRICK DARBY AND
EDUARDO J. MARTINEZ

OXFORD
UNIVERSITY PRESS

Oxford University Press is a department of the University of Oxford.
It furthers the University's objective of excellence in research, scholarship,
and education by publishing worldwide. Oxford is a registered trade mark of
Oxford University Press in the UK and in certain other countries.

Published in the United States of America by Oxford University Press
198 Madison Avenue, New York, NY 10016, United States of America.

© Oxford University Press 2024

All rights reserved. No part of this publication may be reproduced, stored in
a retrieval system, or transmitted, in any form or by any means, without the
prior permission in writing of Oxford University Press, or as expressly permitted
by law, by license or under terms agreed with the appropriate reprographics
rights organization. Inquiries concerning reproduction outside the scope of the
above should be sent to the Rights Department, Oxford University Press, at the
address above.

You must not circulate this work in any other form
and you must impose this same condition on any acquirer

Library of Congress Cataloging-in-Publication Data
Names: Darby, Derrick, 1967– author. | Martinez, Eduardo J., author.
Title: Boxed in : making identities safe for democracy /
Derrick Darby and Eduardo J. Martinez.
Description: New York, NY : Oxford University Press, [2024] |
Includes index.
Identifiers: LCCN 2024006281 (print) | LCCN 2024006282 (ebook) |
ISBN 9780197620205 (hardback) | ISBN 9780197620229 (epub)
Subjects: LCSH: Group identity. | Discrimination. | Equality.
Classification: LCC HM753 .D365 2024 (print) | LCC HM753 (ebook) |
DDC 305—dc23/eng/20240326
LC record available at https://lccn.loc.gov/2024006281
LC ebook record available at https://lccn.loc.gov/2024006282

DOI: 10.1093/9780197620236.001.0001

Printed by Sheridan Books, Inc., United States of America

For Angela and Annabelle

Contents

Introduction   1

PART I   HOW DO WE GET BOXED IN?

1. Boxed In   11
2. Identity Trouble   44

PART II   WHAT DO WE NEED TO BREAK FREE?

3. How Identity Works   75
4. Collective Self-Authorship Processes   105

PART III   HOW DO WE BREAK FREE?

5. Micropolitics   147
6. Macropolitics   185

Conclusion   223

Acknowledgments   227
Notes   229
Index   257

Introduction

Mr. March on Washington

Martin Luther King Jr. is the person most often associated with it, but Bayard Rustin, known to some as "Mr. March on Washington," organized this landmark historical event in 1963. Rustin had many collective identities. He was black, gay, American, socialist, Quaker, pacifist, and he was also a political organizer. These identities come with a social script—a narrative that supplies the content. Rustin was not Jewish, but consider, for example, what he says about Jewish identity: "one is not a Jew because he declines to mix milk and meat in the same pot, or because he's circumcised, or because he follows the law of the Torah. One is a Jew because he stands for social righteousness, is opposed to injustice wherever it is, first of all in himself."[1] We can capture the content of other collective identities, including black identity, in a similar fashion, simply by assigning meaning to the label.

However, when it comes to engaging in collective action to pursue shared projects under an identity—an abiding feature of democratic life—we must understand that group members may depart from these scripts. And these departures are rooted in the inescapable reality of identity group heterogeneity. For instance, black Americans differ according to class, age, geography, and in countless other ways. And Rustin obviously had such differences in mind when he opined: "Only the most supine of optimists would dream of building a political movement without reference to them."[2] Identity optimists contest the claims that identity skeptics make about why identities are bad for politics and for democracy. We

Boxed In. Derrick Darby and Eduardo J. Martinez, Oxford University Press. © Oxford University Press 2024.
DOI: 10.1093/9780197620236.003.0001

2   INTRODUCTION

believe that these claims should be contested. But, in keeping with Rustin's cautionary note, we also believe that optimists must qualify their acceptance of identity. They can do this by acknowledging and mitigating the dangers that collective identities pose for democratic collective action when heterogeneity is not sufficiently accounted for. We are *qualified* optimists because our optimism depends on citizens taking up certain civic responsibilities to account for heterogeneity. Failure to do this invites identity trouble.

Our analysis of the role of identity in democracy is primarily philosophical.[3] But we cannot rely on philosophy alone to capture the complexity and dynamics of identity that Rustin encountered and that citizens engaging in politics encounter today.[4] We draw on research from the social sciences about how identities work, and how they are deployed in social movements, to inform our analysis and provide guidance for the contingent circumstances that citizens encounter.[5] Although we will not provide a comprehensive overview of these research fields, we hope that our endnotes provide useful references for interested readers.

Rustin's Dilemma

Rustin's influential social activist career spanned five decades, beginning in the 1930s as a college student at Wilberforce University. His first noteworthy organizing campaign, which focused on the economic dimension of racial oppression, came during 1941 when he was recruited by A. Philip Randolph to be the youth organizer for an earlier March on Washington movement that never occurred. The aim was to protest racial discrimination in the United States armed services and in employment. As part of a deal that Randolph struck with President Franklin D. Roosevelt, who agreed to sign an Executive Order banning racial discrimination by federal agencies and all unions and companies engaged in defense work, the march was canceled—to the dismay of Rustin and the political rioters who

INTRODUCTION 3

subsequently burned down the movement's Harlem, New York, office.

Racial identity was activated to engage some people to support this march, as part of a shared project to end racial discrimination. But identity-driven collective action, as this case illustrates, also created difficulties as expectations diverged about what kind of action racial struggle demanded of blacks. A difference in perspective about whether to march or not is another instance of group heterogeneity. When building democratic political movements under an identity-like connection to address shared goals, we cannot ignore group differences in background, perspective, or empowerment. And it is important to note that such differences appear within and between groups. In addition to this lesson, as a political organizer, Rustin also learned that when our collective identities are scripted too tightly, which can happen by specifying their meaning in ways that some people find too restrictive, we can become *boxed in*. This is a familiar phenomenon that we aim to understand and address in this book.

Feeling as though one must act in a certain way because one is black, which is illustrative of being boxed in, can be an obstacle to collective action to achieve a shared goal, such as ending economic oppression. On some accounts of what it is to be black, says Rustin, "one is supposed to think black, dress black, eat black, and buy black."[6] And one is also supposed to associate exclusively with blacks (not whites, not Jews), especially when it comes to political struggle on behalf of the race. One complaint that Rustin had about more militant 1960s-era black activists such as Stokely Carmichael and H. Rap Brown, to whom he attributes such views, is that by working with overly restrictive black identity scripts they ignored black heterogeneity, especially along class lines. Rustin believed that this was counterproductive to building a broad political movement to address economic problems in alliance with poor and working-class whites, class-conscious white liberals, and labor union activists, among others.

4   INTRODUCTION

After black people used nonviolent protest to win civil rights, Rustin said: "What had previously been a movement seeking exclusively racial goals was now called upon to challenge the fundamental class nature of the economic structure."[7] And this new agenda required a different and broader alliance of political forces. Rustin was not naive; he understood that a "successful liberal political alliance is enormously difficult to build and, once pieced together, even more difficult to maintain, given the inevitable tensions, rivalries, and antagonisms of the various partners."[8] Still, he believed that forging such an alliance was necessary. Rustin insisted that realizing the goals of a new civil rights agenda meant that blacks needed allies who share "common problems and pursue common goals."[9] And the main challenge was picking the right allies on the basis of their "specific programs and proven willingness to cooperate with a political partner."[10] Part of the sweeping economic reform that blacks could pursue with the right coalition allies included projects such as securing tax reform to redistribute wealth, federal jobs and basic income guarantees, and workforce development. Rustin faced the task of coordinating the collective pursuit of these and other projects in a manner that was attentive to intra- and intergroup heterogeneity. We call this *Rustin's dilemma*. We face this dilemma with all kinds of projects, economic and otherwise.

This is not a story about heroes and villains. Rustin's presumption that militant black activists calling for self-defense condoned the active use of violence in pursuing black rights was itself a case of boxing in with an overly restrictive script. Even he had to guard against this tendency. And it is not a story strictly about success—measured by either the outcome of political movements and coalitions or the uptake of civic responsibilities that it takes to form and sustain them. Rustin believed that successful protests should "produce a feeling of moving ahead" and should win new allies while forcing people to take notice of injustice in the struggle to leverage organized collective power for tangible change.[11] However, our view is that there is much to learn about the challenge of group heterogeneity and how to manage it from both successes and failures of collective political action. This explains why we will attend to case studies that involve both. Overly flexible identity scripts can also create dangers which we discuss, but will not dwell upon, in accounting for the processes that need to be developed and the new ethos that needs to be created to take control of tight identity scripts.

We answer three main questions in this book.

1. How do we get boxed in by tightly scripted identities?
2. What do we need to break free?
3. How do we break free?

By the end of the book, it will be clear why we think that addressing the challenge posed by Rustin's dilemma, thus avoiding the identity trouble that neglecting it invites in the political realm, requires adopting an ethos of collective self-authorship, which guards against boxing in and can support democratic collective action to advance shared projects on small and large scales. This is what we mean by *making identities safe for democracy*.

The Plan

Rustin sought to build a movement to advance economic justice that would advocate for progressive tax reform, job and basic income guarantees, and workforce development. His advocacy for and against particular policies also proceeded from his moral commitments about the value of democracy. For instance, rejecting a policy of total divestment in South Africa during its brutal apartheid regime, Rustin reasoned: "If I am for democracy, and it follows that if democracy exists apartheid must go, then I cannot be against all investment. Because economic chaos has never

6 INTRODUCTION

created democracy! Taking jobs away from people has not created democracy."[12]

Rustin advocated for and rejected different policy platforms based on his moral commitments. We offer guidance about what citizens ought to do, but we do not provide a policy platform to rally around or to reject in this book. Our framework is more general so that those with very different views about policy and morality can embrace our ethos of collective self-authorship and apply it in their own context.[13] And this is in part because any given set of moral and political convictions are insufficient for responding to Rustin's dilemma. Whether Rustin's coalition partners differed about tactics, such as when they needed to decide whether to proceed with plans to march in 1941, or about whether to prioritize tax reform or basic income, they all had to decide whether and how to work together.

Rustin's dilemma was an enduring feature of his life as an activist. It was also dynamic, as the differences in background, empowerment, and perspective he encountered with various coalition partners changed over time. Citizens in democracies continue to face their own versions of this dilemma today. As they seek to coordinate the pursuit of projects with diverse others, whether organizing a protest, an interfaith dialogue, or even a community garden, they run into the challenge of attending to group heterogeneity. And this is especially true in the face of tight scripts for racial, ethnic, partisan, and religious identities, among many others.

When facing Rustin's dilemma, we can, of course, insist on the correctness of our own convictions. But given that heterogeneity persists, we face the further question of what to do next. Once Rustin and his intended coalition partners established their different conceptions of black identity, different policy priorities, or disagreement about protest tactics to adopt, they faced a further question: now what? Should they continue to communicate and negotiate? Should they establish a narrower set of projects on which to coordinate? Should they split up and pursue their projects

INTRODUCTION 7

separately? Identifying their different perspectives, backgrounds, and forms of empowerment was only the start of a longer process.

Alongside the challenge of heterogeneity, Rustin faced this "now what" question repeatedly over the course of his life. Citizens in democracies today also face this question. This book aims to provide guidance about how to address it by defending an account of civic responsibilities that participants in democratic politics must assume. Taking up these responsibilities will lead us to use the right processes, and develop the right ethos, for holding ourselves and others accountable to heterogeneity as we answer the "now what" question. By the end of the book, readers get our big payoff—a practical framework for how to respond both to Rustin's dilemma and the "now what" question to break free from, rather than propagate, tight identity scripts.

Boxed In: Making Identities Safe for Democracy is divided into three parts and six total chapters. Each part comprises two closely related chapters. In Part I, we answer the first main question of the book: How do we get boxed in by tightly scripted identities? Chapter 1 describes the phenomenon of being boxed in by tight scripts and provides an account of why boxing in can be bad for individuals. Chapter 2 extends this analysis by arguing that a political environment where boxing in is pervasive hurts democracy.

In Part II, we answer the second main question of the book: What do we need to break free? In Chapter 3, we analyze identities in terms of three components. We also highlight the importance of the dynamic nature of identities and the heterogeneity they exhibit. In Chapter 4, we describe how our identities and projects lead us to coordinate with others, and how collective self-authorship can be made accountable to group heterogeneity.[14]

In Part III, we answer the third main question of the book: How do we break free? We provide guidance for political engagement to break free from tight scripts as well as the broader identity trouble that plagues democracy. In Chapter 5, we defend a set of civic responsibilities that citizens of democracies should take up

8 INTRODUCTION

to combat boxing in, with a focus on political engagement on a smaller scale. Chapter 6 analyzes and responds to the challenge of engaging in politics at a larger scale while facilitating uptake of these responsibilities. We conclude the book with a word about the importance of continuing to cultivate an ethos of collective self-authorship even when current conditions hampering our political efforts are daunting.

PART I
HOW DO WE GET BOXED IN?

1
Boxed In

Caged Bird

Charlie Parker was no ordinary bird. Wondering what kind he was—goldfinch, mockingbird, or robin—Ralph Ellison remarked: "No jazzman, not even Miles Davis, struggled harder to escape the entertainer's role than Charlie Parker."[1] More than anything else, this Kansas City–born alto saxophonist, who helped usher in the bebop era, wanted to be a jazz musician. It was his answer to the perennial philosophical question, *who am I*?

Parker was nicknamed "Bird." In wrestling with what kind he was, Ellison was seeking insight into the famed jazzman's identity, inclusive of his personality and musical style. Parker's race, gender, nationality, and regional roots also help tell the story of who he was, as does his fondness for movies, classical music composers, and addiction to heroin. But being a jazz musician—not a garden variety collective identity, to be sure, but an identity nonetheless—was central to his life-shaping plan. When he dropped out of high school to devote his life to jazz, this truth was clear to everyone: his mother Abbey, girlfriend Rebecca, and friends. The jazz musician identity gave Parker's life meaning. It served also to define, prioritize, and profoundly shape his projects.

There was a social script for being a jazz musician: master an instrument, learn jazz techniques like timbre manipulation, develop a unique sound, do jam sessions, hit the clubs, entertain the white clientele, and live the musician's life with vices and all. But for jazzmen who happened to be black, improvising in the age of Jim Crow necessitated that entertaining be a salient aspect of the

Boxed In. Derrick Darby and Eduardo J. Martinez, Oxford University Press. © Oxford University Press 2024.
DOI: 10.1093/9780197620236.003.0002

12 HOW DO WE GET BOXED IN?

black jazzman's identity. "Negro" musicians, as they called African American musicians back then, were expected to strongly identify with this aspect of the script. Being able to blow the horn, beat the drum, and tickle the ivory while clowning, grinning, and putting white folks at ease was a way to do this. Black jazzmen were expected to deliver melodic pleasure while acquiescing to their subordinate status in America's white supremacist racial hierarchy.

Rightly or wrongly, some black jazzmen were critical of peers for not resisting this suffocating script. Reflecting on the golden age of jazz, Ellison writes that these critics "were intensely concerned that their identity as Negroes place no restriction upon the music they played or the manner in which they used their talent."[2] And he adds: "They were concerned, they said, with art, not entertainment. Especially were they resentful of Louis Armstrong, whom (confusing the spirit of his music with his clowning) they considered an Uncle Tom."[3]

When Harlem's famous Cotton Club was in full swing during the late 1920s and early 1930s, a decade or so before Bird took flight as a force to be reckoned with in jazz, many people still held a view of nightclubs and black musicians that we find abhorrent today, as Stanley Crouch reminds us:

> The club became a showcase for the hoary tropes of the minstrel tradition, maintained by Negroes entertaining white folks while in tattered plantation attire, or other, equally noxious costumes if the routines called for them. . . . It was a place where white customers could experience so-called "jungle nights" in Harlem, full of what they thought to be the darkies' "natural" behavior—authentically imbecilic, if not amusingly or intriguingly subhuman, much like the thug-and-slut hip-hop world of today.[4]

With the heavy baggage of this fraught history, making entertainment salient to the jazz musician identity, and creating the

BOXED IN 13

demand that they perform in a certain manner, caged the Bird. He wanted to be a master of the art form, not an entertainer. Satchmo, as Armstrong was known, knew how to work the audience and had master skills. But Bird wanted to follow Lester Young's lead, as a purist committed to perfecting the form with a more introspective and focused no-nonsense style. Bird had a different musical project than Armstrong and a corresponding, burgeoning, identity as a pure artist. Scripting the narrative of what it was to be a black jazz musician so tightly, with stifling expectations about how he should behave on stage, left Charlie Parker boxed in. These tight scripts made it difficult for him to pursue a life plan as a black jazz musician and as a pure artist.

Bird and other like-minded musicians did find a way to break free from the tight scripts that boxed them in. Their solution involved the famed Harlem nightclub Minton's, which we will return to at the end of the chapter. And while most of us are not jazz musicians, by the end of the book, we will describe how we can learn from this and other examples to break free from tight scripts as democratic citizens. But before we discuss breaking free or how boxing in with tight scripts poses a danger to democracy, we must first appreciate that it is a familiar phenomenon at an interpersonal level. At some point, it happens to everyone. We do it to ourselves. We do it to others. And it emerges wherever we engage in projects that shape our lives, such as being a jazz musician, rapper, or punk rocker, in coordination with others. And, of course, we can be boxed in by ingredients in the identity politics stew that show up in many of our recipes: race, ethnicity, gender, sexuality, nationality, religion, and partisanship. While it is not always obvious which identities will be instrumental for pursuing collective projects politically, these stock identities often are, and so we will discuss them throughout this book. However, we will start with examples featuring identities that are less salient to illustrate the broad scope of the phenomenon of being boxed in.

14 HOW DO WE GET BOXED IN?

We will proceed by answering three questions in this chapter through the examples we explore:

1. What does it mean for collective identities to be tightly scripted?
2. How do tightly scripted identities box us in?
3. How does boxing in get in the way of our projects?

To answer the third question, we will establish a taxonomy of the different ways we can be boxed in by tight scripts, which will set the stage for us to analyze the distinctive danger this phenomenon poses to democracy in Chapter 2.

Rappers and Punks

Crouch's reference to "the thug-and-slut hip-hop world of today" is unkind and uncharitable. It is unclear whether he is targeting hip-hop generally, or just condemning a segment of it such as Southern trap or gangsta rap. But the truth is that he is not alone in associating hip-hop identity with glorifying thug life and acting out misogyny. Just as Parker pursued the project of being a jazz musician, making the jazzman identity central to his life-shaping plan, many young people, past and present, pursue the project of being a hip-hop artist. They make hip-hop identity central to their plan. Some take up rap, some deejaying, some breakdancing, and others take up different elements of hip-hop culture. The rapper identity became central for those, like MC Rakim, turned microphone fiends. It is their answer to the perennial philosophical question, *who am I*?

There is also a social script for being a rapper: taking in the surroundings, writing rhymes, learning how to flow, forming cyphers, becoming proficient in rap battles, rocking the club and fresh gear. Of course, the content of this script can change over time: new styles of beats with G-Funk synths or 808 bass hits, new flows with

BOXED IN 15

frequent triplets or heavy use of autotune, and new styles with snapbacks or pastel-colored suits and dresses. There are also signs of the increasing flexibility of this script, such as rappers who emphasize melody as much as lyrics, like Juice WRLD, or the prominence of openly LGBTQ rappers, like Lil Nas X.

But throughout much of the history of hip-hop, including today, corporations have fed the white public's appetite—the predominant driver of hip-hop sales—for rap music that portrays gang life with drug sales, guns, and dissing the "opps." And many consumers have come to view these things as part of the rap artist script. During Bird's days, white jazz patrons wanted to be entertained by musicians who would grin and clown while playing. During our time, some consumers of hip-hop want to be entertained by songs about crime and violence. The danger is that scripting the rapper identity too tightly—building all of this into our expectations about rap performance or presuming that the rapper endorses rather than merely reports on this life—can box some artists in.

Jay-Z, a world-famous rapper, tells the story of when he first met Oprah Winfrey. It was about how she boxed him in based on her understanding of the rapper identity script. The queen of talk worked with a script about rappers as too raw, too violent, and all too ready to use the dreaded n-word. Of course, she did not tell him how tightly she scripted the identity. That she had boxed him in showed up in a subtler way. The telling moment was when Jay-Z told Oprah that he read a book about karma which profoundly affected his philosophy of life. It was written by an author who had appeared on her show many times. She was a big fan of the book. Jay-Z noted her surprise. He writes: "She didn't expect that of a rapper. I could tell that the way she saw me shifted in that moment; I wasn't exactly who she thought I was."[5] As evidenced by Jay Z's interpretation of Oprah's expression of surprise, she was utilizing a tight script about how rappers act.[6] In her mind, rappers were not readers or aficionados of "high" culture. They were vulgar, lewd, and profane. She and Crouch worked with a similar script.

16   HOW DO WE GET BOXED IN?

Oprah boxed Jay-Z in, based on meanings she assigned to the rapper identity script. She also believed, mistakenly, that he identified with it. Other hip-hop artists, including Browns Crew, a Milwaukee Latino duo, have felt boxed in, but not by a narrative that builds a gangsta persona or taste for vulgar content into the script. They felt boxed in by narratives about rapper identity that build English-speaking into a tight rapper script. In a search for voices redefining Latino identity, writer Paola Ramos interviews this rap duo. Not only did they resist being boxed in by a script of what it means to be Latino music artists, which says they must do Mexican or Latin music, Browns Crew break free from the script that says they must only rap in English. Ramos, who observed them rapping before a group of third-grade fans, writes: "They sing in English but also in Spanish and Spanglish. They make those schoolkids feel they can break out of *any* box they want."[7]

Rappers have not only challenged expectations about their reading and language habits, but they have also challenged audiences politically. Throughout the history of hip-hop, from Public Enemy and Queen Latifah to Rapsody and Kendrick Lamar, artists have sought to combine other elements of the rapper script with lyrics tackling the social and political issues of the day, such as police brutality and domestic violence. These rappers are not content with songs that just make fans nod and dance along; they also strive to inspire listeners to think critically and act. Some artists and fans have embraced labels like "conscious hip-hop" to describe this set of musical and political projects. But at times, there has been a misalignment between the conscious hip-hop movement's goals and the flexibility of its associated script. For example, as the movement grew in prominence in the early 2000s, some found that new, often white, fans neglected its pro-black political projects. "True fans" were frustrated with the rise of "backpackers" who embraced the conscious hip-hop identity without embracing its politics. One longtime fan notes:

BOXED IN   17

I think also a lot of them just like to listen to hip hop just for the beats and just to go to a party, and I think that's one of the fundamental differences between people who are really into it and backpackers, is that it's less about dancing and partying, it's more about really getting into a movement.[8]

This is an illustration of how scripts that are too flexible can also get in the way of our projects: given the project of using hip-hop to inspire political change, it was too easy for backpackers to embrace a conscious hip-hop identity without promoting conscious politics.

The members of the conscious hip-hop movement needed a more restrictive script to advance their projects. This is an example of too much flexibility getting in the way, rather than tight scripts. That said, as we noted in the Introduction, our focus in this book will be on the danger of tight scripts because this is a more prevalent issue both interpersonally and for contemporary democracies, which we will discuss further in the next chapter. How flexible a script should be will depend on the context, and we will have more to say about how scripts can change over time in Chapter 4. But for now, we just note that excessive flexibility can be an issue, but that being boxed in by tight scripts is a more pressing problem in most cases.

Bird, Brooklyn-bred MCs like Jay-Z, and Browns Crew—jazzmen and rappers—are not the only music artists that get boxed in and wish to break free. Black punks know something about this too. Once upon a time, growing up in a black and brown community and being called a *punk* was a fighting word. This point is not lost on people who write about black punk bands. Writing about Death—a Detroit-based punk band of four black brothers—Katherine Wadkins discusses how failing to fit the script, in white and black communities alike, left them boxed in.[9] They were ostracized. They sought to break free and find their own way in the world of punk rock music. A great irony is that early white punk bands, perhaps owing to dissatisfaction with whiteness and its

18 HOW DO WE GET BOXED IN?

promises, which seemed no longer to apply to them, turned to black culture and black music for creative inspiration. But black punks, like Death, were left boxed in. They were also products of the black music tradition yet felt suffocated by a tight script that did not make room for the sounds, symbols, and styles of punk—a blend of car culture, rock music, and experimental gender performativity. There was no room in the black musician narrative for associating with, or performing, punk.

Death was not interested in adapting everything associated with white punk—no swapping the Afros for spiked-out green colored hair, no replacing blue jeans and white tees with gold lamé—but they did want to tap the punk sound, particularly the rapid pace and rush of unbounded musical energy. "Without any serious musical cohorts, boundaries were not tangible for Death," Wadkins writes, "instead they tried any and every mode of making music and composed complicated tracks that brought listeners from raw, and driving rock energy, to spaced-out jams, and back again."[10] Imagine black third-graders in inner-city Detroit, watching Death rocking and rolling and thinking the same thought as young fans of Browns Crew: "we can break out of *any* box we want to."[11]

We can draw out a few useful lessons from these examples of jazz musicians, rappers, and punks to help us answer the first main question of this chapter: What does it mean for collective identities to be tightly scripted? So far, we have established that collective identities come with scripts. These scripts help us to fill in our life plans and coordinate the projects we pursue as part of those plans, such as discussing books with fellow readers or playing loud music for fellow punks. These scripts also provide norms and expectations for us and others—about how we expect rappers to act and whom we expect punks to associate with. However, the content of identity scripts can be such that they are hard to combine with other identities and projects into a broader life plan.[12] When identity scripts are restrictive in this way, we call them tightly scripted. Parker experienced these restrictions firsthand due to the tensions between prevailing black jazz musician scripts of his time and his aspirations as a pure artist. We have also seen that identities can be more or less tightly scripted and this can change over time, as with the increasing flexibility of the norms and expectations for rappers. And we can bring these changes about with efforts to resist tight scripts, following the example of Death and other black punk rockers. We now turn to additional examples, using thought experiments based on research and reporting, to answer the second question of this chapter: How do tightly scripted identities box us in?

Fútbol Fans

Jimmy and Juan are both openly gay and avid fans of their Mexican *fútbol* team. Being a fan is one of their core projects. This sports fan identity is equally salient for them. And both of them embrace much of the *fútbol* fan script. They wear the gear inside and outside the stadium. They attend the games. And when they can't go, they are either watching on TV with other fans or listening on the radio. They track the gossip about the players and follow the stats. They post, tweet, and comment about the team, the matches, and the opposing teams on social media platforms. But there is a part of the script that strikes one of them as too tight and leaves him feeling boxed in—the homophobic chanting.[13]

In this world, chanting is an elaborate practice of sound, movement, and instrument-playing. It is a socially organized and engineered creation of solidarity and bonding, performing masculinity and dominance rituals. Chanting in this sense defines *fútbol* fans. It is not the whole of the identity. But for many fans it is a salient part of the social script. And they strongly identify with it. Homophobic chants, using words that wound, can unite and divide fans. "While collective sounding-in-synchrony can be uniquely powerful to unite people in feelings of bonding and cohesion," writes one author who follows Argentinian soccer, "it can also propagate

20 HOW DO WE GET BOXED IN?

and normalize profoundly discriminatory ideas."[14] The same identity that brings Jimmy and Juan together, engaging in collective action to cheer on and support the team, also tears them apart.

In the heat of battle, during a match against a hated rival that has beaten them many times before, the visiting team's goalkeeper prepares to receive a penalty kick. The crowd is screaming. The stadium is shaking. And then, seemingly on cue, someone starts the chant, "puto!" "puto!" "puto!" This homophobic slur penetrates the stadium as the ball elevates above the pitch, rocketing toward the net. Jimmy, fully engaged in the moment, lets the slur fly from his lips. But Juan, feeling conflicted and very boxed in, chooses to remain silent. Both are happy that the ball finds its mark, landing high and right into the net. This scene from our thought experiment plays out the same way at every game. It also goes this way when Juan is watching a match at his favorite sports bar with other diehard fans chanting along.

Homophobic chants are not exclusive to Mexico's soccer stadiums. It happens all over Latin America: Argentina, Brazil, Honduras, Peru, and other places. It also happens in Europe: Great Britain, Spain, Italy, Poland, and elsewhere. In British stadiums the slurs are different, "poofter," "fanny," and "sausage jockey," but the aims and effects are the same. There is also a broader story to tell about homophobic chants, not just in soccer but other sports too. Practices and institutions associated with sport play a part in scripting gender roles more generally by masculinizing boys and feminizing girls. Of course "boys" and "girls" or "men" and "women" are themselves collective identities that come with social scripts, which can be too tightly scripted. James Baldwin, lamenting the narrowness of American thinking about manhood, and noting that deviation from the masculinity script is taken to be un-American, makes the point this way:

> The American *ideal*, then, of sexuality appears to be rooted in the American ideal of masculinity. This ideal has created cowboys

BOXED IN   21

and Indians, good guys and bad guys, punks and studs, tough guys and softies, butch and faggot, black and white. It is an ideal so paralytically infantile that it is virtually forbidden—as an unpatriotic act—that the American boy evolve into the complexity of manhood.[15]

The United States does not seem exceptional in this regard. Latin American and European nations as well as African ones may have similar skeletons in their closets. But Jimmy and other *fútbol* fans may say this is beside the point. They may admit that the chants, which intimate that the opposing team goalkeepers or other players are not real men or are softies, as Baldwin might put it, are merely a way to help their team win. The chants are meant to get in the heads of opposing players, take them off their game, and seize an advantage for the home team.

While there may be a broader context that sheds light on homophobic slurs, and there may even be serious problems with homophobia in society, fans like Jimmy will say that in the stadium context, winning the game and helping the team to do so as a loyal fan are all that matters. They see the chants as part of the project of creating an intimidating atmosphere to help their team win. In one study of English soccer fans, who were interviewed about homosexual chants in club football matches, one fan explained a particular incident this way: "I remember we played an away game once [. . .] the other team had a young goalkeeper, about 18. We sung that he 'takes it up the arse' for quite a long time. It obviously affected him, he conceded two soft goals afterwards, and we won the game."[16] Jimmy would say to Juan, "True fans do whatever it takes to win the game. Chanting helps us win. So we chant." But for Juan, who does not leave his ethical consciousness in the stadium parking lot, scripting his *fútbol* team identity so tightly, making this kind of chanting part of it, leaves him boxed in.

When they use homophobic chants, *fútbol* fans deploy a tight script about fan identity that stands in tension with Juan's projects

22 HOW DO WE GET BOXED IN?

as a gay man. This script makes it difficult for Juan to combine his identities, and their associated projects, into one life plan, which leaves him boxed in. The regular use of these chants can also strengthen fans' association between fan identity and the chants. This maintains the tight script, which increases likelihood of future boxing in for others in a similar position to Juan's. As this case demonstrates, deploying tight scripts in our communication, reasoning, and action is what boxes ourselves and others in, in the moment, and creates the conditions for future boxing in.

Trans Soldiers and Black Writers

Less than a week after Joe Biden took his oath to become 46th president of the United States, he lifted a ban on transgender people serving in the military.[17] Ron identifies as trans and checks off many boxes that make him a good fit to be an Army intelligence officer—his dream career. He is physically fit, college-educated, aced the military aptitude test, has exceptional leadership and language skills, and has a spotless record—no criminal history, excellent credit, no drugs, alcohol, or tobacco. He comes from a tight-knit small rural community in America's heartland, surrounded by family, friends, and church members who accepted his identification as a man and fully supported his transition and aspirations to be an Army solider. And being a child of an Army vet, grandchild of a Navy vet, and a sibling of two Marines, Ron is intimately familiar with military life, culture, and norms. But there is one box Ron could not check during the Trump years: the box that asked prospective enlistees to confirm that they did not have a gender reassignment medical history. Ron had costly gender-confirmation surgeries, including a hysterectomy, oophorectomy, vaginectomy, and chest reconstruction. He also completed a comprehensive gender services program including speech and hormone therapy, mental health counseling, and other interventions to facilitate the transition. Prior to President Biden's executive order, transgender people like Ron were prohibited from military service and could be discharged from duty if found to be transgender. So Ron and other prospective trans soldiers welcomed the new commander in chief's willingness to accept their service to country in military uniform.[18]

The characteristics that make Ron a good Army officer candidate are part of the military identity script. Of course, they do not exhaust it. We might add other things such as personality traits of loyalty, courage, and honesty. We can suppose that Ron has all of these too. In fact, his honesty accounts for why he disclosed his medical history knowing that it disqualified him from military service during the Trump years. Another aspect of the military identity script, upheld under the previous administration, excluded persons from service with certain medical conditions taken to compromise their fitness to serve. A Department of Defense regulation held that anyone with a history of "major abnormalities or defects of the genitalia such as change of sex, hermaphroditism, pseudo-hermaphroditism, or pure gonadal dysgenesis"[19] was deemed to have a disqualifying medical condition. The Army added to this its own standard of eligibility for service, stating that "dysfunctional residuals from surgical correction of these conditions does not meet the standard."[20] This ruled Ron out. It also ruled out other transgender people from military service.

Being barred from enlisting or being dishonorably discharged if outed were among the concrete liabilities associated with transgender enlistees and soldiers. Some soldiers managed to officially conceal their trans identity while serving. Yet they were subject to greater risk of harassment, violence, and other forms of abuse. Some soldiers no longer served and need medical care. They could be denied or receive insufficient services—including routine and long-term care as well as mental healthcare—by the Veterans Health Administration system. Some soldiers sought medical care while serving under a "Don't Tell or Don't Get Exposed" regime. They lived with fear that doctors and other care providers would

24 HOW DO WE GET BOXED IN?

not keep their medical record confidential. These concrete liabilities partly explain why persons like Ron found it difficult to combine a transgender and military identity into one life plan.

As the *fútbol* fans case demonstrated, when identities are scripted too tightly it is difficult for their bearers to combine them in a unified life plan. This was also true for trans soldiers like Ron, who were boxed in by a tight script for military identity. In this case, institutional practices and culture, alongside the behavior of individuals within the military, served to draw and reinforce the boundaries between military and trans identities, even though both identities were salient for Ron and for trans soldiers now serving. These mechanisms worked to render these scripts incompatible, leaving trans soldiers boxed in. In this case, practices of dehumanization, stereotype proliferation, and discrimination have served to shape and police LGBTQ and military identities.[21] For instance, not only physical violence such as beatings and sexual assaults, but also language, such as slurs, denigrate the humanity of transgender persons. In one study, Casey, a transgender Army veteran who identified as a lesbian but transitioned later, reports witnessing brutal beatings of soldiers merely suspected of being gay.[22] There was also stereotyping of soldiers: trans and gay soldiers were alleged to have AIDS, to be perverts, and to be weak—all of this in addition to the explicit and official discriminatory military policies that made transgender identities either an obstacle to enlistment or a dischargeable condition and offense. These mechanisms served to shape and police the thoughts and feelings, associations, and actions of military personnel, both ones that identify as trans and ones that do not. These identity-shaping and policing mechanisms contributed to the sense that being a soldier and being transgender (or gay, lesbian, or bisexual) were incompatible identities. This left people like Ron feeling boxed in and wanting to break free.

The identity-shaping and policing mechanisms in this case were created or enabled by institutional policies of discrimination. But we can also imagine identity-shaping and policing mechanisms at work in other cases that operate less formally. For example, stereotyping can serve to shape and police identity behavior in cases that are not primarily institutional but interpersonal, and do not have effects that are as concrete or consequential in derailing or altering an individual's life-shaping plans.

Ralph Ellison shares a personal story about being boxed in as a black writer. He uses an illuminating distinction between "relatives" and "ancestors" to tell the story.[23] Richard Wright, another black writer, was a *relative* because he and Ellison share a common racial identity. Ernest Hemingway, a white writer, was an *ancestor* because he and Ellison share a common interest in writing about the mundane—weather, guns, animals, emotions, and dealing with the impossible. Ellison also considered Langston Hughes a relative and Fyodor Dostoevsky an ancestor. And he noted that writers can choose ancestors but not relatives. Ellison is responding to a critic, Irving Howe, who operates with a stereotype that black writers, or Negro writers as they were called then, should rely upon other black writers for literary inspiration and instruction. He thought that Wright should be Ellison's ancestor or spiritual father, not Hemingway. Howe also thought the same about James Baldwin, and so was critical of both writers, as Ellison notes:

> In his loyalty to Richard Wright, Howe considers Ellison and Baldwin guilty of filial betrayal because, in their own work, they have rejected the path laid down by *Native Son*, phonies because while actually "black boys," they pretend to be mere American writers trying to react to something of the pluralism of their predicament.[24]

Ellison did not deny that black writers could use their craft to protest racial and other forms of injustice. However, he did not want to be boxed in by a black writer identity, scripted too tightly, making it essential that they use or understand novels or writing primarily as political weapons of protest. He argued that literary critics such as Howe could be more at fault for this than Southern politicians. Ellison writes:

> In his effort to resuscitate Wright, Irving Howe would designate the role which Negro writers are to play more rigidly than any Southern politicians—and for the best of reasons. We must express "black" anger and "clenched militancy"; most of all we should not become too interested in the problems of the art of literature, even though it is through these that we seek our individual identities. And between writing well and being ideologically militant, we must choose militancy.[25]

Critics such as Howe were all too ready to operate with stereotypical views about what black writers knew, could imagine or say, views that effectively shaped and policed their identities as writers, rather than with informed knowledge of these things. Ellison writes: "Howe must wait for an autobiography before he can be responsibly certain. Everyone wants to tell us what a Negro is, yet few wish, even in a joke, to be one. But if you would tell me who I am, at least take the trouble to discover what I have been."[26]

So, when we say that someone is boxed in by tightly scripted collective identities, we mean that there are mechanisms at work that make their particular identities, and the projects corresponding to these identities, hard to combine. These mechanisms, which amount to identity-shaping and identity-policing tools, can operate formally and institutionally as in the trans soldier case. They can also work informally and interpersonally as in the writing while black case. However they operate, when this occurs, bearers of the identities in question get boxed in. We now have an answer to our second main question for this chapter: How do tightly scripted identities box us in? In the next section, we introduce an example of how tightly scripted identities can box us in, in ways that inhibit our cooperation with others, to start to answer our third question: How does boxing in get in the way of our projects?

Christian Conservatives and Criminal Justice

John, Joshua, and Josephine White are not real people. However, this thought experiment builds on familiar profiles to illustrate a common form of boxing in.[27] So they may resemble people you have known or have read about. Imagine that they are fraternal triplets born into a tight-knit family of Christian conservatives. They grew up during the 1970s, 1980s, and 1990s in Southern California. Their parents are active in church, community, and politics. All three children are raised to identify with Christianity, conservativism, and a combination of the two that produced a Christian conservative identity. We will call them *Christian conservatives*.

There are different meanings attached to this collective identity. And, as we shall address in Chapter 3, these meanings provide socially constituted scripts, which are used in shaping and pursuing our various projects. Part of the Christian conservative script, used by the Whites and forged by various communities, includes supporting tough-on-crime—particularly inner-city crime—policies and politicians. This orientation infuses much of what they think and believe. It influences their associations. It informs how they behave. They believe that government should direct more money to arm police with military-grade equipment and support creating special units like SWAT to fight urban crime. Giving prosecutors more discretion in charging suspects, imposing mandatory minimum sentences for certain drug offenses, and supporting supermax prisons to lock up violent and nonviolent offenders—mostly black, brown, and poor—are also part of this law-and-order conservative identity. They associate with like-minded folks in their community and join groups committed to realizing these goals. The Whites also feel that Christian ministries, like the one they belong to, which preach an Old Testament message of retribution for wrongdoing and sinfulness that does not shy away from serious punishment when justly deserved, is the best faith home for the family. This is a snapshot of the things they

28 HOW DO WE GET BOXED IN?

believe and some of the things they do. These beliefs, feelings, associations, and actions facilitate a tightening of the Christian conservative script. As adults, one of the triplets, John, would embrace it wholeheartedly. But for the other two, Joshua and Josephine, the script was too tight. They felt boxed in.

Like many white middle-class families, the Whites fled Los Angeles County for the suburbs in the late 1970s. They sought sanctuary and shelter for the triplets from what they described as "the growing urban jungle" in Inglewood, California. The walls that blocked racial integration in South Central, Los Angeles, which the Whites had called home, were crumbling. Blacks and Latino immigrants were moving in. And the Whites feared that desegregated schools, lower property values, and street crime were not far behind. So they joined the white flight.[28]

From the relative safety of their new white picket fence–lined neighborhood in Orange County, with well-resourced white schools protected from court-ordered busing and with white neighbors who shared their conservative values, these Christian conservatives preached about the moral decay of black neighborhoods and the negative effects this had not only on them but on American society. Getting tough on urban crime, from this standpoint, was about applying old-school Christian principles, of letting people reap what they sow, with the promise that this heavy hand would motivate these "sinners" to change course and turn their lives around. Seeing lawbreakers pay, with hard time and long bids, would also be a powerful deterrent: "What worked, conservatives said simply, were long sentences, which would keep those behind bars from preying on society and send a message to those outside that severe retribution awaited them if they violated society's laws."[29] Barry Goldwater, Richard Nixon, and Ronald Reagan—the White family political heroes—towed this line. This way of filling in the script seamlessly linked Christianity and conservativism.

When the triplets were growing up, white fears about street crime, media representations of urban life, and political rhetoric

BOXED IN 29

mutually reinforced the family's law-and-order sentiment about criminal justice. This made it difficult for Christian conservatives like Joshua and Josephine, who came to feel overly constrained by it, to resist this part of the script. However, things were changing in the early 1990s as they were finishing college. Data suggested that crime rates were going down, Democrats were putting their own spin on the law-and-order message; Clinton Democrats pushed gun control in schools and outside of them, leaving some conservatives worried about Second Amendment rights. Some Christian conservatives who had family members entangled in the criminal justice system for nonviolent drug offenses and other crimes got to see some of its problems firsthand. They began to raise objections to federal statutes mandating minimum sentences for drug offenses. They argued that this was too harsh. It led to grave injustices such as excessive punishment not fitting the crime, and insufficient deference to judicial discretion allowing judges to consider factors such as first offenses or defendants' family backgrounds. And a bit later, after 9/11, the public concern shifted dramatically away from fear of urban crime to fear of foreign terrorism—Arab Americans displaced African Americans as the new menace. These are among the numerous macro-level changes in American society and public opinion that created opportunity for departures from the traditional Christian conservative identity script, which left two of the White triplets feeling boxed in.

In light of these macro changes, some Christian conservatives became more open to, and interested in, criminal justice reform. But to engage in politically impactful projects to promote reform, they would have to, as Christian conservatives, work in organizations with others who did not share this identity to hold representatives accountable for policy changes. And for this to happen they had to break free from the overly restrictive script.

The triplets took different paths as adults. Staying true to his upbringing, John stuck with the traditional Christian conservative script. After college he went to law school and became a prosecutor

30 HOW DO WE GET BOXED IN?

who won with a tough law-and-order platform. He sought out coalitions with other like-minded Christian conservatives who doubled-down on the traditional message and argued that urban crime, lawlessness, and moral decay in black and brown communities remained the gravest threats to America's way of life and to its order and security. He did his part to make sure that the prisons remained full and that no deals were cut for lighter sentences. Charging and prosecuting them for crimes, serious as well as minor, was the only way to make them pay and send a strong message that crime does not pay in his jurisdiction. The high costs involved, the harmful impact on families and urban communities, and the well-documented racial disparities in sentencing and time served did not deter John from his law-and-order approach. This put him at odds with his two siblings.

Joshua majored in philosophy, politics, and economics. He wrote an honors thesis entitled, "Libertarian Economics: The Corrective to Big Government." He furthered his studies with a graduate degree in economics from George Mason University under James Buchanan's tutelage. Joshua believed that big government spending was America's root problem. It made government too costly, too inefficient, and too unaccountable. However, following a new generation of Christian conservatives, he extended this critique beyond government spending on social welfare programs to spending on prisons. After graduate school, he moved to Washington, DC, to work for an influential congressional Republican who would become a champion of federal sentencing reform, shrinking the prison population, and shifting the cost of prisons and prisoner support and societal re-entry from public funds to private markets and nonprofit organizations, particularly churches. Joshua thought that economic arguments and arguments for scaling back big government power were decisive in favor of changing course on mass incarceration. And, unlike John, he was willing to work with some liberals who had the same agenda. He was able to do so because he broke free from the tightly scripted Christian conservative identity—with its no compromise law-and-order orientation—that remained salient for his brother.

The same was true of Josephine. She broke free. She volunteered in inner-city after-school programs and homeless shelters with her Christian youth group during high school. She majored in philosophy and religion in college. She continued various kinds of volunteer work during her college years and took a strong interest in social justice activism. She believed that Christian conservatives had a religious and moral duty not only to defend the dignity of the unborn, but to ensure that society's most disadvantaged, which included prisoners, were treated with dignity and respect. Society also had an obligation to address the devasting toll that mass incarceration had on the families and communities of incarceration persons. And it must provide the necessary social and economic supports for formerly incarcerated persons to re-enter society, find work, housing, and get education to support themselves and live normal lives. After college Josephine and several classmates remained in Texas and formed a nonprofit organization devoted to social justice activism supporting families of color impacted by the criminal justice system. Their organization became a highly influential lobby in local and state politics. It added considerable momentum to efforts by some Christian conservatives to reverse the tide of mass incarceration and redirect public spending from supporting and building more prisons to increased investments in education, job training, and entrepreneurship support in communities decimated by incarceration. Like Joshua, and maybe to an even greater extent, Josephine was able to pursue projects with social justice liberals, and even some more progressive types, such as prison abolitionists, by breaking free from the tightly scripted Christian conversative identity embraced by her parents and her brother John.

In the previous section, we established a general answer to the question: How do tightly scripted identities box us in? We noted that tight scripts box us in via identity-shaping and policing mechanisms, which make it difficult to combine different identities into one life plan. This case, which uses a stock identity rooted in religion and political ideology, adds the point that being boxed in by tightly scripted collective identities can be politically impactful. It can inhibit a person's ability to engage in projects with others who do not share the relevant identity. Think about John. But, as this case suggests, the problem is not with the collective identity per se, it is with scripting it too tightly or in ways that do not allow for ingroup heterogeneity. Joshua and Josephine still thought of themselves as Christian conservatives. However, they broke free from a traditional way of understanding this collective identity that enabled them to combine it with a criminal justice reformer identity. And this makes it possible for them to pursue common political projects with a wider array of partners.

Joshua and Josephine both decided to resist tight scripts as they navigated Rustin's dilemma, which we described in the Introduction. This dilemma arises due to the difficulty of coordinating the pursuit of projects while remaining attentive to intra- and intergroup heterogeneity. And when we face this dilemma and establish our differences, we face a further question: Now what? How, if at all, should we continue to work together? Like Charlie Parker in his jazz career, Joshua and Josephine both found that the existing Christian conservative script was too restrictive for the set of projects they wanted to pursue. Their response to the "now what" question was not to abandon their Christian conservative identity, but rather, to push for a more flexible script in order to pursue their projects with others.

In this example, boxing in got in the way of coordinating the pursuit of projects with others. This is one, but not the only way that boxing in can get in the way of our projects. In the next section, we will develop a more general answer to our third main question with a three-part taxonomy of the different ways that we can be boxed in.

Boxed In: A Taxonomy

Rania, Samira, and Farah are Americans of Middle Eastern and North African descent. Like other Americans of similar background, for whom identity is neither black nor white, they had debates in their families and communities over whether to support adding a new box to the 2020 US Census. The proposal to add a "MENA" (Middle Eastern or North African) box would have allowed them to identify themselves more accurately. Of the nearly 4 million persons living in the United States who trace their roots to Middle Eastern or North African nations, roughly 82% are US citizens.[30] Unlike other populations with brown skin, who trace their roots to Asia, Africa, and South America, they are classified as white in America. However, many persons of MENA descent—especially ones who are recent immigrants or part of the post–9/11 generation (like Rania, Samira, and Farah), who identify as Muslim, who have experienced racial discrimination, or who strongly identify with other people of color that have had such experiences—find being categorized as white at odds with their lived experiences in America.

The US Office of Management and Budget is responsible for constructing racial and ethnic categories and has classified MENA populations as white since the late 1970s. The US Census Bureau uses these classifications when it gathers demographic data for the decennial survey. Critics of this long-standing practice of having MENA populations check the "white" box have argued that it does not reflect the vast diversity of this group based on country of origin, language, religion, phenotypical traits, cultural practices, and the like. In addition to not allowing persons of MENA descent to represent more accurately who they are, more importantly, it deprives them and their communities of resources, opportunities, and protections that are afforded to other groups based on racial and ethnic minority backgrounds. For MENA populations, the stakes of breaking free from being boxed in by whiteness are not merely

34   HOW DO WE GET BOXED IN?

symbolic, they are also substantive. A more accurate picture of their numbers can determine whether they get translators in public schools or small business loans in their local communities. So it is not just about expressing one's true identity; it is about claiming rights and opportunities associated with legally recognized and protected identities. These are among the considerations that advocates advanced to support creating a MENA box for the 2020 census.

The proposal called for creating a separate MENA American category listed among seven other options: Black or African American; Asian; American Indian or Alaska Native; Hispanic or Latino; Native Hawaiian or Other Pacific Islander; White; some other race or ethnicity. Census takers would have had the option of checking all of the boxes applying to their identity. Additionally, the survey would have included a fillable box, allowing MENA applicants to make finer-grained specifications of their identities (e.g., "Egyptian American," "Syrian American," or "Arab American"). The Obama administration supported this measure but the Trump Administration did not take it up, so the 2020 census remained unchanged. This will remain a live issue and as of March 2024, the Biden Administration has approved changes to the race and/or ethnicity category on the census along these lines, to be implemented ahead of the 2030 census.[31]

For persons who feel boxed in by having to check the white box, ironically, the proposed MENA option addresses the problem by giving them another box to check. But this has not eliminated disagreement. There are sharp differences in MENA families and communities over whether to support changes to the status quo. And the divisions are generational as well as philosophical. Consider the situation of our trio.

Farah grew up in Arizona and identifies as Egyptian.[32] Samira is from Southern California and identifies as Iranian.[33] Rania, also from this region, identifies as Palestinian and Lebanese.[34] They come from households where the practical advice is to check the "white" box. Rania's father, Marwan, explains that this was the advice he got when he first migrated to the United States from Palestine. He was told to check the white box for everything, including school and work. Rania's mother, Aurora, who migrated from Lebanon, got similar advice. And, mom says, "It's better to be blending in with the rest of the population rather than being cornered, if you want, or subjected to specific climates that [are] going on."[35]

Rania's parents thought this counsel was wise. Checking the white box addressed their desire to be part of mainstream America. They wanted to fit into American society. They wanted to be viewed as good law-abiding, tax-paying, patriotic citizens. Of course this requires much more than checking the white box on a census survey. But for Rania's parents, and many other persons of MENA descent, the act of checking the box was part of accepting the identity. Being white in America was, from their perspective, a good thing. It allowed them to secure the wages of whiteness and white privilege. Farah and Samira's family no doubt held similar views. While the reasons may vary from person to person, ranging from being advised to do so, wanting to assimilate, to survive, or to avoid the stigma of being "othered," an overwhelming majority of persons of MENA descent have checked the white box on past census surveys. According to the *Los Angeles Times*, 89% of Egyptians, 85% of Iranians, 87% of Palestinians, and 94% of Lebanese Americans identified as white in past surveys.[36] So the elders in these families are very much acting in accordance with existing norms within their national-origin ethnic groups.

Studies suggest that older generations of MENA persons are more likely to check the white box.[37] But age is not the only variable that accounts for identification practices within this extremely heterogenous population. Religion, level of educational attainment, and national origin are also important variables: persons of MENA descent who have more education, are Christian, immigrated to the United States before 1990, and have roots in certain regions are more likely to embrace the white identity category. With respect to ancestry, Lebanon and Syria have the longest history of migration to the United States, going back to the late 19th century. This, along with physical appearances similar to persons from Greece, Spain, Italy, and other Mediterranean groups, may partly explain why they are more likely than other MENA populations to announce white racial identity. Although willingness to check the white box is typical of older generations from certain regions, this action does not feel right to many MENA youth. They experience America as persons of color and seek solidarity in fighting discrimination and uplifting communities of color.

With the treatment of MENA populations post–9/11—being added to no-fly lists, subject to travel bans, and state surveillance— still fresh on the mind, Rania speaks of not feeling white in America. Rania also notes that her name, native language, and cuisine preferences make her not feel part of America. Samira recalls being bullied, as a second grader, after the 9/11 attacks. She was addressed with slurs and made to feel that she was not American and did not belong. Farah explains that the real situation is that one is only really white if one has white privilege, and because she does not have this, she is not really white. Coming to terms with this reality created a crisis when it came to checking the white box on the census. She says: "For someone like me, I never know which box to tick. I felt like this tiny checkbox, which in reality shouldn't carry that much value in my life, was picking at me slowly. Taking the one thing I held onto the most: my identity."[38] All three women would agree that in a world where one does not experience life as white, with all the privilege this entails in America, and one is not really seen as white, then the best advice, contrary to the lessons from home, is to "Check it Right, You Ain't White."[39]

These "othering" experiences are all too common for people of color in the United States. And we know that MENA Americans are not beyond the reach of individual, institutional, and societal racial prejudice and discrimination. Still, there are real disagreements among MENA Americans over whether or not to check the white box or, more generally, to take advantage of the hard-fought opportunity to take on generic white identity in America. On the one side, against adding the MENA box, there are some who worry that it would be a troublesome step backward, leading to greater surveillance, profiling, and policing of MENA Americans and their communities.[40] In short, it would be detrimental to their civil liberties. On the other side, in favor of adding the box, there are others who argue that it would help direct much-needed resources and opportunities—educationally, economically, and politically— to MENA Americans and their communities. It would also lead to more accurate data collection to trace health-related trends and assess health-related needs, including ones brought on by COVID-19. In short, it would be beneficial to their civil, political, and economic rights.

When collective identities are scripted too tightly, we can be boxed in. We might do this to ourselves. For example, Rania's parents, Marwan and Aurora, were willing to check the white box. They thought that taking this concrete action was part of assimilating into America. It was about enabling them to gain certain benefits of being white and to avoid certain liabilities of being classified as nonwhite. On the other side, Rania, who would say to them "check it right, you ain't white,"[41] was aiming to box them in by imploring them to take another course of action—checking a different box—that more accurately reflected their MENA identities. So we can box ourselves in or be boxed in by others. The people we box in may be part of our ingroup. Rania may try to box in her parents. John may try to box in his sister Josephine, alleging that she is not a true Christian or not a true conservative by allying with Black Lives Matter (BLM) racial justice supporters or taking up broader social justice causes such a prison abolition. The people we box in may also be part of an outgroup. Rania might say that civil libertarians are anti-diversity and are closet conservatives. John may say that Democrats are too soft on crime and are anti-police.

38 HOW DO WE GET BOXED IN?

Being boxed in is not only about how we act, that is, it is not only about whether to check or not check a box. It can also be about what we think or feel. In trying to convince her father to check the MENA box, if it were an option, Rania appealed to feelings of solidarity with their community. She pointed out the kinds of services linked to money and programs determined by census numbers, for example, language services such as Farsi in hospitals and ballots in Arabic, educational grants, support for local businesses, and protection from race-based anti-discrimination laws. Her point was that persons of MENA descent should feel a sense of solidarity with their group. And her hope was that her father might take a different action based on this feeling. He seemed to be open to this, saying to Rania, "Maybe I'll do it for unselfish reasons, for the rest of the community to benefit, for your generation to gain the benefit. It could be."[42]

Tightly scripted identities might also box us in by dictating whom we should or should not associate with. For persons of MENA descent who worry that civil liberties will be in jeopardy if more people stop identifying as white, choosing instead to announce themselves as Syrian Americans, Palestinian Americans, or Iraqi Americans, it may make sense to associate more with defenders of civil liberties rather than groups lobbying for recognition of generic Arab American identity or more specific identities. And this may seem sensible even if they have other reasons, perhaps stemming from genuine feelings of group solidarity, to view themselves as nonwhite. Likewise, we might imagine a person of MENA descent who thinks more like Rania's parents and who has long practiced checking the white box, but who is also a medical researcher and practitioner. As such, they may understand the need for more accurate identification of MENA citizens to gather important medical information to address disparities in health outcomes and health interventions within MENA communities. They may thus be moved to associate, formally or informally, with groups lobbying for more ways of identifying members of these communities, including by expanding the census survey options.

This three-part taxonomy answers the question: How does boxing in get in the way of our projects? We can be boxed in according to how we act, how we think and feel, and whom we associate with. In each of these circumstances, tight scripts can inhibit out pursuit of the projects that make up our life plan. We have seen this in the case of MENA Americans with respect to projects such as advancing the public health of one's community, assimilating to a new national identity, and working with others to defend civil liberties.

Boxing in is also not something that is carried out solely through the power of individuals. Tight scripts emerge and propagate in the context of certain background conditions. For example, Rania's parents' choice of identification as white, and that of others who reason similarly, does not occur in a vacuum. Their identification is responsive to both institutional features of the environment, such as the Census Bureau's racial classification scheme, and the prevailing social norms, such as expectations of assimilation.[43] We will have more to say about the importance of background conditions in Chapters 5 and 6, but for now, it is worth noting that institutional rules and social norms can serve to enable boxing in. At the same time, institutional rules and social norms alone are not sufficient for sustaining tight scripts and the boxing in they create. They need to be enforced and upheld by people. And it is the deployment of tight scripts by people, whether for themselves or others, that maintains those scripts into the future.

Tightly scripted identities can box us in based on actions, thoughts or feelings, and associations. And this gets in the way of our projects, as we have seen with MENA identities. But it can happen to jazz musicians, *fútbol* fans, and conservative Christians too. It can happen when any identity we share with others is too tightly scripted. Of course, boxing in is not a foregone conclusion. But it is something to worry about. And the worries raised by the

40 HOW DO WE GET BOXED IN?

phenomenon of being boxed in increase exponentially as the political and institutional challenges grow. As this happens, it becomes vital to break free from collective identities that box us in.

How Bird Broke Free

The standard script for being a black jazz musician in America circa 1920s and 1930s, as we noted earlier, was about using one's musical talents to entertain white audiences who paid the bills. Black musicians were expected to clown, laugh, and make white people comfortable while tickling the ivory, beating the drums, and blowing the horn. They were also expected to play music that people could swing and dance to. Of course there were jazz musicians such as pianist Art Tatum and saxophonist Johnny Hodges who deviated from this tight script. Charlie Parker, also known as Bird, greatly admired both musicians but felt boxed in by the standard script and he broke free with musical innovation. Bird wanted no part of the actions it required of him on stage. He wanted no part of the ways it prescribed that he feel or think about his musical craft. And he did not want to associate with musicians that were content with the tight script.

Bird was part of a group of innovative musicians that created a new style of jazz—which they called "modern" music—in the 1940s. We know it as "bebop." "The first generation of jazz players had succeeded as entertainers," writes one author, "and white America was content to celebrate them on that level. But the black jazz players of the 1940s wanted more. They demanded acceptance as artists, as esteemed practitioners of a serious musical form."[44] Improvisation with creative uses of chords, melodies, harmonies, and blazing tempos were among the raw materials that contributed to bebop's technical innovations. Bird became a modern master of bebop. His cutting sound and tone were unique. And his improvisational style set a standard for others to follow. One jazz writer notes: "Parker's tone, slightly shrill, hard-edged, vibratoless and glossy, also tells us we're listening to bebop. Indeed, it formed the basis for virtually every black jazz altoist's sound between 1945 and 1960."[45]

Bird was well aware of his musical gifts, though he made very clear that this was not about natural talent. He became a master of the craft due to countless hours and years of hard work mastering his alto saxophone, learning music, and finding ways to express his innovative musical ideas. Before a gig, when he was feeling especially good, he would say, "The sap is flowing." This meant, "I'm gonna blow my ass off."[46] One place where Bird soared, and the sap flowed, was the legendary birthplace of bebop in 1940, Minton's Playhouse in Harlem, on 118th Street between St. Nicholas and Seventh Avenue. It was the laboratory where jazz heavyweights, including Thelonious Monk, Kenny Clarke, Dizzy Gillespie, along with Charlie Parker and a select group of musicians—playing for predominately black audiences—experimented with elaborate chord changes, intricate harmonies, and improvisation that forged the bebop style. It was the place where you went to play if you wanted a reputation among hardcore musicians and aficionados. "Minton's was," as Miles Davis put it, "the ass-kicker back in those days for aspiring jazz musicians."[47] It was where the real musicians came to showcase their chops, and among this group Bird had no equal. Miles recollected that Bird routinely left everybody else in the dust when he played, often turning fellow musicians into spectators who would forget to come in on time, being so mesmerized by his stunning solos. "They'd be standing up there on stage," says Miles, "with their mouths wide open."[48] Becoming a bebop jazz virtuoso, making technically sophisticated music made for focused listening and music that garnered the respect of serious musicians in Minton's and other jazz venues, is how Bird broke free from the traditional jazz musician script.

Bird was known to like talking philosophy and politics. And some commentators, most notably Amiri Baraka, have interpreted

42 HOW DO WE GET BOXED IN?

the transition from swing to bebop as a form of political expression by black musicians rejecting white expectations and seeking more self-affirming modes of expression.[49] Sounding a similar note, and putting a political spin on Bird's bebop legacy, another writes: "Jazz, especially Bird's bebop, was a model. It highlighted the individual, yet depended on group communication. Its spontaneity and equal partnership on the bandstand opposed bureaucratic rulebooks and refuted segregation."[50]

Other musicians were more explicit about the political stakes involved in breaking free from demeaning jazz musician scripts. Consider legendary jazz bassist and composer Charles Mingus, whose antiracist sensibilities informed his rejection of white normativity and stereotyping of black artists, as well as his musical innovation. We see this in stories of how he criticized white audiences for being phonies as well as in his consciousness-raising with tunes—combining music and politics—such as "Fables of Faubus" protesting segregationist governor Orval Faubus of Arkansas.

So far, we have answered three important questions.

1. What does it mean for collective identities to be tightly scripted?
2. How do tightly scripted identities box us in?
3. How does boxing in get in the way of our projects?

Our answer to the first question is that identities are tightly scripted when the content of their scripts make them difficult to combine with others into one life plan. Our answer to the second question builds on our answer to the first: when we are boxed in, identity-shaping and identity-policing mechanisms make particular identities, and their corresponding projects, hard to combine into a unified life plan. They can work formally and institutionally as in the trans soldier case. And they can also operate informally and interpersonally as in the writing while black case. Our answer to the third question is that boxing in gets in the way of our projects when tightly scripted identities pressure us to take specific actions, prime us to have particular thoughts or feelings, and prod us to pursue certain associations.

At some point, all of us have felt that a particular identity we embrace is too tightly scripted. Not much may ride on this, at times. But at other times, being boxed in by tight scripts gets in the way of projects that are very important for our lives. This is one way that boxing in can be bad for us. But being boxed in can also be bad for us as democratic citizens. The next chapter will identify some of this trouble, along with how identity skeptics and identity optimists respond to it. The overarching worry is that tightly scripted identities that box in—with insufficient regard for ingroup heterogeneity—can inhibit a person's ability, and that of a democratic citizenry as a whole, to engage in political projects with others who do not share the relevant identity.

Think again about John, who embraced the tightly scripted version of Christian conservativism. His siblings, Joshua and Josephine, did not, but still thought of themselves as Christian conservatives. They broke free from a traditional way of understanding this collective identity that enabled them to combine it with a criminal justice reformer identity. And this made it possible for them to pursue common political projects with others. Subsequent chapters will explain, in greater detail, what we need in order to break free from tight scripts (Part II), which is an understanding of how identity works (Chapter 3) and collective self-authorship processes (Chapter 4). They will also lay out how we can break free (Part III) with an account of the civic responsibilities we must take up when engaging in micro (Chapter 5) and macro (Chapter 6) politics.

2

Identity Trouble

Friends and Enemies

Meet Maya and Bailey.[1] They have never met but might feel like they know a lot about one another if they did meet. Both live in the United States and have serious concerns about the political climate. They worry about some of their fellow citizens, whom they see as hypocritical, selfish, and untrustworthy.[2] They are reluctant to socialize with them and may even actively discriminate against them.[3] Both believe that their communities do not receive a fair share of federal government resources while other communities receive more than their fair share.[4] Increasingly, Maya and Bailey's participation in politics by voting, donating money, and volunteering for political campaigns is driven by animosity toward those they see as a threat, rather than by enthusiasm for the political parties or candidates that they support.[5]

Maya and Bailey approach politics with a *friends-and-enemies mindset*. They see some citizens—often on the basis of partisan identity—as friends to trust and support, and they see others as enemies to distrust and oppose. When asked to describe herself politically, Maya identifies as a liberal and expresses concern about the Republican Party and its voters. Bailey, by contrast, identifies as a conservative and expresses concerns about the Democratic Party and its voters. They disagree about policy, but the divide between them isn't just about policy. It's also about identity. These partisan identities are, of course, not the only collective identities that Maya and Bailey identify with, but they are salient to them, especially within the realm of politics. This friends-and-enemies

Boxed In. Derrick Darby and Eduardo J. Martinez, Oxford University Press. © Oxford University Press 2024.
DOI: 10.1093/9780197620236.003.0003

IDENTITY TROUBLE   45

mindset is one of four components of identity trouble we discuss in this chapter. Taken together, they foster what we call an "ethos of boxing in," which we will say more about later.

We can understand Maya and Bailey's division of the world into friends and enemies in terms of a process of *social sorting* with increasingly tightened identity scripts along a range of different dimensions.[6] Partisan identities, and their accompanying social scripts, have become increasingly sorted with respect to other social identities such as race and religion in the United States in the past few decades.[7] But social sorting is not just a matter of finding more black or white citizens, or secular or evangelical citizens, among one's group of partisan friends and enemies. Citizens are also increasingly sorted *residentially* by partisanship, over and above the extensive ethnic and racial segregation in the United States, and this includes micro-level segregation within the same city and neighborhood.[8] In addition to living in different areas, opposing partisans increasingly live distinct social lives: attending different religious services,[9] shopping at different stores,[10] and they are even unlikely to date one another.[11]

As a result of these sorting trends, citizens like Maya and Bailey increasingly do not interact with others with different partisan identities. Because of this they are less likely to have the experience of their own identities being misaligned (where one of their identities is associated with an opposing partisan identity rather than their own). This pattern can serve to further box us in our political life with respect to how we think and feel, how we act, and whom we associate with. Consider, as an example, the phenomenon of what political scientists call *negative partisanship*. Citizens like Maya and Bailey are increasingly motivated to take part in politics (whether by voting in an election, volunteering, or donating to a campaign) by suspicion of, and hostility toward, those they see as their political enemies.[12] Maya and Bailey take part in politics not primarily because of a commitment to a particular policy or platform, but to defeat the opposition that they see

46   HOW DO WE GET BOXED IN?

as a threat to the nation.[13] For them, politics is about combating their enemies.

Given these attitudes, it is perhaps unsurprising that Maya and Bailey do not seek out opportunities to communicate with others with different identities and tend to misunderstand the makeup of their political enemies. When Maya and Bailey engage in political conversations with others, they tend to be in relatively homogenous groups.[14] They also tend to seek out information via partisan-sorted media, which will affirm their prior commitments without much exposure to opposing partisan perspectives.[15] Americans in general tend to have distorted beliefs about the makeup of political parties, and partisans tend to have especially biased perceptions of opposing parties.

A 2018 study found that respondents vastly overestimated the share of Democrats who belong to a labor union (39.3% compared to the actual figure of 10.5%), are lesbian, gay, or bisexual (31.7% vs. 6.3%), are black (41.9% vs. 23.9%), and that are atheist or agnostic (28.7% vs. 8.7%). Similarly, they found that respondents vastly overestimated the share of Republicans who make over $250,000 per year (38.2% vs. 2.2%) and that are age 65 or older (39.1% vs. 21.3%).[16] While respondents tended to overestimate the share of these groups making up their own partisan group, the difference between their perceptions and the actual figures for out-party groups is higher. This same study also found evidence that these misperceptions contribute to perceptions of the extremity of opposing party supporters' views and feelings of social distance from them.

When those motivated by negative partisanship encounter those with misaligned identities in their community, rather than establish robust lines of communication, they can initiate negative interactions that range from unwelcoming to active hostility. The writer Silas House describes the negative interactions he has faced around the country given that he is from Kentucky, such as being asked if he is ashamed of being from Kentucky and suggesting that he is complicit in obstructionism from Kentucky senator Mitch McConnell.[17] The tight scripts that others deploy about Kentuckians lead to a perceived tension between his pride in his Appalachian roots in eastern Kentucky and his commitment to progressive politics. He writes, "I am ashamed of McConnell, but I am never ashamed to be a Kentuckian. My state is a complicated, beautiful place with a rich heritage and people who have contributed a huge amount to the American experiment. I will defend the state to all outsiders, even as I complain about its flaws."[18]

House calls attention to the work of Kentuckian activists and organizers that have led to the growth of Pride events across the state, environmental conservation, and rural protests against police brutality. Of course, the majority of Kentuckian voters are Republicans and voted for Donald Trump in the 2020 presidential election, including the overwhelming majority (over 80%) of voters in the county where House grew up. When he encounters attributions of blame for political outcomes to his home state, House thinks about "the 17 percent—4,883 souls—back home who cast ballots against [Trump]. They made a principled stand against enormous peer pressure that people outside the region cannot possibly understand. Some who voted against McConnell and Trump were even accused of being 'traitors' and 'murderers.' As a gay man, I left home to feel safer and more comfortable. I think of the 4,883 there who are fighting back, and I am thankful for each one."[19] House calls attention to the hostility faced by those working on progressive causes in areas where they are seen as political enemies by most people around them, as well as the ways that he is boxed in by partisan conceptions of regional identities as signifying whether one is a friend or foe.

This division of fellow citizens into friends and enemies, and the accompanying animosity, distrust, and limited communication are not exclusively an American problem. Political scientists have begun to investigate the degree to which citizens in different countries dislike or distrust opposing partisans and have a favorable

48   HOW DO WE GET BOXED IN?

view of their co-partisans. This research suggests that while there are countries with lower levels of these attitudes than the United States, such as those in northern Europe, there are also countries with higher levels of these partisan attitudes, such as those in southern and eastern Europe.[20]

To illustrate the danger of some of the more extreme forms of partisan distrust and animosity, consider Hungary. It is a country with a very high degree of partisan animosity and distrust and where politics are currently characterized by a stark divide between friends and enemies. Hungary transitioned to electoral democracy from communist rule in 1989 and initially elected a parliament with six parties. These parties differed along multiple dimensions that crosscut one another, most notably, a religious versus secular cultural dimension and a socialist versus pro-market dimension.[21] So, unlike the current circumstances in the United States, voters' salient identities did not all align along one partisan dividing line between friends and enemies. However, over time, the political landscape shifted to a strict left versus right divide. Political parties tended to use more "us versus them" rhetoric and left-right symbolism, which led voters to perceive greater differences in platforms than really was the case, and parties became increasingly unwilling to work in coalitions with one another across the main left-right dividing line.[22] Much like in the United States, citizens started to feel boxed in with respect to their partisan identities even in nonpolitical contexts, to the point that there were distinct left- and right-wing magazines for hobbies like fishing and bird-watching.[23] Hungary's governing party, FIDESZ, and its supporters see the electoral opposition as enemies, and have changed electoral rules to their advantage.[24]

Once we start to see our political opponents as enemies, untrustworthy, and perhaps irredeemably corrupted, we can see how we might come to justify stopping them from taking power by any means. As a result, this friends-and-enemies approach to politics takes hold to the point that democratic institutions, such as free elections and press, are undermined. For this reason, many commentators now see Hungary as an authoritarian state, rather than a democracy.[25] While the political environment in the United States has not reached the extremes of Hungary, it is a useful illustration of the stakes of boxing in as part of the political domain.

Identity scripts are a powerful tool to mobilize voters to make change and to win power. But when deployed irresponsibly, these scripts can be used to box ourselves and others in, in ways that amplify the alignment of our identities, and exacerbate forms of distrust and animosity that threaten the core institutions of democracy. The more we find ourselves boxed in by tightened identity scripts, the greater likelihood that we will squarely face Rustin's dilemma as democratic agents. We see this dilemma in action with Silas House's effort to coordinate the collective pursuit of projects for progressive causes in a manner that is attentive to group heterogeneity.

Once we sort everyone into camps of friends and enemies, we lose sight of possible cooperation across that divide, and come to see politics as solely a matter of winning at the expense of the losers. The more that Maya and Bailey, and those like them, come to approach politics in these terms, the greater threat we face of losing our democratic institutions altogether in the name of winning against the enemy.

Winners and Losers

Roberto and Michael, like Maya and Bailey, are on opposite sides of an identity-cleavage. They both like to watch baseball, but they support rival teams. Again, much like Maya and Bailey, identification with their team is not just a matter of supporting their own, but also a form of opposition to the competition. Roberto and Michael both own shirts that express their dislike of their rivals: Roberto's reads "I support two teams, the Yankees and whoever beats the Red Sox," and Michael's reads "Keep Calm and Hate the Yankees."[26]

50   HOW DO WE GET BOXED IN?

While they both support their respective teams, their dislike for their rivals often exceeds their feeling of warmth toward their own team. If you run into Michael and Roberto during the baseball season, you are especially likely to find that this is the case when their team is performing worse than their rival.[27] Since the Red Sox and Yankees play in the same division, a successful season often requires consistently defeating one's rivals. And since there can only be one champion per season, winning the ultimate prize requires performing better than their rivals.

In this context of a sports rivalry, Roberto roots for his Yankees to win at the expense of the Red Sox and their fans like Michael, and vice versa. Their sports fandom amounts to a matter of winning and losing, and winning necessarily comes at the expense of their rivals. We can call this situation *zero-sum* because the Yankees winning only comes at the expense of the Red Sox losing and vice versa (assuming away other teams in the league, for a moment). Like sports, politics can also be competitive: activists compete to shape policy platforms and candidates, and parties compete to win elections. However, as we sort ourselves into friends and enemies, we make the mistake of seeing politics solely through the lens of competition. When the world consists of friends and enemies, and we sort ourselves into political rivals, rooting for our team at the expense of our enemies, democracy becomes solely a matter of winning and losing.

The sociologist Arlie Hochschild conducted a series of in-depth interviews to examine the perspective of Tea Party supporters in Louisiana and uncovered a winners-and-losers approach to politics. Based on the interviews she conducted, she put together what she calls a "deep story," which her respondents affirmed captures their experience—how they *feel*. The story centers on a metaphor about cutting in line:

> You are patiently standing in a middle of a long line leading up a hill, as in a pilgrimage. Others beside you seem like you—white,

older, Christian, predominantly male. Just over the brow of the hill is the American Dream, the goal of everyone in line. Then, look! Suddenly you see people cutting in line ahead of you! As they cut in, you seem to be being moved back. How can they just do that? Who are they?

Many are black. Through federal affirmative action plans, they are given preference for places in colleges and universities, apprenticeships, jobs, welfare payments, and free lunch programs. Others are cutting ahead too—uppity women seeking formerly all-male jobs, immigrants, refugees, and an expanding number of high-earning public sector workers, paid with your tax dollars. Where will it end?

As you wait in this unmoving line, you're asked to feel sorry for them all. People complain: Racism, Discrimination, Sexism. You hear stories of oppressed blacks, dominated women, weary immigrants, closeted gays, desperate refugees. But at some point, you say to yourself, you have to close the borders to human sympathy—especially if there are some among them who might bring harm.

You're a compassionate person. But now you've been asked to extend your sympathy to all the people who have cut in front of you. You've suffered a good deal yourself, but you aren't complaining about it or asking for help, you're proud to say. You believe in equal rights. But how about your own rights? Don't they count too? It's unfair.

Then you see a black president with the middle name Hussein, waving to the line cutters. He's on their side, not yours. He's their president, not yours. And isn't he a line-cutter too? How could the son of a struggling single mother pay for Columbia and Harvard? Maybe something has gone on in secret. And aren't the president and his liberal backers using your money to help themselves? You want to turn off the machine—the federal government—which he and liberals are using to push you back in line.[28]

52 HOW DO WE GET BOXED IN?

This deep story suggests a zero-sum form of reasoning, much like the rivalry between Roberto and Michael. According to the deep story, one has to wait in line to fulfill the goal of the American Dream. For those who experience politics this way, the perceived success of immigrants, refugees, black Americans, and some women involve a form of line-cutting. Members of those groups get their shot at the American Dream at the expense of white Americans living in rural white Louisiana. So, much like the Red Sox aiming to win the championship, their success can only come at the expense of their rivals. Making things better for people like them, and those they see as their political friends, necessarily involves winning at the expense of their political enemies.

Hochschild emphasizes that this story is a matter of feeling-as-if. As we saw in Chapter 1, tight identity scripts can box us in with respect to how to feel, and this can coincide with scripts about how to think, how to act, and whom to associate with. In this case, certain political scripts, such as being a Tea Party activist or being a "true" Republican, may come with the expectation of feeling that the government has let others cut in line. Furthermore, attempts to chastise those who feel this way may simply lead them toward other parties, candidates, and groups who will affirm their feelings. For example, Hochschild describes one respondent's view that political commentators on television, such as Christiane Amanpour of CNN, implicitly scold viewers like them and tell them how to feel. In this case, she was telling them to feel responsible for forms of global poverty.[29] Whether justified or not, it seems that a sense of being told how to feel can serve to affirm one's sense of the boundaries between friends and enemies and the feeling of loss at the expense of one's enemies.

These political emotions of winning and losing can shape public debates about policy. Consider immigration, which has been a hot button issue in the United States for many years. A belief in zero-sum relations between groups is associated with negative attitudes toward immigration.[30] As in the deep story, immigration-skeptics

IDENTITY TROUBLE 53

may worry that immigrants may gain access to opportunities for success, such as jobs, education, and government resources at the expense of native-born citizens. Yet there are some reasons to doubt that immigration is a zero-sum game. For example, some economic historians argue that high-immigration counties in the 19th- and early 20th-century United States greatly benefited from immigration, which contributed to increased industrialization, productivity, and innovation.[31] So, unlike two rivals competing for the same, singular championship, immigration could contribute to a better set of circumstances for all (or at least for many via economic growth). If this is the case, a winners-and-losers approach to immigration policy may actually inhibit forms of cooperation between different citizens who share goals like economic stability that are commonly associated with the American Dream.

These forms of zero-sum thinking and feeling about immigration can also contribute to further divisions between friends and enemies that threaten democratic stability. For example, some radical political parties, like the AfD (Alternative for Germany) in Germany, have leveraged these responses to immigration to draw support away from mainstream parties.[32] Some commentators have raised concerns about the AfD as a threat to democratic institutions in Germany. For example, some AfD members have drawn attention by trivializing Germany's Nazi past, and its leaders' rhetoric about refugees has been blamed for political violence.[33] Unlike FIDESZ in Hungary, the AfD is still in the minority in the German parliament, but it has presented enough of a threat that the German Federal Office for the Protection of the Constitution decided to place the party under surveillance.[34]

Of course, the economic effects of immigration are hard to determine, and economists continue to debate its effect on wages based on historical data.[35] But we do not have to settle on one particular view about the economics of immigration to accept the danger posed by approaching politics solely in terms of winners and losers. Unlike Roberto and Michael in their baseball fandom, winning

54 HOW DO WE GET BOXED IN?

at the expense of our rivals is not the only goal of politics, and we can impose serious costs on ourselves when we lose sight of this. When we come to see our co-partisans as enduring friends that always share in our victories at the expense of opposing partisans, who serve as our enduring enemies, we can miss out on the opportunities to advance initiatives that benefit co-partisans and opponents alike. We can also resist political compromises, whether on immigration or with regard to other policy debates around trade or economic inequality,[36] and be reluctant to cooperate with political rivals on shared goals, where zero-sum thinking is prevalent, but might be misleading. Finally, we can fail to address threats to key democratic institutions as long as they benefit our side, as is the case in Hungary. In other words, our desire to come out of an election as winners can supersede the importance of other goals, including sustaining democracy itself.[37]

Signals without Solutions

Rafael and Gianna are both enrolled in a survey, which they are initially told is about how people learn. After being screened for some basic mathematics and statistics skills, they are presented with a hypothetical study on gun control.[38] The study reports crime data in cities that did and did not ban concealed handguns in public. However, they are both presented with results that challenge their prior commitments. Rafael is a proud gun owner and values the ability to carry a concealed weapon, while Gianna is in favor of increased gun control and thinks that concealed carry should be banned. In the hypothetical study presented to Rafael, cities with concealed carry bans experience crime rate decreases, while cities where concealed carry is permitted do not. In the hypothetical study presented to Gianna, cities where concealed carry is permitted experience crime rate decreases, while cities where concealed carry is banned do not. Both Rafael and Gianna answer subsequent *factual* survey questions about the data they are presented with in ways that are inconsistent with the hypothetical study, but which confirm their prior commitments. So, despite the fact that the results presented to Rafael suggest that concealed carry bans decrease crime, he answers questions in accordance with the opposite trend. Despite the fact that the results presented to Gianna suggest that concealed carry bans increase crime, she answers questions in accordance with the opposite trend.

So far, Rafael and Gianna's survey responses are consistent with the explanation that they either do not understand the results they were presented with, or are biased in how they learn new information. That very well might be true for some people. But recall that Rafael and Gianna were screened for math and statistics skills—they do not lack the ability to make sense of the data they are presented with. And some research by social scientists suggests that had Rafael and Gianna been given a modest incentive, such as ten cents to one dollar per correctly answered question, they would have been much more likely to answer correctly.[39] At least in some cases, this research suggests, their answers are a way to express their support for or opposition to gun control.[40]

This phenomenon, expressive responding, need not even be tied to a particular commitment about a policy issue like reducing crime. Citizens can also be motivated to express a sense of belonging to a group in accordance with an identity script. For example, responses to survey questions about whether one "accepts" evolution may not indicate differences in understanding of evolution, but instead serve as a way of expressing a commitment to a particular conception of being religious or the proper respect for science.[41] Expressive responding can even extend to fairly superficial matters, such as the respective size of crowds attending the first presidential inaugurations of Barack Obama and Donald Trump.[42] Supporters of Donald Trump could clearly see in side-by-side comparisons that the crowd for Obama's first inauguration was larger, but answering otherwise served as a way of expressing

56 HOW DO WE GET BOXED IN?

their support for Trump and antipathy to his and their perceived opponents.

Even in cases that are not purely a matter of expressive responding, our group-identity attachments can hinder our ability to factor important information into our reasoning about politics. Some political psychology researchers argue that differences in public perceptions of scientific evidence of risks and expert consensus can be explained by the influence of our identity-defining cultural commitments. When we encounter evidence about, for example, the risks posed by climate change or nuclear power, we tend to formulate our beliefs in ways that will affirm our cultural worldviews.[43] When someone—who in virtue of their political group attachments ties rejection of anthropogenic climate change to their identity—encounters a question about the scientific consensus on climate change, they can experience this question as asking them "whose side are you on?" rather than as a genuine question about what they know.[44] This can make determinations of public understanding of science more difficult, but it also limits our ability to learn about and discuss scientific information. Our drive to affirm our group commitments makes us worse learners and reasoners.

This tendency toward expressing, or *signaling*, our group membership, and the commitments that align with our identities, can inhibit our ability to productively contribute to democratic politics. According to some theorists, democratic decision-making is valuable because it allows us to bring the variety of perspectives and sources of information spread throughout a society to bear on solving common problems.[45] Of course, we often disagree about how to solve problems, how important a given problem is, or even whether it is a problem at all. But the hope is that through information-gathering, discussion, experimentation, and then continued discussion, we can learn and develop solutions to shared problems over time. When we are boxed in by tightly scripted identities, our ability to contribute to shared problem-solving

IDENTITY TROUBLE 57

breaks down.[46] We see some forms of information, or perspectives that do not conform to our scripts, as threats. And, at times, we prioritize expressing our commitments in accordance with identity scripts *at the expense of contributing to problem-solving.*

Even if it turns out that either Rafael or Gianna is correct about the relationship between concealed carry and the crime rate, they both may have useful information bearing on developing solutions to related issues. Citizens like Rafael may provide information about the costs of additional forms of gun control and how those might be mitigated if further restrictions are put in place. Similarly, citizens like Gianna may provide information about the costs of existing conditions of gun accessibility, and how those costs might be mitigated even in the absence of levels of gun control that Gianna would prefer. But if Rafael and Gianna instead report factual judgments, whether in polls or in discussions with others, in ways that are meant to signal their identities, forms of input and discussion lack this nuanced information and fail to contribute to problem-solving.

Philosophers have also called attention to the costs of the related phenomenon of moral grandstanding. Often, political issues involve discussing questions of right and wrong and what we owe to one another. To address these issues, we need to discuss, and debate, matters of morality and not merely empirical matters about the expected effects of public policy. Moral grandstanding arises when citizens abuse moral talk and engage in it for the purpose of self-promotion.[47] Moral grandstanding can involve identity-signaling when self-promotion involves appearing as an especially devoted or impressive member of one's group. For example, when a representative, Bob Ney, had the US congressional cafeteria change the name of french fries to "freedom fries" due to French opposition to the US invasion of Iraq.[48] This sort of action allowed Ney to signal his patriotic identity and perhaps his partisan identity as a Republican, at a time when the war in Iraq was a source of both domestic and international political debate. It also allowed him to

58 HOW DO WE GET BOXED IN?

castigate those who were opposed to the war in Iraq, suggesting that they were opposed to freedom, and thereby making a moral mistake. While changing the names of foods in the congressional cafeteria can serve as a clear moral and political signal, which can be useful for politicians engaging in self-promotion, it does not contribute much to the kind of moral debate and discussion required to solve shared problems.

Philosophers disagree about their overall assessments of moral grandstanding and related phenomena like virtue signaling.[49] But when we engage in moral and political discussion in ways that prioritize signaling in contexts where boxing in is pervasive, the problems it poses are especially acute.[50] Because tightly scripted identities restrict the number of perspectives that are compatible with a particular identity, they may extend the list of commitments one must signal to be recognized as a "friend" to co-partisans. Rafael and Gianna may not just express their commitments on gun control with counterfactual responses to questions, they may do so with other issues to affirm their partisan and other sorted identities. And insofar as being perceived as true members of the corresponding groups is a source of social status, they have further reason to prioritize signaling over contributing to a search for solutions. When politics is seen as a matter of securing victory for one's friends at the expense of one's enemies, it can seem more important to signal our allegiances than to find solutions that can be accepted by our friends and some of our enemies.

The People? Which People?

In December 2006, then presidential-incumbent of Venezuela, Hugo Chávez, closed out his campaign with a speech referencing his standing with the people: "you are not going to re-elect Chávez really, you are going to reelect yourselves, the people will reelect the people. Chávez is nothing but an instrument of the people."[51] To Chávez's supporters, like Daniela, this was an engaging reminder to take part in the electoral process and left her with a sense of political empowerment that she had not felt before, given Venezuela's history of political corruption and the lack of political influence of poorer citizens. However, to Luís, who worked for a newspaper, this was a sign that his concerns about recent changes in media regulation, which could serve to limit public criticism of the government, placed him squarely outside the ranks of "the people" of Venezuela.[52]

The difference between Daniela's and Luís's reactions highlights the challenge posed by this rhetorical appeal to "the people." On the one hand, talk of empowering "the people" in contrast to corrupted elites can be a useful tool for mobilizing supporters. Previously alienated citizens, like Daniela, can become motivated to take part in political action that they would otherwise be unlikely to take, and feel that their concerns are being heard rather than ignored. On the other hand, such rhetoric can amplify the costs of boxing in by crowding out discussions of how and why different people disagree, as well as reinforce dismissals of one's political opponents as perceived enemies not worth engaging with. Citizens like Luís might share some concerns with Daniela about the history of political corruption, but if Chavez is understood by his supporters as "nothing but an instrument of the people," it is difficult to take up Luís's concerns about media regulation without being seen as an enemy of the people.

Some scholars have raised these sorts of concerns about a phenomenon called "populism." There is an ongoing debate about how best to define populism and what its core elements are. Minimally, it is an approach to politics whereby "the people" are understood to be "in a morally charged battle against the elites."[53] For example, one especially prominent use of the term "populist" refers to the People's Party, an influential third-party alternative to the Republicans and Democrats in the 19th-century United States. The

60   HOW DO WE GET BOXED IN?

People's Party assembled a coalition including indebted farmers, temperance activists, and urban wage workers in labor unions behind a policy platform including currency reforms, government ownership of railroads, and redistribution of wealth.[54] The People's Party claimed to be a party worthy of the people's trust, in contrast to the corruption and concentration of wealth represented by the two dominant parties.[55] In other words, they saw their role in politics as waging a morally charged battle on behalf of the people against the elites. This kind of mobilization of alienated constituencies to advance their (shared) interests demonstrates the power of populist politics and its associated rhetorical moves, which Daniela felt in Venezuela over one hundred years later.

While they may not be used in every instance of populist politics, populism is associated with tight scripts about "the people" and their interests, which should make us wary of populism despite its potential mobilization benefits. In their portrayal of "the people" opposed to the elites, populists can misleadingly portray the people as homogenous and dismiss those who disagree with them as illegitimate, thereby glossing over forms of disagreement and diversity that should be discussed and negotiated.[56] Much like Chávez's description of being an instrument of the people, it is commonplace for elected officials to speak of their support in terms of "the will of the people." For example, when discussing migration and refugee policy, Viktor Orbán, the prime minister of Hungary, called for stronger borders by stating that "Europeans have a clear will," and that "2018 will be the year of the restoration of the will of the people in Europe."[57]

Public opinion polling in 2018 suggested a more complicated picture. While there were clear signs of disapproval of how the European Union had handled refugee issues, there were also signs of substantial support for "taking in refugees from countries where people are fleeing from violence and war." While it is true that the citizens of Orbán's home country expressed opposition to this idea at much higher rates than in other parts of Europe, even

IDENTITY TROUBLE   61

32% of Hungarians polled expressed support. Orbán's statement masks this difference of perspective. This concern also applies to his statement about Europe because there were much higher rates of support for taking in refugees, in Spain (86%), the Netherlands (83%), and Sweden (81%). Those in support of taking in refugees were also citizens of the EU and were part of "the people" taking part in political decision-making. As in this case, populist rhetoric can serve to sidestep engaging with this more complicated set of perspectives by dismissing those who disagree as out of step with the "will of the people."

In addition to reinforcing a friends-and-enemies mindset, populist tight scripts' misleading portrayals of "the people" can also lead us to misunderstand our shared problems and political disagreements. In the United States, one kind of friends-and-enemies divide is the urban-rural divide. Urban America is seen as racially diverse and Democrat-supporting, while rural America is seen as white and Republican. This divide can then serve as the basis for populist political mobilization. Rural citizens are mobilized with appeals to "real Americans" in contrast to the morally corrupted elites thriving and/or relying on wasteful government spending in urban centers. Urban citizens are mobilized to combat political elites, who have duped ignorant rural voters into stopping American progress toward a more cosmopolitan and diverse ideal. In both cases, "the people" are called to take part in a morally charged struggle against corrupted elites, of one kind or another.[58] Yet these scripts box us into a limited understanding of "the people" in urban and rural areas. These scripts are not conducive to discussing the interests of the 21% of rural Americans who are people of color, the economic interdependence of rural and urban areas, or the shared challenges in both rural and urban areas posed by persistent poverty.[59] By trying to mobilize *the* people, we end up focusing on our perception of who counts as *our* people, and lose sight of the diversity and similarities of *many different* groups of people.

Skeptics and Optimists

In light of the phenomena we have described—sorting ourselves into friends and enemies, winners-and-losers mindsets, prioritizing identity-signaling over crafting solutions, and restrictive scripts about "the people"—many authors worry that democracies face identity trouble. They worry that the pervasive influence of collective identity scripts on political reasoning and action threatens the stability and success of existing democracies. We call these authors "identity skeptics" because they are skeptical that our identity attachments contribute to democracy.

These skeptical concerns take a few forms. First, some skeptics worry that our identity attachments make us worse political reasoners.[60] Like Rafael and Gianna, we can end up placing priority on signaling loyalty to our perceived political friends over learning about how to advance our goals through political action, and how policy proposals or political candidates may offer solutions to our problems. We may seek out information that we expect to give us good news about ourselves and make us feel like we are on the winning team, but which may actually give us a biased impression of the evidence about different policy proposals. When tight scripts box us in with respect to how we think and feel in the political domain, we can be left in a worse position to figure out how to advance our goals and address our problems through political action.

Second, skeptics worry that our identity attachments make collective action more difficult.[61] When we are tightly sorted into camps of friends and enemies, it can be difficult to work together in large coalitions with many stakeholders to address complex challenges such as climate change and economic inequality. Many challenges in the political domain require working with many diverse others, and when we are boxed in with regard to whom we associate with, it can be difficult to do so successfully. Although we need not embrace such identities to work with others, these skeptics worry about us losing sight of the superordinate identities that bind us together despite our differences, either at the national level as Americans and Australians, for example, or at the international level with shared commitments to protect human rights, for instance.

If our identity attachments make us worse reasoners and cooperators, this would seem to make our democracies less effective. But as these phenomena are sustained and grow increasingly severe over time, they may start to undermine the stability of democratic institutions themselves.[62] When we get swept up in populist narratives about enemies of the people, we can start to deride our political opposition as illegitimate and start to question the legitimacy of elections themselves. Without much contact and learning from those whom we perceive as enemies, we can become less likely to support their political rights. So, in the extreme, identity skeptics worry that our attachments to our identities can supersede our commitments to sustaining democratic institutions altogether.

These identity skeptics are challenged by identity optimists, who emphasize the ways that identity scripts facilitate our political reasoning and activity.[63] While some identities can be too tightly scripted, identity attachments also help us to navigate complex informational environments. It can be difficult for individual citizens to know how to evaluate candidates for political office or the particular policy proposals they endorse. Identity-based cues can help us to learn about candidates and policy platforms. Learning that an individual or organization we trust, such as a local community leader or a labor union, has endorsed a candidate or policy proposal might tell us about whether it aligns with our own goals and values. For example, there is some evidence that endorsement of non-black candidates by black leaders in local US elections increases black voter support for those candidates.[64]

Even partisan identities, which some skeptics are especially concerned about, can provide voters with helpful information about the policies that particular candidates are likely to support. Such cues can even serve as a source of information of whom

64   HOW DO WE GET BOXED IN?

not to support. For example, researchers found that a liberal advocacy group's endorsement of and canvassing for Democratic candidates in Pennsylvania elections helped Republican voters determine whom not to vote for, and helped those with less awareness of politics vote as if they were better informed.[65] For this reason, many voters, perhaps especially those who feel most alienated by the political domain, would face a tougher challenge when deciding how to vote and take political action without partisan cues.[66]

As we saw with populist rhetoric, identity scripts can also be useful for mobilizing citizens to take political action, especially among groups who have been alienated and marginalized. For this reason, some optimists appeal to the value of identity attachments for mobilizing citizens to take part in political decision-making, such as by voting or contacting elected officials. Candidates who share a salient identity with a certain group of voters have been shown, at least under certain conditions, to increase electoral turnout among those voters. For example, black Democrat candidates tend to increase black voter turnout in congressional elections.[67]

Sharing a salient identity can also lead to greater voter contact. Barney Frank, the first congressperson to publicly come out as gay, described being contacted by LGBTQ citizens across the country, even when they were not his constituents.[68] Optimists can also point out that these identity-based connections are not merely symbolic. There is evidence that elected officials in the United States who share identities with racial, gender, and veteran constituencies work to advance the goals of those constituencies, even in work that is less public-facing, such as contacting administrative agencies.[69] In addition to helping citizens learn about their political environment, optimists argue that identity attachments can also help to increase valuable political participation, especially among marginalized groups and especially when the political rights of marginalized groups are under threat.[70]

IDENTITY TROUBLE 65

To take stock, identity skeptics take a look at the challenges posed by tightly scripted identities and conclude that our identity attachments leave us worse off in the political domain. Optimists, in contrast, argue that identity attachments are an indispensable tool, as they enable us to learn about and take part in political decision-making. This debate is not merely about assessing our current situation. It is also about what we should do in response to it. If we reach a skeptical conclusion, we may conclude that we should try to limit the influence of our identity attachments on our political decision-making. We should de-emphasize attempts to organize ourselves on the basis of identities, perhaps especially those that have become tightly scripted. Or if that is not possible, we may grow more pessimistic about the prospects for democracy and try to limit the scope of democratic decision-making.[71] If the optimists are right, these forms of action would be misguided. By trying to diminish the influence of identity scripts, we can make taking part in politics harder, and perhaps diminish the voices of those who are most marginalized. To settle this debate about the value of identity attachments in politics and to figure out what to do about them, we first need to get clear on what we want democracy to do for us, and why we should think we are facing identity trouble under our current circumstances.

Shared Goals

What is it about tightly scripted identities that leads to identity trouble in politics? After all, as we saw in Chapter 1, people can be boxed in when working as jazz musicians and when supporting their favorite sports teams, so boxing in is not unique to political matters such as voting, talking about politics, or protesting. One answer is that a friends-and-enemies mindset, as well as the other phenomena we describe in this chapter, is especially concerning in light of the *stakes* of political activity in a democracy. Sometimes,

66 HOW DO WE GET BOXED IN?

due to environmental, economic, or political crises, democratic citizens and their governments must engage in collective problem-solving. One major instance in recent memory was the advent of the COVID-19 pandemic at the end of 2019 and beginning of 2020. The pandemic posed a major threat (of illness and death) and a corresponding set of challenges for governments, which had to formulate policy responses and communicate guidance to citizens, and for citizens themselves, who had to make decisions about their own behavior and evaluate public officials' responses.

In the United States, some citizens (including government officials) were boxed in by tight identity scripts, which inhibited a successful response and the ability to learn over time about how best to do so. The familiar social fault lines of partisan division re-emerged with respect to citizens' behavior, support or opposition to policy responses, and evaluations of the government. Republicans were less likely to wear masks and engage in social distancing than Democrats, who were more likely to do so.[72] Signs of protective behaviors could then be used to identify friends and enemies and interact accordingly: a laboratory experiment conducted during the pandemic found that maskless participants were more likely to cooperate with those without masks (and vice versa).[73] Public health-related behaviors became ways of signaling group loyalty and, as we saw with Rafael and Gianna, when this happens our attention turns away from finding solutions. Instead, the pandemic became another battleground through which citizens felt they could secure victories for their friends at the expense of their enemies.

Political science research on the start of the pandemic also suggests that these tight scripts were advanced and strengthened by political elites.[74] Much like the danger posed by populist rhetoric, public officials and public political commentators shaped how we talked about the challenges we faced and how we responded to the different perspectives, values, and goals of different groups of citizens. And many public figures doubled down on our friends-and-enemies fault lines and promoted or encouraged tight identity scripts; this left us further boxed in.

Tragically, the COVID-19 pandemic caused many deaths. Some were preventable with better democratic problem-solving. If public health measures could have been discussed, communicated, and adopted without the influence of tight identity scripts, such as whether Republicans or Democrats wear masks and social distance, we would have all been in a better position to advance a crucial goal that we all share—to protect our health and safety. Despite what an approach to politics in terms of winners and losers suggests, the pandemic was not a zero-sum situation. Everyone stood to gain from a better environment for determining the best responses to health and safety threats posed by the pandemic.

The United States was not the only country that experienced a troubling response to the pandemic. Brazil provides an especially striking example of polarizing elite rhetoric, which has coincided with threats to the stability of democracy itself. The Brazilian president, Jair Bolsonaro, repeatedly downplayed the severity of the COVID-19 virus, comparing it to a "little cold" or "little flu" and mocking mask-wearers with a homophobic slur. Then, after contracting the virus in July 2020, Bolsonaro attributed his mild case to hydroxychloroquine, a discredited remedy. These forms of rhetoric were accompanied by a series of conflicts between different branches of the government, which have raised concerns about the ongoing stability of Brazilian democracy. Bolsonaro repeatedly quarreled with the health ministry. He replaced the health minister in April 2020. And due to further disagreements, this new minister resigned four weeks later. In addition, Bolsonaro encouraged and joined protests calling for the forced closure of the legislative and judicial branches due to disagreements about the policy response to the pandemic.[75] Perhaps unsurprisingly given this institutional backdrop, Brazil's policy response to the pandemic was unsuccessful, and into 2021, Brazil was seen as one of the epicenters of

68   HOW DO WE GET BOXED IN?

the pandemic with high numbers of deaths and severe strains on hospital capacity.[76]

When our politics are shaped by tightly scripted identities, we are left unable to respond to crises. This prevents us from achieving a key function of democratic decision-making: collective problem-solving to advance shared goals.[77] This is an instance of democratic failure. Rather than functioning as a way to collect public input and solve problems in a justified manner, democratic decision-making resulted in an identity-driven competition that left us all worse off. At the start of the COVID-19 pandemic, we failed to advance even a fairly basic shared goal of protecting citizens' health and safety. Given the way that identity scripts inhibited the response to this crisis, we should not be so naive as to think that the path to identity optimism is straightforward, despite the potential benefits of our identity attachments. The identity trouble in contemporary democracies like the United States and Brazil is perilous. When the stakes are high in times of crisis, we face serious consequences if we do not address it.

Is Unity All We Need?

To overcome these challenges—to restore the soul and to secure the future of America—requires more than words. It requires that most elusive of things in a democracy: Unity. Unity. Unity. . . . Today, on this January day, my whole soul is in this: Bringing America together. Uniting our people. And uniting our nation.

This quote comes from Joe Biden's inauguration speech in January 2021. He gave this speech after a highly contested presidential election, following an attack on the US Capitol meant to stop the certification of its results, and facing the democratic failures of the nation's response to the COVID-19 pandemic. While the absence of

IDENTITY TROUBLE   69

unity may have been especially salient under these circumstances, a call for unity was not completely new. Calls for unity, of one kind or another, are hallmarks of elected officials' public statements. They are not wholly empty either. As we have seen, there is something valuable about being able to maintain our commitment to democratic institutions and our shared problem-solving capacity despite deep-seated social divisions.

Some skeptics suggest that we can solve identity trouble by focusing on what unifies us rather than what which divides us.[78] This might involve dropping identity-talk in politics as much as possible and focusing instead on a superordinate identity that unifies us, such as being Americans. This line of reasoning has a clear appeal; if democracies are facing identity trouble, they should excise the identities that are causing that trouble. It is also an approach that many citizens find intuitively appealing, as evidenced by its ubiquity in political speeches.

One problem with an approach merely focusing on unity is that it can lead to constraints similar to those imposed by populist rhetoric. Much like appeals to a homogenous conception of "the people," emphasizing unity can lead to failures to be responsive to the interests of those who do not match the dominant conception of who "the people" are. This can be true even in relatively small communities. For example, Jane Mansbridge has written about the use of direct democracy in a small Vermont town, where its residents meet to make decisions about matters such as taxes, recreation services, and zoning.[79] While everyone in the town had the formal opportunity to attend these meetings, she found that the interests of different members of the town were not equally represented. This was in part due to differences in comfort speaking during the meetings, as some residents feared being made fun of, or concerns about intragroup conflict, as well as differences in availability for meetings held during the day.[80] When interests between residents conflicted, long-time residents, older residents, and wealthier residents tended to be better represented.[81]

70   HOW DO WE GET BOXED IN?

However, Mansbridge found that working-class residents found it useful to meet the night before meetings to discuss strategy and offer mutual support.[82] By identifying themselves as a distinctive group apart from the broader array of residents of the town, these working-class residents were better positioned to reason about their particular goals (and their relationship to the broader goals of the community) and empower themselves to represent their perspective to the broader community. Yet Mansbridge notes that because the residents of the town had a hard time recognizing conflicts of interest, they often failed to take conscious action to reduce disparities in representation.[83]

A more general lesson we can draw from this example is that it can be valuable for like-minded citizens or similarly situated ones to collaborate in spaces separate from the broader community. This can allow subsets of citizens to better understand their situation and make their perspective more salient when it has not been adequately represented.[84] Identity scripts provide a means of organizing around a shared perspective or similar situation. However, for this form of internal grouping to be most effective, it also requires uptake from and engagement with the broader community. Otherwise, disparities of representation can go unaddressed and a friends-and-enemies line of division can emerge. A unity response to identity trouble risks the former while attempting to avoid the latter. If this issue arises in small towns in Vermont, it should be all the more pressing in much bigger and more diverse populations.

So, while appeals to unity can be useful for elected officials looking to preserve commitments to democracy in the face of disagreement, these appeals do not provide a sufficient response to our identity trouble. When identity differences align with differences in empowerment, reflect differences of backgrounds, or express differences of perspective, we cannot expect an emphasis on unity to provide a path out of being boxed in. We can expect citizens to cling to their identity attachments, as they are communicating an important set of facts about the current political landscape, and even if not, a unity strategy risks replacing one limitation of democracy with multiple others.

Mapping the Trouble

Tightly scripted identities constrain how we think and feel, how we act, and whom we associate with. We have seen that being boxed in by tight scripts is not just a concern for our lives as individuals. It is also a major concern for our lives as political agents. When it comes to politics, the costs of boxing in occur on a mass scale and can be amplified. This chapter highlights four tendencies of political behavior and reasoning. And we have analyzed them as constitutive components of identity trouble. We sort ourselves into pervasive fault lines by adopting friends and enemies. We fall into the trap of zero-sum reasoning and try to secure victory for our perceived friends at the expense of our perceived enemies—resulting in a winners-and-losers mindset. We focus on and prioritize signaling our group loyalty rather than working to find solutions. We mistakenly think of the true people as homogenous and start to discredit our perceived enemies as morally illegitimate.

These four components of identity trouble lead to a "boxing in ethos." And there is a reinforcing loop at work here: an environment where boxing in via tight scripts is pervasive is an environment of identity trouble, and individuals within such an environment can adopt a boxing in ethos that carries the identity trouble into the future. So, when this ethos is operative in the political domain, not only are we individually constrained, but our ability to advance shared goals now and in the future is diminished too. Boxing in, in the political domain, makes us worse problem-solvers and this can be a high cost to pay, especially in times of crisis.

Responding to identity trouble requires a way to restore and maintain our problem-solving capabilities, by sustaining

72 HOW DO WE GET BOXED IN?

successful democratic cooperation, despite the threat of tightly scripted identities. We have seen identity skeptics propose a way out of the trouble by aiming to reduce the influence of identities in the political domain, but this approach is not properly responsive to all of the benefits that our identities realize or to the central role that they play in organizing our lives. In addition, given the magnitude of the identity trouble we currently face, we cannot be satisfied with a naive path to optimism about our identities either. This book charts a narrow path forward, hoping to avoid the real dangers that both sides of this debate have identified. We respond to identity trouble, and the ethos of boxing in, without diminishing identities altogether.

As we will discuss in the next two chapters, collective identities are complex and dynamic. This makes successfully using them to engage in political reasoning and activity very demanding. To settle this debate between skeptics and optimists, we must know more about what we need to break free from being boxed in.

PART II

WHAT DO WE NEED TO BREAK FREE?

3

How Identity Works

Collective Identities

"Latinx soy yo, Abuelo," said Paola Ramos, when coming out as Latinx to Grandfather Carlos.[1] Ramos, a political correspondent, writes about not using the word "gay" to describe preference for lovers, not fitting in at "Hispanic Group Meetings," and about questioning Latina identity notwithstanding having Mexican roots and growing up in Madrid and Miami's Cuban community. Ramos had no problem with using the labels "queer," "Latina," "Cuban," "Mexican," and "first-generation American," but did not really own them as capturing the whole self. The label "Latinx" was liberating. Ramos says: "That addendum, the 'x,' set free the parts of myself that had deviated from the norms and traditions of the Latino culture I grew up in."[2]

A lesson here is that collective identities provide a socially developed script that individuals may feel obliged to follow. But this script, which is associated with a label with assigned meanings, can leave them feeling boxed in. And when individuals deviate from the script, trouble may arise. A person may experience dissonance associated with flouting settled norms or expectations. However, as Ramos makes clear, breaking free from these norms can be a source of liberation. Although labels contribute to how we view ourselves, how we answer the question "who am I?", and how we are viewed by others, a particular label may not tell the whole story or, as in this case, it may be in tension with other ways of understanding who we are.

Boxed In. Derrick Darby and Eduardo J. Martinez, Oxford University Press. © Oxford University Press 2024.
DOI: 10.1093/9780197620236 003.0004

76 WHAT DO WE NEED TO BREAK FREE?

The presence, or absence, of the feelings of dissonance that Ramos experienced can lead to different degrees of identification with an existing identity label. For example, in a 2013 survey, respondents were queried about their beliefs regarding white Americans in the United States, and their responses indicate a variety of levels of identification with white identity. Consider the contrast between these two responses:

- "Because I identify and am proud to be white, I see all the struggles that minorities go through and I thank god every day that I do not have to face those types of situations."
- "Maybe my identity as a member of specific European ethnicities is significant to me, but not the color of my skin. That's just asinine. The only people who are ever 'proud' of being white are neo nazis, KKK members, or various unaffiliated hicks."[3]

These respondents differ with respect to the role that white identity plays in their self-understanding. The first respondent notes that their white identity is salient to them in light of the advantages they experience relative to minorities. They not only identify with but also take pride in their white identity. In contrast, the second respondent rejects white identity as insignificant to them, in contrast with their identification with specific ethnicities. This is an example of how two individuals who might both fit the script for a given identity label can have different degrees of identification with it.

Apart from serving as sources of identification, the labels we use to identity one another can also make a difference to how we are treated by others. Moreover, being boxed in by a collective identity that is too tightly scripted may be a serious obstacle to taking up shared projects with others. The day after Joe Biden was sworn in as president, the *New York Times* ran a piece on the three types of Republicans that would fight for the future of the party.[4] The premise was that the party was fractured, and members had sharp political differences. The "Never Trumpers" were anti-Trump from the beginning and claimed that he was the wrong choice for the party. The "RINOs" (Republican in name only) were not anti-Trump but did things that went against his wishes or were viewed as "spineless" and "soft" by his followers. This included political officials who refused to stop the formal certification of the 2020 election or to support efforts to void votes in contested states. The "Trump Republicans" supported him fully as well as his efforts to spread claims of voter fraud and to prevent Biden from assuming the presidency. The latter treat those in the first two categories with more hostility and contempt.[5] Moreover, the tightness of these scripts about what it is to be a Republican may be an obstacle to the pursuit of shared projects, such as getting particular legislation passed.

Being Latinx, white, or Republican are—along with other illustrations we have discussed—instances of collective identities we share with others. Breaking free from identities that are too tightly scripted, and avoiding the identity trouble associated with this phenomenon, requires a deeper understanding of how identities work. This chapter provides it by drawing on an illuminating taxonomy that describes three core practices around which identities take shape. We use it to make the point that collective identities are dynamic. Identity group members will be situated differently based on variations in labeling, identification, and treatment-as practices. The intragroup heterogeneity that results from this variation poses challenges for the collective pursuit of life-shaping projects. But it also provides opportunities for collective self-authorship, which is vital for making identities safe for democratic accountability. Before we can address what collective self-authorship processes involve and identify the tools we need to break free from tight scripts (Chapter 4), and how we actually break free with them by taking up certain civic responsibilities (Chapters 5 and 6), we must comprehend how collective identities work and why their dynamic nature cannot be ignored.

An Illuminating Taxonomy

Charlie Parker's drive to become a jazz musician was a choice about how to shape his life. It served to define, prioritize, and profoundly shape his projects. Mastering the alto sax, playing techniques, learning tunes, understanding music theory, and doing other things that musicians do became projects central to his life-shaping plan. Choosing how to shape the one life we have to live is an act of *self-authorship*.[6] It is a manifestation of our agency. Philosophers could be concerned with understanding the nature of self-authorship per se or, more specifically, with understanding the relationship between self-authorship and collective identity categories. We are most interested in the latter. Specifically, we ask: How do collective identities contribute to how we shape our lives? When we understand this, we can appreciate why identity heterogeneity needs to be managed successfully if we are to engage in the collective pursuit of certain life-shaping projects.

Bird's choice to become a jazz musician was an act of self-authorship. The same can be said of Jay-Z's choice to become a rapper and—later in life—a music mogul. This also goes for Ralph Ellison's decision to be a writer. These choices also gave rise to projects that became central to their life-shaping plans. As authors of our own lives, we pursue projects and with this, a story unfolds about who we are and what we want. One way to think about the relationship between self-authorship and collective identity categories, which we find insightful, is to see the latter as providing the social raw material that we use to shape our lives and tell our stories. Bird identified as a jazzman. Jay-Z identified as a rapper. Ellison identified as a writer. In so doing, each man had an answer to the question: Who am I? Each could rely upon content carried by these ready-made categories to author their respective life-shaping plans and to write their stories.

Of course these identities do not tell the whole story of who they are or what they wanted out of life. Bird, Jay-Z, and Ellison identified with other identity scripts. But these are important ones for understanding their lives and stories, nonetheless. Identities can be more or less central to our overarching life-shaping plan. And over time they can change in relative importance to this plan. Still, we identify ourselves and others in many ways that develop these biographical stories and give content to our life plans.[7] We identify as jazz musicians, rappers, and writers. We also identify as black and as white, as Puerto Rican and as Cuban American, as Protestant and as Catholic, as union members and as entrepreneurs, as New Yorkers and as Tejanos, as liberals and as conservatives, as Democrats and as Republicans, as men and as women, as gender-conforming and as transgender, and in countless other ways. Some ways of identifying are familiar, other ways of identifying are less familiar. Some ways of identifying are more consequential politically and socially, while others are less so.

In Chapter 1 we argued that individuals can be boxed in when our collective identities are scripted too tightly—making it hard to combine some identities into a unified life plan. Being boxed in is not only about how we act. It is also about how we think or feel and about who we should or should not associate with. For example, recalling a case we introduced in the previous chapter, novelist Silas House may be pressured by his fellow Democrats not to associate with fellow Kentuckians who have more conservative leanings, which may leave him boxed in. Part of the trouble with collective identities stems from their being overly restrictive. And this happens when they are scripted too tightly. Our account of how to break free from tight scripts that can box us in, and how to avoid the identity trouble that arises from this, relies upon a philosophical understanding of how collective identities can contribute to resisting being boxed in through what we call collective self-authorship. This extends the notion of self-authorship to efforts to coordinate our life-shaping projects with others. Before laying this out in the next chapter, here we consider three general features of collective identities to describe how they work, drawing

80 WHAT DO WE NEED TO BREAK FREE?

on a taxonomy found in the work of philosopher Kwame Anthony Appiah.[8]

According to Appiah, the structure of our identities, which shape our individual and collective projects, emerge around three core practices: *labeling, identification,* and *treatment-as*.[9] We affix labels such as black and white, men and women, veterans and non-veterans, Ewes, Jains, or *kothis* that carry public meaning. Our labeling can be imprecise. It can evolve. Yet labeling invokes criteria by which we recognize ourselves or others as members of some group. Internalization happens when someone owns a label and views themselves as part of the group identified by it. We can also describe this as a label being "salient" for its bearer. For instance, the first white respondent in the aforementioned survey clearly internalized the label. This can happen to a greater or lesser extent, making labels more or less salient to their self-understanding. Internalization influences how someone sees the world, how they behave, and how they respond to others. Whether or not someone internalizes a label, being publicly recognized as a member of a group bears on how one is (or is not) treated. Being treated as black, for instance, can lead to victimization by police brutality—even if one only weakly identifies with being black. These three core practices, or features, partly account for what makes collective identities complex and dynamic.

Race, ethnicity, nationality, gender, religion, and sexuality are among the most salient and politically consequential collective identity attachments. However, all identities, including ones rooted in sports rivalries, such as the one between fans of US college football teams, the Michigan Wolverines and Ohio State Buckeyes, are tools for shaping our lives. If life-shaping is a process of self-authorship, as Appiah maintains, collective identities provide ready-made scripts we use to write the story, and the three core practices help us do this. They help us do the work of collective identity construction. We use them to define ourselves and others. They are vital to our agency.[10] We use them to shape our life

HOW IDENTITY WORKS   81

plans—in self-interested ways, at times, and working collectively with others, coordinating our life plans through collective projects, at other times. This latter point is crucial for the next chapter. There we will expand on how to manage the heterogeneity that comes into view after applying Appiah's taxonomy to understand the structure of identities. Another task at hand is to reference these three core practices to illuminate the dynamic nature of collective identities. And later, in Part III of the book, this work will inform our account of the civic responsibilities that citizens should take up to make identities safe for democracy.[11]

There are two kinds of self-authorship: individual and collective. Appiah stresses the value of pursuing a mode of living in which one is self-authored. *Individual self-authorship* amounts to selecting one's own life plan. In the course of engaging in individual self-authorship, we often need to coordinate with others; for example, sports fans coordinating on particular banners and chants to cheer on their team, or labor union members coordinating on a campaign to bargain for a new contract.

We engage in *collective self-authorship* (CSA) when we coordinate with other self-authors to pursue life-shaping projects under the banner of an identity or with an identity-like connection. An identity-like connection involves one of the three components of Appiah's taxonomy: a shared label, mutual identification, and/ or shared treatment-as. We note this possibility because some processes of CSA do not quite reach the level of establishing a fully formed identity, yet still involve the coordinated pursuit of projects. For instance, workers at the same job site might face similar treatment from management and mutually identify, but they may not have a distinctive label under which to unify their bargaining campaign. These workers could still engage in CSA by pursuing collective projects, such as fighting for better working conditions, with their identity-like connection binding the group together. Yet we could also imagine that through repeated struggles for better conditions, the workers at this job site come to identify with their

82 WHAT DO WE NEED TO BREAK FREE?

union local, which then becomes a significant collective identity for them. So CSA is often pursued under the banner of an identity, but sometimes it is just one or two parts of the taxonomy of identity-shaping practices that bind the group together.

We shall have much more to say about CSA in Chapter 4. Indeed, as we will argue, it is essential for understanding what is required to break free from identities that are overly restrictive. But first we must consider each element of the taxonomy in more detail.

Labeling

Paola Ramos is not alone in preferring to use the label "Latinx." It was liberating. For others, using this label rather than "Latino" is also a matter of respect and inclusivity. A black college student from the South attending school in California, and using the label "Latino" to describe friends back home, recalls being corrected by a white student who remarks: "We say 'Latinx' here because we respect trans people."[12] For any of the labels that we use to mark collective identities, whether they be garden variety labels referring to ethnicity, gender, race, or sexuality or others that do not first come to mind, such as musicians, rappers, writers, or artists, we must ask certain questions. What do these labels mean? How do we apply them? What value do they have? Understanding what these labels mean is vital for determining who does and does not count as the type of person captured by the label. But this is not always a simple matter. And applying labels is not without controversy. It is tempting to think that the black student was making a mistake—using the wrong label to identify friends back home. But if we dig deeper we might find that they had good reason to use Latino rather than Latinx to refer to friends back home. The labeling practices in the American South may vary from those in the American West. So geography may matter. Politics may also matter. And both may factor into illuminating the meaning and usage that accounts for why the black student used "Latino" and not "Latinx."

In recent years, much has been made of the growing support of the GOP by Hispanic voters, and the difficulties that Democrats have had in getting their support at the polls. Some of these voters describe feeling "alienated by progressive labels and mottos like 'Latinx'" and they use this to explain the rightward drift of Hispanic voters.[13] Moreover, it has been argued that this label, created as a gender-neutral term, most commonly used by media, political, and educated elites, is far less common in Spanish-speaking communities, where only 3 percent of Hispanics use it, according to a 2020 Pew Research study.[14] Some Hispanic voters who reject the Latinx label as a fitting description of their group identity, have explained their partisan preferences as motivated by what they see as a closer alignment between what they most value, God, family, and country, and the issues that they care about, jobs, immigration, and education, and the conservative agenda.[15] And, in some cases, Hispanics are moving to the extreme right, aligning themselves with Trump Republicans, who they believe more closely support their values and are more committed to defending them.[16] The black student's friends back home in the South may refer to themselves using the label "Latino" and live in Hispanic communities where this is the dominant linguistic usage. And their reasons for using this label may be similar to the ones listed here.

Of course geography and politics are not the only factors that shape the meaning we assign to labels and how we apply them. We are now seeing how world events, particularly the war in Ukraine, is impacting the use of labels that identify persons by nationality.[17] Because collective identities also bear on how we are treated by others, anti-Russian sentiment has made immigrants from the former Soviet bloc anxious about being called Russian, despite shared language, culture, and history. Some of the 1.2 million immigrants from the former USSR living in the United States now prefer using labels identified with their countries of origin,

84   WHAT DO WE NEED TO BREAK FREE?

such as Ukraine, Belarus, Uzbekistan, and so forth. As one immigrant from Moldova put it, when asked about this rethinking of identity, "The old self-identity crumbles under the weight of the unthinkable and unimaginable. A new self-identity as Ukrainians, Moldovans, and Georgians emerges." And another immigrant from Ukraine to the United States, upset about the Russian invasion and concerned about being associated with the aggressor because she speaks Russian, had this to say: "I have always loved Russian culture, music, dance. But I don't want to be called Russian anymore." On the other side, Russian president Vladimir Putin justifies the invasion by claiming that Ukrainians are part of the Slavic Russian nation precisely because they are united by language, culture, and blood. So, for him, the Russian-Ukrainian war is about consolidating an ethno-national identity.[18]

To further illustrate the controversy that can crop up in assigning meaning to labels, consider the case of Ritchie Torres. In the aftermath of the George Floyd murder by Minneapolis police officers, mass protests against police brutality sprang up across the United States and around the world during the summer of 2020. We also witnessed large numbers of Americans looking to join forces with others in the battle for racial justice and political change. At the time, Ritchie Torres, a Democratic candidate for New York's 15th Congressional District, expressed a frustration captured by the title of his *Washington Post* op-ed: "I'm Afro-Latino, but I can't join both the black and Hispanic caucuses in Congress. That must change."[19] Torres wondered whether he would be accepted for who he was— a gay man, an Afro-Latino, and a millennial—when he joined his Congressional colleagues. Although he does not take this up, some of his constituents may have similar concerns about whether they should accept Torres as their representative.[20]

Torres knew that not everyone sees eye-to-eye on who is or is not black in America. When asked, "Who shall be among us?" and "What is required of us?" individuals who self-identify as black or who are identified by others as black will surely have different

HOW IDENTITY WORKS   85

answers to these questions. Indeed, some may draw a hard distinction between African Americans and Afro-Latinos, notwithstanding the fact that the latter may be born and raised in the United States. Torres uses the label "Afro-Latino." This is how he self-identifies. However, this label has social meaning about which there might be disagreement. And he anticipates that members of the Congressional Black Caucus will reject his membership due, in large part, to disagreement over what it means to be black in America. They will impose an either/or binary—you are black or Latino but not both—that Torres categorically rejects as being at odds with how he understands the meaning of the label, as well as with how he identifies himself and with his treatment in the real world. He identifies with the racial and ethnic aspects of this label; both aspects are salient for him. As he puts it, "I am both black and Latino—there's no need to artificially barricade one from the other."

Settling the meaning behind labels can be complicated. Appiah gives us many colorful examples of collective identities and the labels used to describe them; for example, the label "Ewe," which is used to identify persons who speak dialects of "Ewe," a language spoken by most people living in Ghana or Toga.[21] In some cases, the meaning of ethnic labels can be cut and dry. So, for example, if both of your parents are Ewe, then so are you. But, as Appiah notes, complications can arise, as when we must decide whether someone who has only one Ewe parent, and who has never learned an Ewe dialect, can be rightly described as Ewe. We might draw an analogy, though not a perfect one, with Afro-Latino by seeing a complication in meaning when someone has only one parent who identifies (or is identified) as black, and another who identifies (or is identified) as Latino. Much goes into thinking about the meaning of labels or, as we might also say, the scripts associated with them. It can include characteristics like ancestry, language, and culture. But it can also include information about what bearers of the label are like—what they believe or feel, how they act or whom they associate with, as well as how they are, or should be, treated. The set of

86 WHAT DO WE NEED TO BREAK FREE?

characteristics linked to the label, although varied, serve to define the meaning of it in a rough-and-ready way. But that is all. These meanings cannot be set in stone.

Associating the meaning of a label with a set of beliefs or complex ideologies, rather than with features of race or ethnicity or nationality, is a particularly illuminating way to illustrate the dynamic nature of collective identities due to variations in meaning. For example, the label "Black Nationalist" may mean different things depending on how one understands black nationalism. One might emphasize building a black nation within America— something once advocated by the Republic of New Afrika president Imari Abubakari Obadele—or building one in Africa, as famously defended by Marcus Garvey, founder of the United Negro Improvement Association. The former may mean "internal nationalism" and the latter "external nationalism." Both versions could be subsumed under the heading of "separatist nationalism" holding that genuine black autonomy is only possible with black sovereignty over land, whether in America, secured as part of a long overdue reparations payment, or land on the African continent offered by a sympathetic government ready to receive African Americans in their ancestral homeland. Separatist nationalism can be distinguished from "community nationalism" which stresses black control over institutions such as schools and banks within black communities.[22] The content, and ultimately the salience of the label "Black Nationalist," may thus turn on whether one thinks that black community autonomy over its social, political, and economic well-being should be secured on black-controlled land within the internal borders of the United States, beyond them, or less radically by working within America's legal jurisdiction to develop institutional structures that serve blacks and are controlled by them.

Understanding that we have variation in the meanings of collective identity labels, which partly explains the group heterogeneity that we believe must be taken seriously to vindicate the utility of

HOW IDENTITY WORKS   87

identities for democratic cooperation, is only part of the recipe for understanding how identities that are too tightly scripted can box us in and cause identity trouble. There are two further ingredients that explain their dynamic nature.

Identification

Assigning a meaning to labels is not the only thing that we do with them. Labels, and their assigned meanings, are also things that we can actively identify with, and identifying with them—whether strongly or weakly—has ramifications for our beliefs, preferences, actions, and the like. All of this further illustrates the dynamic nature of collective identities and helps us account for why intragroup heterogeneity must be taken seriously if we are to make identities safe for democracy.

Some people who bear a label such as Latino, white, Republican, or Dallas Cowboy fan may internalize some of the meaning—the stereotypes—associated with these labels. They may take on some of this meaning in ways that inform the narrative that they tell about themselves, who they are and why they do what they do. For example, as a Dallas Cowboy football fan, they may internalize that part of the identity script that requires them to hate Pittsburgh Steeler and New York Giant football fans. As a Republican, they may take on the stereotypes that portray Republicans as anti-abortion and pro-guns. Identifying with an identity label may shape how a person thinks and feels, whom they associate with, and how they act. When identity labels are internalized, and shape these things, we have grounds for saying that the identities are salient for the individual that bears them. Appiah captures the relationship between identity labels and action by saying that our identification with a label gives us *reasons* to act in certain ways.[23] So, for example, being a devout Muslim gives one reasons to profess the faith (*shahada*), pray (*salat*) facing Mecca five times a day, give alms (*zakat*) to those

88   WHAT DO WE NEED TO BREAK FREE?

in need, fast (*sawm*) during Ramadan, and to undertake a pilgrimage (*hajj*) to Mecca. So another way to explain what makes an identity salient for a person is to say that such reasons for acting become their reasons. "I pray five times a day facing Mecca," a person may say, "because I am Muslim."

Label self-selection can be complicated. One source of complication stems from how the other identities a person bears may affect whether they identify with a particular label. We see this, for example, in the case of biracial labels such as Asian-white, Latino-white, and black-white and the role that other identities (gender, class, religion) play in racial labeling decisions. One research study examines how non-racial identities such as gender, socioeconomic status, and religion shape the labeling decisions of biracial individuals.[24] Drawing on a fairly large national survey of more than 37,000 biracial persons of part-white parentage in the United States, political scientist Lauren D. Davenport argues that their identification decisions are highly contextual. They are based, in varying degrees, on "interpersonal encounters, neighborhoods, and places of worship."[25] The main findings of this study are: (1) biracial women are much more likely than biracial men to identify as multiracial, (2) biracials with ethnic religions are more likely than non-religious biracials to identity with only one racial group, and (3) biracials with affluence are more likely than biracials without affluence to identity as white.[26] If the biracial identity script provides reasons for acting, this study suggests that whether these actually become reasons for a particular person who bears the label may depend largely on what other identities the person holds. Identification is a complex matter indeed.

Consideration of empirical research offers additional insight about the category of identification. Some identity researchers distinguish between how a person self-describes and how a person is described by others.[27] Some researchers use the term "identification" to designate the former (self-description) and the term "ascription" to designate the latter (other-description). Furthermore,

HOW IDENTITY WORKS   89

these researchers also call ascription "group membership," which refers to assigning a person to a group because they bear particular properties possessed by members of the group. Applying a particular label to a person is a way to facilitate this kind of ascription. Identification or self-description, in contrast, is closely related to individual psychology and behavior. Here we must ask: To what extent is an individual aware of being part of the group, and how attached are they to it based on having shared attitudes, ideas, interests, or emotions with other group members?[28]

Identification, in this sense, may also be described in terms of *salience*.[29] Social psychologists who study identity salience aim to measure how relevant some aspect of a person's self-concept is to them at a given time and in a certain situation. Some aspect of a shared group identity may be more relevant to one individual and less relevant to another. And the degree of relevance may vary situationally. For instance, being the only woman in an all-male boardroom may make gender salient for one woman, while another may not consider it all.[30] However, finding themselves in a hospital maternity ward as patients may make gender equally salient for both women. Attention to salience matters because it can partly explain ingroup variation in behavior, attitudes, and decisions, helping us appreciate the dynamic nature of collective identities. So, for example, in the boardroom case, the woman for whom gender is salient may be more likely to attribute being constantly interrupted by a male colleague when speaking as sexism, while the woman for whom gender is not salient may attribute it to something else, such as that person being rude.

To take another example, research on political behavior has shown that strong salience relations among Jewish voters, union members, and black voters has strengthened their preference for the Democratic Party compared to their respective group members for whom these identities are not as salient.[31] In addition, there is evidence that in the case of gender, when this identity is more salient for women, they exhibit more liberal or left-leaning policy

90   WHAT DO WE NEED TO BREAK FREE?

preferences and views on matters such as abortion, same-sex marriage, welfare spending, and job discrimination than women for whom gender is less salient.[32] And some research finds a strong correlation between participation in forms of activism such as women's rights activism and the politicization of collective gender identity.[33] Identity salience, and the politicization of particular identities, can stem from a variety of influences.[34]

Variations in the meaning of labels such as Latinx, black, Russian, Ewe, Afro-Latino, or Black Nationalist partly account for the dynamic nature of our collective identities. But so does variation in the strength of our identification with these labels. Regarding the Black Nationalist label, for instance, one can ask: How strongly does someone identify with this label, and which meaning of it is most salient for them? Is it separatist nationalism or community nationalism? Researchers have shown that other aspects of identity, including age, gender, and class, bear on these questions.[35] These two dimensions of black nationalism—separatism and community—find proponents among different black subgroups. Young blacks, black men, and working-class blacks and ones living in poverty are found to be more attracted to the former (separatist nationalism), while older blacks, black women, and blacks with greater upward social and economic mobility are more attracted to the latter (community nationalism).[36]

Appreciating that how strongly or weakly we identify with a label has ramifications—as empirical case studies show—is another way to illuminate Appiah's observation. What we are calling salience maps onto what he describes as the internalization of an identity label. And in line with empirical literature in social and political psychology, we can subsume both designations under the heading of identification. This second dimension of the taxonomy helps us account for another source of intragroup heterogeneity. Appiah makes clear that one sense in which identities matter is that they give us reasons to do things. In other words, being normatively significant, identity labels can guide our actions. To this we add that

HOW IDENTITY WORKS 91

identity labels can also matter more or less to their bearers; consequently, the reasons that they give us to do things may be more or less action-guiding. This will ultimately depend upon how salient these identities are for their bearers. Hence we can add this to the list of things that account for intragroup heterogeneity in addition to contestation over the meaning of group identity labels and over their normative significance.

How we self-identity, what aspects of our identity we make salient, is partly about making self-authorship choices. Of course, these choices can be shaped by many factors and are, therefore, highly contextual, as the Davenport biracial labeling study and other studies show. In some cases, when we are confronted with self-authorship choices about how to understand our identities, and choices about what aspects to make salient, we may need to be guided by pragmatic concerns, such as what constitutes a useful political strategy for our diverse communities. Philosopher Linda Martín Alcoff makes this point in arguing for treating Latina/o identity as a racial identity and for making race more salient on such grounds.[37] Ritchie Torres may have some sympathy with this point, especially insofar as he seeks to cooperate politically with the Congressional Black Caucus and wants to see his black roots as making such cooperation seem apt. However, Torres is not naive. Not only is he concerned about being rejected by this Caucus, but he also certainly appreciates that other mixed-race Latinos may make different self-authorship choices, including ones that make race less salient. Although Torres decides to make his Afro-Latino collective identity salient in his self-authorship, others may not. An Afro-Cuban or Afro-Chicana may more strongly identify with their national origin heritage, either downplaying or entirely ignoring their African roots. Still, as Torres rightly points out, in line with Alcoff's philosophical pragmatism about identity, the world may see things a different way.[38]

Additional complexity regarding the meaning and salience of identity is added when we consider that *Latino* designates

92 WHAT DO WE NEED TO BREAK FREE?

individuals with diverse backgrounds. They can be of African, European, and Asian descent and can have indigenous heritage or, like Torres, they can be mixed-race. And this raises further questions about which form of Latino identity—national origin, pan-ethnic, or race—is most relevant to political participation.[39] It has been argued that the latter has a significant impact on voter registration and local political involvement. Race consciousness may account for why Latinos like Torres, who identify with their black racial background and the experience of being discriminated against, take up antiracist political action.

He acknowledges that this racial identity is socially given, that is, the scripts that go with it are ready-made, but that the choice to embrace it in his life-shaping projects is his alone. Yet Torres further notes that he has been subject to treatment-as that does not depend on his identification. As he notes, he was treated as black as one "among the hundreds of thousands who were humiliated at the hands of the New York City Police Department during the height of stop and frisk."[40] This observation that our identities also have consequences for how we are treated by others, irrespective of whether or not we self-identify in a particular way or whether an aspect of our identity is salient for us, calls attention to a final component of the taxonomy in describing how identity works.

Treatment-As

Ritchie Torres reports experiencing "the pain of colorism" within the Latino community, even within his own family.[41] Novelist Alice Walker coined the term "colorism" to describe the practice of prejudicial or preferential treatment within and between racial and ethnic communities, whereby light skin is privileged over dark skin.[42] And Torres's experiences highlight the term's relevance for the Latino community.[43] A recent Pew Research Center study confirms this point.[44] It finds that Hispanics with darker

HOW IDENTITY WORKS 93

skin are more likely than those with lighter skin to report being discriminated against or treated unfairly because of their race or ethnicity. It identifies various types of treatment: being treated with suspicion; being treated unfairly in hiring, pay, or promotion; being unfairly stopped by police; being subject to slurs; and being treated as if one were not smart. In each case, darker-skinned Hispanics report experiencing the type of treatment at higher rates than lighter-skinned ones. Here is a sample of the data. More than half of Hispanics with darker skin surveyed (55%) reported being treated as if they were not smart, compared with 36% of those with lighter skin. More than half (53%) of Hispanics with darker skin reported being subject to slurs, compared to about one-third (34%) of lighter-skinned Hispanics. And about 30% of Hispanics with darker skin reported being treated unfairly at work in hiring, pay, or promotion, compared to 19% of those with lighter skin.

There is also a perception, perhaps widely shared within Hispanic communities, that colorism also operates within popular culture and industries such as film. This point was made by those who criticized the producers of the Hollywood film *In the Heights*. Critics complained that this Hollywood adaptation of the Broadway musical, set in the New York neighborhood of Washington Heights, known as the Little Dominican Republic, failed to cast dark-skinned Latinos, which was tantamount to erasing Afro-Latinos.[45] This omission was especially reprehensible in this case because the neighborhood where the film is set is predominately Afro-Dominican. One person interviewed about this controversy, who is among the nearly 90% of Dominicans of African descent from this New York community, summed up the complaint this way: "Hollywood has long valorized and highlighted fair-skinned Latinos over Afro-Latinos, often denying the latter roles that reflect their culture. It's a limited and inaccurate representation of Latinos, who are diverse in culture and complexion."[46] This same person recalls the history of how Spain set up a racial caste system on Hispaniola that placed Europeans and

94   WHAT DO WE NEED TO BREAK FREE?

mixed Europeans higher up in the system and afforded them better treatment.[47] He then notes that there are still vestiges of this white supremacist legacy in how black Latinos are viewed and treated in comparison to lighter Latinos. He says: "[Afro-Latinos] are more impoverished and have less access to a quality education, housing or health care than fair-skinned Latinos. By erasing them onscreen, we are perpetuating this harm and furthering the narrative that only white is right."[48] Some people involved with the film, most notably Lin-Manuel Miranda, apologized for coming up short in "trying to paint a mosaic of this community."[49]

There is also evidence that Latinos' political views and self-perceptions of skin color are intertwined. Social scientists Mara Ostfeld and Nicole Yadon find that Latinos who overestimate the lightness of their skin tone, relative to a spectrophotometer measure, are more likely to assert conservative positions regarding racialized policy debates than those who do not overestimate the lightness of their skin tone.[50] Furthermore, they find that "moving from those who were most likely to overestimate lightness to those who were most likely to overestimate darkness reveals a 37 percentage point gap in support for President Trump," and they find a similar relationship with respect to attitudes toward police.[51] So, in addition to differences in how they are treated, individuals who identify with the same label (Latino), but vary in color, may hold different political views that align with differences in self-perceptions that are especially relevant to heterogeneous treatment.

Another person interviewed by the *New York Times* about the *In the Heights* controversy observed: "Colorism in the Latino community manifests itself similarly to how it does in the Black American community."[52] Indeed the phenomenon of colorism—perceived differences in treatment as well as measurable differences in outcomes, opportunities, and obstacles based on skin color and morphological traits—has been studied extensively for this community. Research on colorism suggests that darker-skinned blacks bear a disproportionate share of anti-black prejudice. Whites have more negative affective reactions to blacks with darker skin tone and Afrocentric phenotypes such as thicker lips and wider noses.[53] And there is evidence that the more stereotypically black the features, the more threatening the person appears, no matter the person's facial expression or demeanor.[54] This evidence shows that colorism is not merely about differences in color. It extends to differences in morphological features.

Such findings also shed light on the depth of differences in treatment-as that blacks experience due to colorism. For instance, there are variations in severity of punishment both in school and in the criminal justice system: darker-skinned African American females are suspended at a rate of three times greater than ones with light skin;[55] African Americans with more stereotypical Afrocentric features are sentenced more harshly within the criminal justice system than those with less of these features,[56] and in capital cases involving white victims they are more likely to receive a death sentence.[57] Colorism also impacts economic outcomes for African Americans and for darker-skinned immigrants.[58]

Research regarding ingroup and outgroup colorism affecting African Americans exhibits multiple layers of complexity. There is evidence that light- and dark-skinned African American men perceive more discriminatory treatment by other African Americans than medium-skinned men, although their experiences with outgroup discriminatory treatment are very dissimilar. Dark-skinned African American men perceive the worst treatment from whites, while light-skinned ones perceive the best.[59] This finding reveals a double layer of complexity regarding how racial identity works. It shows that skin tone variation can affect perceived treatment, and that depending on the context, this variation can be advantageous or disadvantageous. Blacks who are very light-skinned can fare better in white company, but less well in black company that looks at them with suspicion as potential racial sellouts or with a less robust commitment to black uplift. The color dynamics play out differently in the case of black women.[60] As with

96 WHAT DO WE NEED TO BREAK FREE?

lighter-skinned black men, similarly hued black women are treated more favorably by the white outgroup. However, within the black ingroup, lighter-skinned women have been perceived as more attractive. This has been advantageous within the racial ingroup, as it garners them more attention from potential partners, though it can hurt relations with darker-skinned women, who are regarded as rivals. Notwithstanding these findings about colorism, some social scientists have argued that in the United States, mobilization around anti-black racism is primary and trumps mobilization around colorism. This might make it more difficult to address disadvantages based on colorism, especially if policy remedies to combat racial hierarchy, such as black political representation and affirmative action, tend to benefit light-skinned black Americans.[61]

Although colorism has been well documented in the case of blacks, and there is more and more research on colorism in Latino communities, it is important to note that colorism is not just a black or Latino thing. For example, Asians also deal with colorism. This includes members of Asian American communities descended from China, Japan, South Korea, and other parts of East Asia, as well as South and Southeast Asia, such as India, Singapore, Thailand, Philippines, and Vietnam.[62]

After developing this illuminating taxonomy of how identities work, using his own examples and cases, Appiah acknowledges a point that we have sought to highlight, namely, that social identities are more complicated than is typically supposed and that this complication has much to do with their dynamic nature. He concludes: "In sum, identities come, first, with labels and ideas about why and to whom they should be applied. Second, your identity shapes your thoughts about how you should behave; and, third, it affects the way other people treat you. Finally, all these dimensions of identity are contestable, always up for dispute: who's in, what they're like, how they should behave and be treated."[63] We agree. And, as we now argue, taking seriously the group heterogeneity that emerges from this contestability is essential for

HOW IDENTITY WORKS 97

appreciating why identity optimists must take greater care to vindicate collective identities and to make them safe for democracy.

Taking Heterogeneity Seriously

Collective identities can be epistemically useful in political reasoning and activity, a point we made in Chapter 2 when we introduced "identity optimists." There we highlighted how collective identities come into play for individuals serving in various roles, including as leaders or representatives in organizations, and as constituents served by them. Constituents can identify individuals with shared experiences and perspectives, who might be better positioned to understand their own, facilitate communication between members of the group, and communicate shared perspectives to others outside the group in different domains. On this basis, it comes as no surprise to advocates of descriptive representation—who champion the importance of constituents being represented by people who are descriptively "like them"— that there are some advantages of a shared identity between constituents and representatives. For example, a research study finds that US congressional representatives who are women, racial/ethnic minorities, and veterans are more likely to intervene on behalf of constituents with the relevant shared identity in the relatively unobserved context of engaging with federal agencies on related issues.[64] In this case, constituents for whom these identities are especially salient features of their life plans have a reason to trust descriptive representatives to advance collective goals, even when active public monitoring is more difficult.[65]

However, as the taxonomy of how identity works shows, shared group labels can also obscure substantial group heterogeneity. Light-skinned Latino descriptive representatives (and even those with different self-perceptions) may not share experiences of colorism (or hold different interpretations of their experiences) that

98   WHAT DO WE NEED TO BREAK FREE?

are deeply felt and consequential for darker-skinned constituents. Black American representatives may have different understandings of the degree to which black Americans share a linked fate and endorse different strategies for responding to commonly experienced discrimination as a collective project. While collective identities can communicate useful information for constituents and representatives, a full appreciation of how they operate empirically suggests that they also heighten epistemic demands on constituents and representatives due to these multiple forms of group heterogeneity. Taking such data to heart, while embracing a more dynamic analysis of these identities, makes it difficult for us to maintain unqualified optimism about the prospects of identity scripts facilitating political reasoning and activity. Our position is best described as a qualified optimism.

In addition to helping us illuminate how identities work, Appiah's taxonomy helps us illustrate, more concretely, the heightened epistemic demands that follow from taking group heterogeneity seriously. Labels are one aspect of collective identities that can increase the epistemic demands of deploying these identities in political reasoning and activity. Group members, despite enduring some common experiences and sharing some common goals, may disagree about the appropriate labels. Consider, as an example, contemporary debates about collective identity labels among Latino Americans. Motivated by the experiences of gender nonconforming group members, some Latino Americans have advocated a shift to the label "Latinx," which avoids the gender binary of the Latino/Latina label. Recent survey results suggest that few of the intended targets of the label identify with it, and the choice of term has become a discussion in the broader public sphere with some commentators suggesting the label will not become widely adopted due to the sense that it is imposed by those with activist or academic inclinations that are not widely shared among group members.[66] This situation poses a challenge for group members: representatives may face a trade-off between acknowledging consciousness-raising efforts related to the gender binary and representing fellow group members' goals in terms that they will recognize as their own.[67] It may not be obvious how best to advance group members' projects in light of this disagreement, and resolving it may require regular consultation with a diverse array of group members, as their own self-perceptions and views on collective goals change over time. In Part III, we will return to this theme of consultation, as well as the theme of communication, when we provide concrete guidance on what representatives can do to counteract the phenomenon of being boxed in by tightly scripted identities.

Preserving a collective identity label through the acknowledgment of group heterogeneity can also serve a communicative role. Kamala Harris's emergence as the vice presidential candidate for the Democratic Party spurred discussion of her identification as black American.[68] Harris has Tamil ancestry through her mother and African ancestry through her father via Jamaica, which led some political commentators to question her identification as black. In an op-ed, Jamelle Bouie argues that Harris's embrace of the label "black" reflects her ancestry, her upbringing in the black American community in Oakland, California, the history of Afro-Caribbean leaders in black American political movements, and the realities of American racism. This is a nuanced and informative picture that reflects particular subsets of black American experiences, while challenging some conceptions of the boundary of the label, as in the case of Ritchie Torres discussed above. Harris's choice to foreground her identification as black and black constituents' embrace of this identification reflect a choice about how best to represent the diversity of experiences. Labeling practices might have emerged such that ADOS (American Descendants of Slavery) became especially salient given discussions about reparations from the United States government, where they might have been distinguished from Afro-Caribbean descendants of slavery and African immigrants to the United States. Emphasizing these more specific labels might be useful for achieving goals that most directly apply

100   WHAT DO WE NEED TO BREAK FREE?

to these particular subsets of black Americans. The decision to preserve or emphasize particular labels through the acknowledgment of heterogeneity again requires extensive consultation with differently situated members of the group and strategic decision-making about shared and disparate goals.

The identification component of Appiah's taxonomy can also introduce further epistemic demands in light of the possibility of toggling between different labels. Citizens, whether acting as representatives or not, may find it useful to foreground particular collective identities in particular contexts. This is especially salient in regard to pan-ethnic identities, such as Latino or Asian American, whereby social movement leaders and advocates may face a tension between affirming subgroup identities and a sense of metagroup unity.[69] For example, some Latino and Asian Americans report a stronger identification with their national origin identities, as Mexican or Korean Americans, than with pan-ethnic identities. Relatedly, rates of pan-ethnic identification and conceptions of pan-ethnic consciousness differ among national origin subgroups of Latino and Asian Americans.[70] Latinos who primarily identify with their national origin are significantly more likely to report feeling represented by congressional representatives from another state who share their national origin, as opposed to officials described simply as "Hispanic."[71] Given these differences in identification, descriptive representation on the basis of pan-ethnic, as opposed to national origin identities, may appeal to and engage different subsets of citizens, and may coincide with different life-shaping projects.[72]

Aside from toggling between collective identities for the purposes of political activity and coalition-building, citizens may also toggle to make situational distinctions. Julie Dowling's description of the nuanced situational deployment of different labels by Mexican-Americans in Texas illustrates this point:[73]

Mike usually identifies as "Hispanic," a term that he defines as someone of Mexican ancestry who was born in the United

HOW IDENTITY WORKS 101

States. At times, he also calls himself "Mexican American," but he explains that he is not "Mexican" because he is not an immigrant. When someone insults people of Mexican heritage in his presence, however, he asserts a "Mexican" identity strategically in that context. Moreover, when he is speaking Spanish, he refers to himself as "Mexicano." But Mike is also definitely an "American," and he never uses "Latino" because "it sounds like someone who isn't from here." He is a "Texan," but he would not typically use the Spanish corollary "Tejano" as a self-referent because he associates the term with styles of music and working-class cultural expressions among Mexican Americans in Texas that do not suit him. Yet, when someone asks in Spanish where he is from, "Soy Tejano [I am Tejano]" is his response. So, in sum, Mike is Mexicano but not Mexican, Texan but not really Tejano, and Hispanic because he is not an immigrant. To outsiders this might seem confusing and even rather contradictory. However, among Mexican Americans in the study I found remarkable consistency in many of the distinctions in labeling that Mike identifies here.[74]

Some of this reported situational toggling is used to reflect cultural distinctions that may not be especially salient to political behavior. However, Dowling finds that some contextual identification seems tied to political attitudes and experiences related to discrimination and assimilation. For example, some respondents who reported rejecting the label "Mexican" shift to identifying with the label when reporting discriminatory episodes.[75] As these additional examples demonstrate, constituents and representatives seeking to coordinate social and political behavior cannot assume the stability of identification with particular labels with which they might describe or communicate about such efforts, which again adds to the challenge of reliably deploying them in political reasoning and activity.

Our discussion of colorism and the relevance of differences in treatment-as within identity groups also tells against unqualified

102   WHAT DO WE NEED TO BREAK FREE?

optimism about collective identities facilitating political reasoning and activity. However, we admit that similar experiences of treatment-as can also serve as the basis for the formation and strengthening of new, overarching, identities to facilitate coalition-building. Drawing on W. E. B. Du Bois's defense of democracy, Derrick Darby has argued that forms of class-identity can form the basis of successful egalitarian movements to improve the functioning of democracies, despite contemporary concerns about their stability and functioning.[76] Identifying shared forms of treatment-as despite group differences can serve as a precursor to addressing shared challenges and advancing group members' projects. However, such efforts also cannot ignore the dynamics of contextually shifting labels and identification, which might threaten the stability of such a coalition. In addition to familiar concerns about racial attitudes among white Americans, differences in a sense of commonality between Latino and African Americans might also threaten the prospects for coalition-building between members of each collective identity group, despite some shared forms of discriminatory treatment-as.[77] Given the various forms of group heterogeneity and the dynamic complexity of label-identification, successfully coordinating class-based political engagement on the basis of shared treatment-as is a daunting epistemic task.

Looking Ahead

In this chapter, we have drawn on Appiah's illuminating taxonomy to explain how identities work. Our main takeaways are that collective identities are dynamic in that they change over time and that they are complex in that they are connected to one another, and to our life plans, in many different ways. As a result, there can be considerable heterogeneity in the attitudes, actions, and associations of group members. Just knowing that a generic identity label can be applied to someone does not reliably allow us to predict how they will act, what they will think or feel, or how they will associate. Collective identities change over time and they do not have hard and fast boundaries. This is because the meaning assigned to identity labels varies, as does the extent to which someone identifies with a label and how they may be treated by others both within and outside of the ingroup. Identity-group heterogeneity raises challenges for identity optimists, especially when we consider the role of identities in political reasoning and activity.

Proceeding as if the black American population is monolithic, for example, in how they define the meaning of being black, the extent to which they identify with being black, and how they experience being treated as black can lead to faulty predictions about matters of representation, such as predicting that black Americans would support Kanye West for president no matter the alternatives. Group heterogeneity, stemming from variations in the meaning of identity labels, their salience, and how individuals are treated, dictates against imposing homogenizing scripts on persons. Glossing over these differences can box us in, and contribute to us boxing others in, making identities unsafe for democracy. We follow a tradition of thinking about collective identity and taking group heterogeneity seriously that goes back to W. E. B. Du Bois's groundbreaking sociological study of *The Philadelphia Negro*.[78] Anthony Appiah's analytical taxonomy, which we have deployed here, is particularly useful for our purposes because it allows us to illuminate the dynamic nature of collective identities. In sum, identity heterogeneity must be taken seriously because (1) it helps explain how we can get boxed in by tightly scripted identities when identity-shaping and identity-policing tools—formal or informal—make it hard for bearers of identities to combine their various identities into a unified life plan, and (2) it holds the key for breaking free.

Collective identities per se are not the problem. The problem is with scripting them too tightly or in ways that do not allow for intragroup heterogeneity. Not only does this make it harder to

104 WHAT DO WE NEED TO BREAK FREE?

formulate and follow our self-authored life plans, but it can also get in the way of pursuing common life-shaping projects with others, as we saw with Rustin's dilemma in the Introduction to this book. Fortunately, being stifled in pursuit of such projects by tight scripts is not inevitable. Group heterogeneity can and must be successfully managed. We can overcome Rustin's dilemma with the right tools. As we will discuss in Chapter 4, it is up to us to answer two key questions—namely, who should be among us? and what is required of us?—to determine the flexibility or restrictiveness of our collective identities. And we can answer these questions, as well as change our answers to them together, by engaging in collective self-authorship processes. By taking part in this coordinated exercise of agency, in ways that are responsive to group heterogeneity, and holding ourselves accountable for it, we can collectively take control of tight scripts and break free from them. Where there are tight scripts and identity trouble, we can use our agency to get greater flexibility in how our identities are understood. This allows us to open up space for more successful pursuit of our life-shaping projects. Making clear exactly what we need to do to make this happen and identifying what tools we need to do it successfully are the main tasks of the next chapter.

4

Collective Self-Authorship Processes

My Projects Are Our Projects

Efrain Estrada was raised on a farm in Puerto Rico but it was only after moving to the South Bronx in New York City that he chose gardening as part of his life plan years later. Choosing a life plan, which constitutes an exercise of our agency, is an act of individual self-authorship. This choice provides insight into who we take ourselves to be and what projects matter to us. Because our sense of these things can change over time, individual self-authorship is *dynamic*.

Collective identities—ready-made scripts—provide the raw material through which we fashion our life plans and engage in individual self-authorship. The gardener identity serves this purpose for Estrada and others, like Sue Stuart-Smith, a member of a community garden in England and a psychiatrist who touts the positive effects of gardening on psychological well-being. "To be a gardener," on her view, "you need to tune in to how the plants are doing, and attend to what they need."[1] Of course this is not all there is to it. You must also know how to protect your garden from invasive insects like lanternflies. But being able to discern how the plants are doing and what they need is certainly a familiar element of the gardener script. And this identity script helps Estrada, Stuart-Smith, and other gardeners answer the questions: Who am I? and What are my projects? This chapter will explain the processes involved in making "my projects" become "our projects" to mark the shift from individual to collective self-authorship (CSA). Our thesis is that we need CSA processes to make ourselves accountable

Boxed In. Derrick Darby and Eduardo J. Martinez, Oxford University Press. © Oxford University Press 2024.
DOI: 10.1093/9780197620236.003.0005

106   WHAT DO WE NEED TO BREAK FREE?

to group differences, along with an understanding of how identity works, to break free from being boxed in by tight scripts.

Because of Estrada's decision to be a gardener, working with neighbors to convert a vacant city lot into space for a community garden, preparing his individual garden plot, deciding what to grow, where to shop for seeds, tuning in to how the plants are doing, fighting off lanternflies, and deciding what to do with his harvest became life-shaping projects central to pursuing his life plan. Of course, being a gardener is not his only identity. Estrada is also a family man and youth mentor. And over time, after the community garden got more established, he took up other projects relating to how the garden space might be used for other things, including festive family gatherings and hosting educational programs to teach his young mentees about gardening. These projects, which relate to other parts of his life plan, combine seamlessly with his projects related to being a gardener. And we can imagine the same thing being true of his fellow gardeners.

They may also be environmentalists, educators, entrepreneurs, political activists, health professionals, fitness instructors, and mentors. And these identities may also serve to define, prioritize, and shape the projects they undertake within the community garden. One of Estrada's fellow gardeners may be a mental health professional and want to use garden space as a place where clients can visit for peaceful meditation as part of prescribed therapy. One of them may be a salsa instructor and want to use it for salsa lessons. Another one may be a Christian youth mentor and want the garden to be a retreat for at-risk youth in the neighborhood. Because Estrada and his fellow gardeners have many collective identities, as do we, which illuminate who we take ourselves to be and what projects matter to us, and because these projects can connect in different ways to inform their life plans, individual self-authorship is also *complex.*

The various identities that Estrada and other gardeners might use to fashion a life plan—in exercising individual self-authorship—integrate their life purposes and values over time.

COLLECTIVE SELF-AUTHORSHIP PROCESSES 107

And the overarching framework of identities, serving these ends, gives content to their life plans. Each gardener may have different life plans that make sense of their pursuit of gardening. One gardener may be on a spiritual quest for enlightenment through meditation, while another may be on a quest for fame through writing unforgettable novels. The identities they embrace, which include the gardener script, integrate these life purposes into a unified life plan. Although they have different life plans, these two gardeners may have similar projects.

For example, both may be interested in creating a space in the community garden for quiet reflection, where one can meditate and the other can write, and this becomes their shared life-shaping project. It contributes to the realization of their respective life plans. Over time, these gardeners and others who are also interested in making space in the garden for quiet reflection—for reasons having to do with their individual life plans—may come to have an identity-like connection: they might adopt identity labels (e.g., the Peaceful Gardeners), may identify with these labels to varying degrees, and may be treated as such by their fellow gardeners and by others. If this new script becomes too tight, some gardeners may even find themselves boxed in.

When Estrada became a founding member of the United We Stand Community Garden in the 1990s, he recalled saying: "This corner is going to be my garden. Now I'm going to make a garden on my own with what my father taught me. I had farming in my blood."[2] If we were members of this community garden, Estrada's garden would also be *our* garden. It would equally belong to the mental health professional, the salsa instructor, the Christian youth mentor, the enlightenment seeker, the novelist, and to the Peaceful Gardeners. It would also belong to the political activists among us—always eager to fight political battles on behalf of community gardens and their members.

That the garden belongs to all of us means, above all else, that we must coordinate with one another to pursue our various

108   WHAT DO WE NEED TO BREAK FREE?

life-shaping projects that relate to the garden space. Collective self-authorship processes that include *communication, representation,* and *exit,* as we will explain, facilitate such coordination in ways that hold us accountable to group heterogeneity. We will have to coordinate the use of community garden tools and supplies, watering schedules, taking care of shared expenses, and the like. We will have to work with others to determine how to deal with pests like lanternflies. We will have to coordinate to plan activities within the garden and to set schedules. Estrada will want to work festive family events and gatherings for his youth mentees into the schedule. The salsa instructor will want to work in salsa lessons. And the Peaceful Gardeners will want time in the garden for quiet reflection. Some of us may not have farming in our blood like Estrada, and we may come to gardening for different reasons, but because the community garden is our shared space, and pursuing our particular life-shaping projects requires coordinating with others, it is easy to see how "my projects are our projects."

We cannot complete our life-shaping projects, as part of our life plan, without pursuing them with others, which we do by contributing to CSA processes. With these processes, we can vary the projects that we take on collectively and prioritize over time. And they can facilitate the pursuit of loftier projects. We can move from using them to pursue the project of making space in the garden for quiet reflection, for instance, to using them to wage a political campaign against the commercial development of garden space in black and Latino urban neighborhoods, or even to fight city budget cuts that affect public bus access to community gardens for some members. As we pursue loftier projects, working within our smaller identity group may not be enough to achieve our goals. Our group might be too small relative to the broader population or we might need information and expertise that members of other groups have. Under such circumstances, we may need to extend CSA processes outside of our group by working in a *coalition.* Forming and sustaining coalitions, which allow us to coordinate

COLLECTIVE SELF-AUTHORSHIP PROCESSES   109

activity across multiple identity groups, is vital to pursuing our life plans and life-shaping projects—especially as we scale up to working with more agents, as we will discuss in Chapter 5.

The present chapter explains how CSA unfolds over time through various processes. We start by attending to how group differences create challenges as well as opportunities for coordinating our life-shaping projects with others. Then, after explaining how identity scripts can become too flexible or too restrictive, we contend that we can take control of them by varying our answers to the questions of "who is among us?" and "what is required of us?" We then discuss the role of CSA processes, which include accountability mechanisms and chains, in helping us take control before considering intersectionality—an alternative approach to addressing group heterogeneity—and concluding the chapter.

Shared Projects, Group Differences

Differences in perspective among gardeners, for instance, over how to control invasive insects like lanternflies are inevitable. And when matters of dispute connect with politics—something that can thwart our life plans—we may need to take part in collective self-authorship in the political domain. But here group differences in perspective, among other differences, which we will outline in this section, can create challenges as well as potential resources for successful collective self-authorship.

The spotted lanternfly, a gray and red insect native to Asia and capable of laying 30 to 50 eggs at a time on everything from trees, trains, to tractor trailers, arrived in New York City in the summer of 2020. The harm they cause to plants and trees and their potential economic harm to various industries, including wineries, account for why the US Department of Agriculture encourages us to kill lanternflies. Neil Weisman, a member of the Roosevelt Island Community Garden, who serves on its pest mitigation committee,

110   WHAT DO WE NEED TO BREAK FREE?

has a vested interest in this problem.[3] But so does his fellow gardener, Pia Doane, who may have a different perspective on how to control the lanternflies. Cities like New York, where they live, worry about the negative economic impact of these invasive pests and also have strong interests in dealing with the problem.

Imagine that the city proposes legislation to mandate the use of a toxic pesticide to kill lanternflies in community gardens on city property. Now suppose that some members of the garden applaud this legislation and want to comply, while others like Pia, who prefers organic plant-oil-based spray to control the insects, are strongly opposed to this mandate. Further suppose that some of these members, who are also activists and environmentalists, want to drag the Roosevelt Island Garden into a political battle with the city, and that some fellow gardeners strongly oppose this action, wanting the garden to be a politics-free space. These differences in perspective, amplified by the background change in city regulation, pose a challenge because they threaten to drive members away from the garden, who may have been vital to pursuing our shared life-shaping projects. But this outcome is not a foregone conclusion. Under the right conditions, where community garden members have a means to manage these and other group differences, successful CSA is still possible. Below we explain the role that CSA processes play in turning our differences into opportunities to advance our shared projects. This will depend, in part, on using the accountability mechanisms of communication, representation, and exit. But first, relying on three case studies, we will identify types of group differences that can serve as challenges to, and opportunities for, successful collective self-authorship.

Consider the case of Naakh Vyosky and his emergence as a local leader in his community of low-income, predominantly immigrant, seniors in the Brighton neighborhood of Boston.[4] Vyosky grew up in eastern Europe, fought the Nazis during World War II, and eventually moved from Ukraine to the United States in 1979, fleeing anti-Semitism. He and his wife, Klara, arrived in Brighton

COLLECTIVE SELF-AUTHORSHIP PROCESSES   111

with a large wave of immigrants coming first from the former Soviet Union and then China. They assumed leadership roles in their building, helping other immigrants get settled.

Naakh Vyosky's project of helping his neighbors did not initially involve pushing for policy change or involvement in electoral politics. But that changed in 1996 when Congress passed a welfare reform bill. This bill threatened the disability and food stamp benefits that he and his neighbors had come to rely on. In response, the Vyoskys helped organize study groups so that they, and their neighbors, could pass the citizenship test and fight for their benefits as citizens. Naakh Vyosky eventually become a spokesperson advocating for immigrant benefits. He spoke to local media and even gave a speech at the National Press Club in Washington, DC.[5] Eventually, the Vyoskys and their Brighton neighbors became a valuable voting bloc in local politics. Naakh became a coveted endorsement for local politicians looking for support from seniors. He started with the project of helping his fellow immigrant neighbors adjust to life in a new country and ended up acting as a representative for his community in the media and in formal politics.

Vyosky and his neighbors had to engage in political activity together, despite being a heterogenous group. They had different health problems, financial situations, home countries, and spoke different languages.[6] In other words, they had *different backgrounds*. And this influenced how they pursued shared projects. It also made communication between them challenging, at least at first, with neighbors having different perspectives on the group's problems and goals. It is also not clear that Vyosky and his neighbors coalesced around a distinct group identity label. There are multiple relevant identity labels, including: senior citizens, immigrant seniors, or seniors of Brighton. Were their collective community activity to continue, and were building residents to develop a strong level of identification, a more cohesive identity could become salient. The ongoing pursuit of life-shaping projects with others can create and change identity labels over time.

112   WHAT DO WE NEED TO BREAK FREE?

The pursuit of our life-shaping projects may call for direct confrontation with others, and an identity group or one with an identity-like connection can form for this purpose. Consider the Chipko movement in the Himalayan foothills of India during the 1970s and 1980s. Logging and related commercial activities driven by government development programs in the region threatened local residents' access to trees used to make agricultural tools. It also threatened the sustainability of the local environment. The movement emerged as a response to these threats to local residents' way of life. Movement activists organized nonviolent protests, including ones where they stood in front of trees, at gunpoint, to protect them.

The movement was also notable because women played a prominent role in pioneering its protest tactics.[7] However, despite coming together to pursue this shared life-shaping project, there were important differences between men and women's initial motivations to participate in the movement. Early challenges to the government's development scheme in the area, and subsequent commercial activity, focused on lack of employment and benefit for local people, and tended to engage male workers. However, as the movement began to push for relief from recurring floods and landslides, more women were mobilized.

Women were especially likely to have an ecological perspective, noting the connection between logging activity on nearby mountain slopes and the recurring floods and landslides that threatened their survival.[8] This was in part due to the fact that women were responsible for most agricultural work on local farms, while men tended to travel for paid work. However, men tended to be property holders and hold political office, and so had more authority and decision-making power.[9] Participation in the Chipko movement thus created opportunities to challenge gender hierarchy while also protecting the local modes of living threatened by industrial logging. In some cases, women took part in Chipko demonstrations despite complaints and defamation from men in village councils.[10]

COLLECTIVE SELF-AUTHORSHIP PROCESSES   113

The Chipko movement is indicative of another way that group differences can be relevant for CSA, especially when politics gets in the way. Members of a group can be *differently empowered* within the group. Either due to historical or currently existing forms of hierarchy, the interests or voices of some group members can be prioritized over others, and this can affect the degree to which they are taken up during collective self-authorship. However, through CSA processes, marginalized group members can become more empowered, like women in the Chipko movement. Starting from shared life-shaping projects related to a sustainable surrounding environment, residents of the Himalayan foothills took part in political confrontations as part of CSA. This, in turn, led to a new form of identification around the Chipko movement. As part of this new form of identification, and its associated political activity, an opening was created for using CSA processes to change gendered differences in empowerment.

In other circumstances, group differences arise from disagreement about whether our CSA requires political engagement, and if so, what kind. Consider disagreements about the Eritrean government among Eritrean Americans. The Eritrean government is controversial in the international community, as it has not held national elections since its independence in 1993. United Nations reports have catalogued human rights abuses in the country including arbitrary arrests, detainment, and torture.[11] Political disagreements about the Eritrean government, and whether it merits support, have fractured the Eritrean American community. One 2011 newspaper report from California notes: "Many Bay Area Eritreans would prefer to stay neutral, but decisions about what local Eritrean café to patronize, or which church to pray at, or whether to attend certain cultural events can be interpreted as taking sides on political affairs."[12] This political disagreement has notably affected the spiritual life of Eritrean Americans who practice their faith in Eritrean Orthodox churches. Members of these church communities, including clergy, have different attitudes

114   WHAT DO WE NEED TO BREAK FREE?

toward the Eritrean government and its influence on the Eritrean Orthodox Church. As a result, even churches in the United States have split in two, with separate services for communities with different orientations to the Eritrean government.[13]

This is an example of group heterogeneity in the form of *different perspectives* about how best to pursue a group's life-shaping projects. Eritrean Americans in the United States have different perspectives on how best to practice their culture and, in some cases, religion. While some Eritrean Americans see their cultural and religious commitments as involving a relationship with the Eritrean government, others reject that view or may even understand these commitments to call for opposition to the current Eritrean government. In this case, we have a disagreement about the meaning of an already existing identity—being Eritrean American—and what relationship it requires to particular institutions like the church and the state.

This political disagreement and the ensuing social divide limit participation in non-political aspects of Eritrean American CSA. The same 2011 report includes this telling quote from Nunu Kidane, an Eritrean American from Oakland, California: "People are conflicted. They want to express their need to be Eritrean, to be part of these communal events.... But people are afraid that if they speak out, they will be cut off—not from their country, but from their culture."[14] This quote suggests that some Eritrean Americans have been boxed in by this situation. Taking part in communal events is a crucial part of the script of being Eritrean in the United States, and this satisfies an important need for Eritrean Americans given their life plans. However, a friends-and-enemies mindset has taken hold, and those with different views on the Eritrean government risk being ostracized from their local communities, which can undermine the robustness of religious and cultural CSA activities.

These cases illuminate three kinds of group heterogeneity: different backgrounds, differences in empowerment, and different

COLLECTIVE SELF-AUTHORSHIP PROCESSES 115

perspectives. Each one can create challenges and opportunities for CSA. Of course these categories are not mutually exclusive. Different members of a group might be disempowered on the basis of their background, as in the case of racial or ethnic disempowerment, or on the basis of their perspectives, as in the case of marginalizing heterodox political views. Similarly, different perspectives can be informed by different backgrounds and kinds of (dis)empowerment, while different backgrounds can be characterized by shared forms of (dis)empowerment and perspectives. We should expect heterogeneity of some kind when faced with the task of CSA. Identity groups will exhibit each type of heterogeneity to some degree. To ensure the successful coordination of life-shaping projects, over time, group members must attend to these forms of heterogeneity, look out for instances of boxing in, and utilize the CSA processes, which we will outline shortly, to take control of overly flexible and restrictive scripts.

Flexibility and Restrictiveness

"Traitor." "You bring dishonor to your family." These were the comments Tram Nguyen, a Massachusetts state representative, saw on a video she posted to her Facebook page declaring support for the Black Lives Matter movement. This was not the sort of reception she was used to: "I represent a purple district," she noted, "but I've never had this sort of attack thrown against me before."[15] For Nguyen, a Democrat, it was not solely her partisan affiliation that drew the ire of some of her constituents. It was that her political stance, as a Vietnamese American, was seen by others in her community, especially older Vietnamese Americans, as in tension with the Vietnamese American script. For some, the Vietnamese American script involves a commitment to avoid or oppose left-wing politics (or anything with such an association). This is informed by personal experience with, or family histories of, fighting

116   WHAT DO WE NEED TO BREAK FREE?

communist guerrillas in the Vietnamese civil war and subsequent experiences as refugees. Some Vietnamese Americans also understand their identity as being threatened by China (or at least the Chinese government's position in geopolitics), given a history of contested borders between the two countries, and continued fears of territorial encroachment.[16]

In light of a tumultuous political history accompanied by political traumas, many Vietnamese Americans see anything associated with left-wing politics as a betrayal of the life-shaping projects of the community. For some Vietnamese Americans, like Nguyen, these scripts have become overly constraining. They do not see voting and activism in support of progressive policies, or Democratic Party candidates, as in tension with their identity, nor do they see it as entailing support for communism.[17] In their eyes, vigilance against communism has become a way to shut down any left-leaning policy preference. A "common joke among young Viet progressives is that you're bound to be called a communist, or cộng sản, once you openly express any left-leaning political views."[18] This sort of political environment can be stifling.

It may not be obvious which policy choices will best serve Vietnamese Americans, even assuming a shared interest in combating communism and Chinese foreign policy influence on Vietnam. And some Vietnamese Americans believe that an unwillingness to consider progressive policies prevents the group from advancing its own interests, such as interests in protecting public health or combating poverty. Some younger Vietnamese Americans see the tight scripts their parents have internalized as so restrictive that they do not see any viable path forward for political discussion and exchange. In a Facebook group called "Asian Americans with Republican Parents Support Group,"[19] one member noted: "My frustration toward the older generation of Vietnamese Americans being entitled, hypocritical, racist, homophobic, transphobic, misogynistic, and every other kind of bigotry under the sun, has more or less boiled over into nothing short of pure disdain.... It's gotten

COLLECTIVE SELF-AUTHORSHIP PROCESSES 117

to the point where I flat out don't care about what they think of me or say to me."[20]

These sentiments are driven in part by concerns about the influence of partisan news and misinformation, including both English- and Vietnamese-language sources. As these sources amplify a friends-and-enemies mindset regarding partisan and racial identities, some progressive Vietnamese Americans worry that they are losing, or have already lost, a communicative pathway to the older generation. Once these sentiments become widespread, it is hard to see how the group's CSA can continue effectively.

In this case, progressive Vietnamese Americans feel boxed in with respect to identity scripts about how they should act in the political domain.[21] They feel that they cannot promote policies that will advance some of their life-shaping projects without being accused of betraying their Vietnamese identity, and simultaneously losing the ability to communicate effectively with the older generation. The restrictive situation experienced by progressive Vietnamese Americans stems from the requirements that group members impose on one another. In any context of collective self-authorship, demands will be made on group members, such as volunteering a certain number of hours each week in a community garden. In a larger and less formally organized group like an ethnic group, while these demands are often contested and context-sensitive, they are made, nonetheless. We see, therefore, that one determinant of the flexibility or restrictiveness of an identity is how those who identify with it answer the question: What is required of us, as members of the group?

In addition to making demands of one another, we can also make identities restrictive or flexible with our conceptions of who is eligible to be a group member. And we do this with our answer to another question: Who should be among us? Consider, for instance, differences in eligibility requirements for enrolled members of federally registered Native American tribes in the United States. Many tribes use "blood quantum" criteria for membership. This measure

118   WHAT DO WE NEED TO BREAK FREE?

is calculated based on the proportion of an individual's ancestry that descend back to the tribe's enrollees with the federal government in an earlier census.[22] It originates from government policy,[23] and continues to be used by the US Bureau of Indian Affairs to determine eligibility for social services (usually the threshold is a blood quantum of ¼ or higher).[24] While one does have to establish ancestry dating back to a 19th-century Cherokee census to enroll, unlike many other Native American tribes, Cherokees have no minimum blood quantum.[25] This is one reason why the Cherokee Nation has an especially large, multiracial membership with a wide range of blood quanta (with some as low as 1/2,048).[26] In this case, the Cherokee have a relatively flexible answer to the question "who should be among us?" as compared to tribes with stricter blood quantum criteria. It is worth noting that answers to this question are not inevitable. In the Cherokee case, it is the result of a longer history of disagreement and contestation, including about the place of freed black slaves, intermarried white Americans, and people adopted in the tribe from other tribes like the Shawnees, as well as the descendants of all of these groups.[27] In any context of CSA, there will also be ways of answering the group membership question, even in a community garden where members may debate whether having a commitment to pesticide-free gardens should be a criterion of membership.

The Vietnamese and Native American cases illustrate that the flexibility or restrictiveness of a particular identity, with its associated scripts, is neither automatic nor fixed. Rather it is the result of how group members interact over time, through CSA processes, to answer two key questions: (1) Who should be among us? and (2) What is required of us? To coordinate their pursuit of life-shaping projects and take collective action, groups need to have some sense of who can be in the group and what is required of its members. But there are many possible answers to these questions. And some can lead to tight scripts that we encounter and deploy with respect to how we act, how we think and feel, and whom we

COLLECTIVE SELF-AUTHORSHIP PROCESSES   119

associate with. While our identity scripts can be overly flexible, the identity trouble we face most urgently is, on our view, primarily a matter of being boxed in by tight scripts. These overly restrictive scripts make it more difficult for us to formulate and enact our life-shaping projects in coordination with others. Fortunately, our answers to the key questions, which determine the flexibility or restrictiveness of collective identities, are under our control.

Taking Control of the Script

We have established two questions that determine the flexibility or restrictiveness of an identity script: (1) Who should be among us? and (2) What is required of us? The answers are rarely up to us as individuals: we can change the answers, over time, through our participation in collective self-authorship processes. Much like Charlie Parker and the punk rock trailblazers in *Death*, whom we encountered in Chapter 1, we can take control of the tight scripts that box us in. And we change them so that our identity scripts work better for us—to advance our life-shaping projects.

Taking control of tight scripts sometimes occurs over time by building on the work of those who preceded us. Think back to the members of *Death* and their work to make the punk rocker script more flexible, as we discussed in Chapter 1. The challenge they faced in 1970s Detroit was that black youth were not seen as eligible to be punk rockers—white punks did not see them as "among us." James Spooner took up this resistance to tight scripts and built on it by providing different answers to the question of what is required to be punk. Spooner describes feeling dissatisfied with the punk movement even though he shared many of its core values:

[D]espite being a vegan, and politically progressive person of color, and like, being a 16-year-old vegan feminist that was down with gay rights, I felt like the punk scene wasn't addressing my

120 WHAT DO WE NEED TO BREAK FREE?

needs. And it wasn't really addressing my needs as a black dude. It was a hard spot to be in due to my love of punk at a core level.[28]

In response to this experience of tight punk rocker scripts, Spooner set out to interview black punk rockers, often though chatrooms and message boards. Eventually, he put together a documentary, "Afropunk." He found that the documentary, and the community he tapped into through his interview process, addressed an unmet need for many others: "What it did was create connection and community in ways I never knew it would. It resonated.... The message board scene kids were meeting up on their own. It felt like we were not only suiting a need but helping those that needed it and were marginalized culturally."[29] From their experience of being boxed in by tight scripts, Spooner and others built a new community as Afropunks within the broader punk scene. In this scene, they could embrace and express the punk values and style of music that attracted them, while also discussing and making music about experiences of race and racism that had historically been neglected by the punk scene. When the punk script was too tight, they took control of the script and refashioned it.

In some cases, taking control of scripts to advance life-shaping projects requires much broader collective action than the Afropunk scene. For some activists in radical left politics in the 1960s and 1970s, their projects required challenging racial and gendered division, misunderstanding, and hatred to overcome inequality and oppression—a task they saw as challenging the structure of American society. Groups like the Black Panthers sought out like-minded groups organizing in other communities on the basis of other identities to push collectively for structural change. Here is how Kathleen Cleaver, a prominent member of the Black Panthers, described this task:

In a world of racist polarization, we sought solidarity. . . . We organized the Rainbow Coalition, pulled together our allies,

COLLECTIVE SELF-AUTHORSHIP PROCESSES 121

including not only the Puerto Rican Young Lords, the youth gang called Black P. Stone Rangers, the Chicano Brown Berets, and the Asian I Wor Kuen (Red Guards), but also the predominantly white Peace and Freedom Party and the Appalachian Young Patriots Party. We posed not only a theoretical but a practical challenge to the way our world was organized, And we were men and women working together.[30]

Cleaver's goal of solidarity across all of these groups challenged tight scripts about who to associate with, and provided a more flexible answer to the question of "who should be among us?" It also added content in response to the question of "what is required of us?" The structure of the coalition, with its identity-based member organizations, reflected the importance of groups engaging in intragroup CSA. But with its emphasis on solidarity, the coalition also added expectations that coalition members would support mutual struggles in the interest of intergroup CSA. For Cleaver and other radical activists, the answer to "who should be among us?" was not only people of the same race or living in the same neighborhood or only the men of a given group, but anyone facing oppression. And their answer to "what is required of us?" was not just contributing to ingroup struggles, but also mutually supporting the CSA of coalition partners. In this way, these activists worked to take control of the scripts about association that inhibited broad collective action and instead made intergroup solidarity a core component of their identity scripts.

Our point in this section is not that these individuals and groups are good or successful in all respects. There is certainly room for debate in most cases.[31] Moreover, it may not always be obvious how much flexibility or restrictiveness is best for a particular group or CSA process. Coalitions can fail to be responsive to their members and can break down, which could happen in a community garden when members who strongly oppose killing lanternflies with pesticides threaten to withdraw from the garden if a more

122 WHAT DO WE NEED TO BREAK FREE?

environmentally responsible control method is not adopted. And there can be legitimate reasons to conclude that one's identity group has become incompatible with one's own life plan, leading to a decision to disengage. Instead, what these examples demonstrate is that tight scripts are not inevitable. It is up to us to answer the key questions that determine how restrictive or flexible an identity will be: (1) Who should be among us? and (2) What is required of us? We can engage in CSA processes via discussion, disagreement, and contestation to change scripts over time. In a social environment characterized by tight scripts and identity trouble, or by an ethos of boxing in, we can use our collective agency to push for greater flexibility to support a more successful pursuit of our life-shaping projects.

Accountability Mechanisms

Identities exhibit heterogeneity and change over time. Failure to account for this can make CSA more difficult. To take control of identity scripts, we need a means of remaining responsive to our differences while sustaining CSA and coalition-building. Recall our community gardeners who have different backgrounds, perspectives, and who may be differently empowered within the group. They need tools to account for these differences so that they can be successful in coordinating shared life-shaping projects—everything from managing the garden schedule, to deciding how to control invasive pests, and whether to involve the community garden in political battles such as fighting budget cuts affecting public bus access to the garden. We propose to think about the tools they need to do this as "accountability mechanisms." We can manage group heterogeneity, and realize its value in CSA, by holding one another accountable for attending to our differences and life-shaping projects. Deploying these mechanisms is part of a process of CSA that unfolds over time. We identify three types of mechanisms.

COLLECTIVE SELF-AUTHORSHIP PROCESSES   123

Norms and expectations of *communication* constitute one type of accountability mechanism. Alicia Garza, a political organizer who co-created #BlackLivesMatter, discusses the organizing failures and successes she faced when engaging in multiracial coalition-building in California.[32] Noteworthy, for our purposes, is the role that communicative accountability mechanisms played in successful coalition-building. One challenge that Garza encountered was the pervasiveness of stereotypes among the people she was working to organize, as she explains:

> Stereotypes and prejudices fly around from all sides as people try to make meaning out of their conditions and seeming powerlessness. When I was organizing in San Francisco, I would hear these accusations exchanged between people with no organized or systemic power to change their own conditions: "Damn Mexicans," Black people would mutter under their breath. "¡Pinches negros!" Latinos would exclaim.[33]

When she would go door-knocking to talk with people about their shared problems, and ask them to get involved in advocacy, she would often hear misconceptions about people with other backgrounds. She reports hearing from black residents of San Francisco: "Look, I don't have nothing against nobody, but here's what I don't understand about these Mexicans.... How can so many of them live in one house?... They're loud, and the men be getting drunk and fighting on the weekends."[34] Similarly, Garza's friends reported similar misconceptions in their conversations with Latina domestic workers: "I don't understand why Black people are so lazy.... There was a movement in this country to get justice for Blacks.... But for what? What are they *doing* with that freedom they fought for?"[35] This mutual misunderstanding between black and Latino San Franciscans is an impediment to coalition-building. It can prevent people of different backgrounds—but with reasons to engage in CSA—from approaching one another in the first place,

124 WHAT DO WE NEED TO BREAK FREE?

and if they do communicate, that communication can be more difficult in light of these misconceptions.

Garza describes using communicative accountability mechanisms to address such stereotypes. She would avoid silencing or shutting down the person she was speaking with, as this might end the conversation without addressing the situation. Instead, she would elicit an explanation for the statements by asking questions to discern their reasons. And she notes that asking questions is important tool because it "is how we get to know what's underneath and in between our experiences in communities."[36] So, in response to the comment about many Mexicans living in one house, she would ask the commentor what they thought it might be like to live in a house with so many people, and why Latino families might be living under those conditions. Eventually, these questions could lead to a conversation about immigration policy and concerns about affordable housing.[37] And the hope was that addressing these matters could become shared life-shaping projects for these groups. Garza helps us see how we can hold one another accountable for being attentive to heterogeneity through communicative action—asking for explanations, justification, and calling for responsiveness to our perspectives.

To be sure, the kinds of conversations that Garza describes are not easy to initiate. And their impact can be short-lived without additional communication and action. Individuals making communicative demands on one another may not, in the end, suffice to take control of scripts and maintain successful CSA. But our influence can be amplified by coordinating CSA through organizations. This can make our activity more sustainable while creating additional opportunities for collective action.[38]

An example of how organizations can facilitate accountability over time is the ACT (Allied Communities of Tarrant), an advocacy and community service organization in Fort Worth, Texas. The ACT was founded in 1982, primarily drawing on membership from Christian churches across the city. The organization

COLLECTIVE SELF-AUTHORSHIP PROCESSES   125

emerged in part out of a desire to establish cooperation between Christians of different races and from different parts of the city after church leaders found that working within race-specific organizations had been ineffective.[39] Common religious values and identity provided an initial connective tissue for the organization and helped its members see one another as taking part in shared projects. Political scientist Mark R. Warren notes the following about the ACT: "In a society so fractured along racial lines, people from different racial groups often have difficulty seeing a common interest. A set of common beliefs, a shared identity as people of God, helps people to identify themselves as members of the same community."[40]

One early effort spearheaded by the ACT targeted an under-resourced and dysfunctional school "located in an area from which most of ACT's black churches drew members."[41] The ACT organized both teachers and parents to collaborate on reforming the school. They facilitated meetings to collect input from parents on obstacles to getting involved and then worked with parents and staff to identify, and address, their needs. Some initiatives that emerged in response included a free after-school program, parental training programs for helping students with their homework, and public recognition of student achievements. The program was successful: within two years, student test scores had improved, and a few years later the school won awards from the Texas governor and education agency.[42]

Communication was crucial for the success of this campaign, as it allowed the ACT, school staff, and parents to identify problems and strategies for problem-solving. But it also involved the expectation of certain forms of action, such as creating programs to address perceived problems. Had the ACT and school staff not followed through on these expected actions, they could rightly be held accountable by parents, who could disengage from the campaign. This marks a second type of accountability mechanism at our disposal in CSA processes—the *threat of exit*.

126   WHAT DO WE NEED TO BREAK FREE?

The school reform campaign was led by black participants in the ACT, but crucially, it was supported by Hispanic and white members.[43] The communication, cooperation, and mutual support for the education reform campaign established the basis of mutual trust which enabled ongoing collaboration for future challenges. It is important to note that trust-building and the mutual learning that accompanies it are not only things that happen within coalitions over time. They can also be facilitated by taking up the civic responsibilities we discuss in Chapter 5.

Communication and trust were valuable when the ACT crafted a proposal to apply for funds from the city to bring resources to underserved neighborhoods. Member churches put forward projects for their neighborhoods, but then had to negotiate among themselves for what to include in their joint proposal. With well-functioning mechanisms of accountability, and a strong basis for mutual trust, some members felt comfortable forgoing their projects in exchange for future support. As a result, the members of the ACT were able to collaborate on a joint proposal to put themselves in a better position to secure resources for their neighborhoods, rather than succumbing to a winners-and-losers mindset.[44] Without an organization through which to facilitate collective action and sustain knowledge from previous campaigns, this robust trust and attentiveness to the different members' needs would have been much more difficult to sustain. And with this organization in place, enforced by the threat of exit, the ACT was able to advance the life-shaping projects of their different church community members while remaining attentive to their differences.

CSA processes through organizations such as the ACT often involve forms of representation where some members assume the task of speaking and acting for the broader group. This is also a feature of CSA processes taking place outside of the government; even our Peaceful Gardeners can find themselves with group representatives that speak and act for the group, either at community garden board meetings or at officer meetings for a citywide council of Peaceful Gardeners. Representation was crucial to the ACT, with members of the clergy representing the projects and perspectives of their congregations in ACT meetings. Every constituent cannot be present in every meeting and it can be harder for groups to speak and act cohesively without delegating tasks to individuals who can speak and act for them. This is especially salient in governmental formal decision-making where elected officials, such as senators, as well as unelected public officials, such as judges and bureaucrats, make decisions about public policy on behalf of their constituents. These representatives are more likely to have a clearly defined constituency, such as a particular legislative district, or domain of representation, such as the Environmental Protection Agency's responsibility to protect the environment. These cases call attention to a third type of accountability mechanism—*actions to select and support representatives*.

Voting is a familiar action of this kind, such as when elected officials are selected through an electoral process by their constituents. Unelected officials, such as bureaucrats, can also be held accountable by elected officials who authorize their funding and influence their leadership when fielding complaints from constituents who can decide whether to re-elect them in the future. One may worry that any of the three accountability mechanisms we have identified can be manipulated, especially by elected or unelected elites or those with influential communication platforms like Rupert Murdoch, Elon Musk, and Mark Zuckerberg, to shape how people answer the questions of "who is among us?" and "what is required of us?" The truth is that these accountability mechanisms can be used to tighten scripts and to support a boxing in ethos. However, they can also be used—by elites, influencers, and non-elites—to create more flexible scripts and to support the alternative ethos we describe in Chapter 5.

The foregoing cases show, more generally, that we use accountability mechanisms when we make demands or express expectations of one another through CSA processes. We can demand forms of

128 WHAT DO WE NEED TO BREAK FREE?

communication, such as discussions about why a local school is underperforming, or we can demand particular outcomes, such as an after-school program. We can also sanction others, whether representatives or fellow constituents, when they fail to live up to these demands or expectations. For instance, we can leave groups or coalitions that are insufficiently responsive to our projects, and we can elect new representatives or legislators if the incumbents are not meeting our needs. All of these mechanisms of accountability pertaining to communication, representation, and exit are crucial for ensuring that representatives and organizations are attentive to the heterogeneity of the groups they serve.

Accountability Chains

Accountability mechanisms offer hope for making identity heterogeneity a coalitional strength. But the four distinct challenges posed by identity trouble (presented in Chapter 2), and the ethos of boxing in that they foster, are wide-ranging and deeply embedded. They extend beyond any one identity to threaten the stability and effectiveness of democracy itself. And to address this problem, given its immense scope, our accountability practices must extend beyond any one organization or coalition.

Think back to our community garden example. We raised the possibility that group members may have different perspectives on whether the garden should get involved in local politics either to pushback against a city pesticide mandate or protest changes to public transportation funding that would make it difficult for bus-riding members to access the garden. On the one hand, their different perspectives could cause the group to break down and become less effective with fewer members. On the other hand, if the group could find a way to make decisions about political involvement in ways that were attentive to their differences, it could become an informative and influential voice in the local

COLLECTIVE SELF-AUTHORSHIP PROCESSES   129

political scene because of the diversity of its membership. This attentiveness could be secured through the use of accountability mechanisms: the gardeners could host meetings to communicate their different perspectives and priorities and decide on a decision-making procedure. They could add more structure to their organization to facilitate these processes, such as by electing an executive committee tasked with making decisions, communicating with other organizations in the community, and consulting with the membership as needed.

To take another step in this collective self-authorship process: if the members of the community garden adopt larger projects, such as contributing to sustainability and food security nationally, they will need to work with other persons and organizations in other contexts. They may need to engage in coalition-building with community gardens in other cities to share knowledge of sustainable practices, conduct outreach to populations they have not already engaged, and push for changes to public policy and food systems. At this point, the community garden members cannot just concern themselves with internal accountability mechanisms focusing narrowly on attentiveness to the projects of its membership. They must extend these mechanisms externally so they can be responsive to coalition partners' projects too. In addition, they must contribute to holding other organizations accountable in their collective endeavors, and to holding other representatives, such as elected officials, accountable to the projects associated with sustainability and food justice. With this broader scope in mind, the community garden members must consider how its CSA processes can also contribute to chains of accountability within the broader environment in which they must operate to pursue larger projects.

Much like the community garden's projects of sustainability and food justice, the project of responding to identity trouble and securing democracy is wide-ranging. It is not specific to one particular tight script or one local context, but instead arises out of the interaction of multiple scripts and contexts. But like the community

130   WHAT DO WE NEED TO BREAK FREE?

garden, as agents committed to democratic problem-solving we can aim to responsibly engage in accountable CSA processes in our own contexts in ways that contribute to broader change and facilitate other forms of collective action. We will have more to say about how the micro and macro scale connect to one another in Chapters 5 and 6, but it is worth saying a bit now about how we can contribute to chains of accountability to respond to identity trouble in the political realm.

One example of increased accountability that changed tight scripts comes from the recent history of the AFL-CIO. As the labor movement has diversified in the past several decades, with increasing numbers of immigrant members speaking multiple languages, the leadership of the AFL-CIO and its member unions has had to become more attentive to this diversity in a few ways.[45] With respect to communicative accountability, national union conventions are increasingly multilingual. This facilitates the ability of representatives to learn about the needs and projects of their constituents who speak different languages and the ability of their diverse constituents to make demands for explanations and outcomes.

In addition, the change in labor movement demographics spurred the AFL-CIO to support pro-immigration legislation and regulatory policies. In this case, the AFL-CIO was responsive to the ways that politics could get in the way of the life-shaping projects of their immigrant members and needed to advance those projects to secure continued support through leadership elections and financial support in the form of dues. These changes in communication and political activity also coincide with changes to the AFL-CIO member script. In light of these changes, AFL-CIO scripts are flexible enough to permit, and make visible, the substantial contributions of immigrant, non-English-speaking members in the labor movement. Whereas taking part in CSA in particular immigrant communities and being a member of the AFL-CIO may have seemed in tension, in the same way that being an Afropunk in the 1970s might have been, this added flexibility allows these

CSA processes to be complementary. In addition, with the various accountability mechanisms at their disposal, the members of the AFL-CIO have tools to push for continued attentiveness to their heterogeneity as the membership continues to change in the future. The change in demographics first visible among union locals, through an accountability chain, led to increased accountability to immigrant union members at the national level.

It would be a mistake to conclude on this basis that consensus and cooperation involving all citizens in a democracy are required to combat identity trouble. That would be much too demanding. But to combat the troubling mindsets we discussed in Chapter 2, such as a friends-and-enemies conception of the social environment, and the boxing in ethos fostered by this and other components of identity trouble, we do need greater flexibility to formulate different coalitions and different life-shaping projects. With more citizens taking control of tight scripts, we should expect a greater variety of organizations with different conceptions of their identities to emerge and contribute to political contestation and debate. And these organizations can provide different models of political activity for citizens with different backgrounds, perspectives, and levels of empowerment.

For example, during the 1960s and 1970s, a variety of radical and more moderate Mexican American organizations took on anti-Mexican discrimination. Some Mexican American organizations, such as MEChA (Movimiento Estudiantil de Aztlán), were motivated by ideals of ethnic and cultural self-determination and embraced confrontational protest tactics. Others, such as MALDEF (Mexican American Legal Defense and Educational Fund), were motivated by more moderate ideals such as national equality and pursued it through organizing for election turnout, lawsuits against segregated school districts and to protect voting rights, and lobbying elected officials.[46]

Despite these differences in perspectives and strategy, these organizations, and many others, coexisted in an ideologically diverse

132 WHAT DO WE NEED TO BREAK FREE?

landscape of Mexican American political activism. This landscape provided many different models of political engagement such that Mexican Americans with different life plans were not constrained to a narrow band of political activity to contribute to the shared project of combating discrimination. These organizations thereby facilitated the political activity of their constituents to hold policymakers accountable to their life-shaping projects. They also contributed to accountability chains by holding one another accountable insofar as members of one organization that was proving ineffective could exit to join another.

In addition to providing more flexibility with regard to political activity in Mexican American CSA, this diversity of perspectives contributed to a more robust overall social movement that combated discrimination through social, cultural, economic, and legal means. Using this diverse political landscape of Mexican American political organizations as a template, it is clear that we do not need one overarching coalition, and that all citizens need not converge on the same political perspective, to combat identity trouble. In fact, preserving the flexibility to shift between different coalitions and different kinds of political activity can contribute to more successful CSA, while combating the strict lines of division on which our current form of identity trouble relies.

What about Intersectionality?

My feminism will be intersectional or it will be bullshit.[47]

This isn't just the white climate kids' movement anymore—this is an intersectional movement for justice.[48]

The identity politics that come from intersectionality are designed to separate people into different social groups with different ratings of privilege and grievance.

COLLECTIVE SELF-AUTHORSHIP PROCESSES 133

Military units must be one team—in complete unity—or
Americans die and America fails.[49]

"Intersectionality," an academic term originating from legal scholarship about anti-discrimination law, is now a widespread feature
of political and cultural debates in the United States. These quotes
are instances of its use. You may have seen the first quote on tote
bags or magnets. And the others illustrate how the term appears
in political and cultural battles under our current conditions of
identity trouble. All of this is indicative of the current salience of
intersectionality in public discourse, where it is a familiar framework for talking about heterogeneity within and between identity groups. Critical readers may ask: (1) Why should we bother
thinking about identity scripts and accountability mechanisms
when we already have intersectionality? (2) Is there any tension between our discussion of how identities work and their role in CSA
processes, on the one hand, and intersectionality on the other?

To answer these questions, we must clarify what "intersectionality" means in its original academic context. It was first
introduced by the legal scholar Kimberle Crenshaw to describe
shortcomings in anti-discrimination law as well as feminist and
anti-racist social movements. Black women faced a dilemma with
respect to anti-discrimination law, according to Crenshaw, as they
were simultaneously seen by courts as insufficiently similar to
white women and black men to reliably secure anti-discrimination
protection in the workplace, while courts did not recognize discrimination as black women as falling under a protected class.[50]
Similarly, feminist and anti-racist movements tended to assume
that race and sex could be analyzed in isolation, and as a result,
tended to focus on the experiences of class-privileged white women
and black men.[51]

Crenshaw compares discrimination to a traffic intersection. Traffic can flow from multiple directions so when an accident occurs, it can be caused by cars traveling from any of the

134   WHAT DO WE NEED TO BREAK FREE?

directions leading into the intersection and sometimes all at once. The discrimination faced by black women is analogous: they can experience race discrimination, sex discrimination, as well as distinctive discrimination as black women.[52] On this basis, Crenshaw concluded that it was a mistake to analyze race and sex (as well as class) as distinct axes that can be isolated. In contrast, an intersectional approach recognizes the need for anti-racist theories that include analyses of patriarchy, as well as the need for feminist theories that include analyses of racism.[53]

When "intersectionality" is used according to Crenshaw's initial formulation, it is both compatible with, and complementary to, the framework we have articulated here.[54] Intersectionality, in this sense, calls attention to the discrimination and oppression that people experience in virtue of the interaction between certain identities they inhabit. Heterogeneity in the form of differences of empowerment—a category we illustrated above with the Chipko movement case—can arise because of these dynamics and should be attended to in CSA processes, or else they may fail to be responsive to disadvantaged group members' projects.

For an example of this complementarity, consider Patricia Hill Collins's work on intersectionality and participatory democracy. Hill Collins puts forth a notion of "flexible solidarity," which she argues has been practiced by black women in social movements. When engaging in flexible solidarity, activists work in coalition with others in a context-sensitive manner, and do not accept existing hierarchies, such as gender hierarchy in black American organizations, as permanent features of their cooperation.[55] Hill Collins argues that flexible solidarity can facilitate *both* intersectional efforts to resist interlocking forms of oppression and participatory democratic efforts to promote equality among citizens.[56] These insights are compatible with our perspective on CSA processes, as practicing flexible solidarity can also promote accountability to differences of empowerment and contribute to democratic problem-solving.

COLLECTIVE SELF-AUTHORSHIP PROCESSES   135

The term "intersectionality" garnered heavy academic and public use following Crenshaw's work, but it is not always used clearly and consistently. A 2019 academic article notes: "[r]arely has one term been asked to do so much. It has been described as a lived experience, an aspiration, a strategy, a way to analyze inequality, and even a movement."[57] One ambiguity concerns the scope of intersectionality. Some use the term to refer specifically to structures and experiences of oppression such that there are specific intersectional identities, such as black woman or disabled person of color. Others use intersectionality more broadly to refer to any confluence of identities.[58]

Despite the compatibility between our argument in this book and the work of intersectional theorists such as Hill Collins, intersectionality theory is ultimately insufficient for addressing the problems posed by tight scripts and identity trouble. There are a few reasons for this. First, not all forms of heterogeneity that matter for CSA are reducible to differences of oppression. For example, the differences of perspective we discussed between Eritrean Americans and between different Mexican American political organizations are not fully captured by differences in oppression. They reflect, at least in part, different conceptions of what is required of group members or what will best advance the group's life-shaping projects, independently of any differences of oppression experienced by group members.

Second, some forms of boxing in can still contribute to identity trouble without constituting oppression. For instance, in Chapter 2, we discussed Silas House's experience of being boxed in by fellow progressives when they find out he is from Kentucky. House's experience reflects that others were treating him according to restrictive and misleading scripts about being a Kentuckian, but it is not clear that these experiences mean he is oppressed. So, intersectionality that refers specifically to oppression is not general enough to account for the full scope of the challenge posed by heterogeneity and our concerns about identity trouble. This is not necessarily a defect

136   WHAT DO WE NEED TO BREAK FREE?

of intersectionality theory, as it was not designed to address this problem, but it does suggest that public discussions of group heterogeneity should extend beyond intersectionality to address the wide scope of identity trouble.

Sometimes "intersectionality" is used more broadly to refer to any confluence of identities, without necessarily referring to oppression.[59] As an example, consider Martina Avanza's research on women activists in the Italian Pro-Life Movement. Avanza argues that using intersectionality as an interpretive framework allows her to "account for the heterogeneity of the women" she met during her fieldwork.[60] She notes that "[n]ot all pro-life women have lived the same lives: some have children but some do not, some have careers while others are housewives, many are married and have a conservative lifestyle (stay-at-home mothers), while others had children out of wedlock or had an abortion."[61] It is clearly important for movement participants to recognize and be accountable to such heterogeneity.[62] But it is not clear that the confluences of identities that Avanza identifies are reducible to oppression. For example, the difference between childless women and women with children might be an important source of heterogeneity, but it may not amount to a difference of oppression.

While this broader usage is a better fit for the more general scope of identity trouble, it is still inadequate for our explanatory purposes in this book. One issue is that it is not clear that all impactful forms of heterogeneity arise from an intersection of two or more identities. For instance, we noted that Naakh Vyosky's organizing of his neighbors as a voting bloc was a form of CSA that did not quite give rise to a coherent and salient identity label, but which depended on some identity-like connection. Yet their participation in this CSA process seems to be a distinctive feature of their life plans that would distinguish them from other Massachusetts voters, other Bostonians, and other senior citizens.

Relatedly, group members with different perspectives on the meaning of an identity label may not have corresponding

COLLECTIVE SELF-AUTHORSHIP PROCESSES   137

differences of intersecting identities, or even different life experiences, that explain their different perspectives. Consider the different perspectives on Black nationalism that we discussed in Chapter 3: some black nationalists emphasize black control of institutions such as schools or banks, while others emphasize black sovereignty over land. We can imagine activists that endorse each view disagreeing about the proper content of the label "Black Nationalist," and this disagreement could be impactful for future prospects of coalition-building between them without the disagreement amounting to a difference of the confluence of their identities, let alone a difference of oppression. At the very least, then, it would be confusing to use intersectionality theory to refer broadly to all forms of group heterogeneity that are important for accountable CSA processes, and doing so may also lead us to mischaracterize the range of heterogeneity that is present.

In summary, we should not conclude that intersectionality can or should account for all forms of identity heterogeneity. And we should not conclude that it is in tension with the perspective we articulate in this book. Instead, intersectionality theory seems complementary to our view given its insights about the complexity of oppression and differences of empowerment. Having offered this assessment of the relationship between our view and intersectionality as a theory, we now turn to intersectional political practices to examine potential complementarities and tensions with our view.

Intersectional Tight Scripts

"Unfortunately, when I encounter conversations about intersectionality online, the term is often uttered merely as cultural shorthand, the social justice equivalent of 'You go girl!,' ready to be GIFed, Tumbled, or tee-shirted."[63] Latoya Peterson, writing in the *Washington Post*, worries that the content of intersectionality

138 WHAT DO WE NEED TO BREAK FREE?

theory has been lost in its transition from the academic to the public sphere. She reports flinching at the term "intersectional feminists" because identifying as such involves taking "a term designed to complicate our understanding of society and flattening it into a label."[64]

Whether or not its content has been flattened, intersectionality has certainly emerged as a label with which activists identify. With that transition come both opportunities for collective self-authorhip and the risks of being boxed in. And while intersectionality has served as a site of cultural contestation, many public debates about intersectionality focus on practices associated with the theory and whether they are justified or not, rather than debates directly about the theory itself.[65] For example, some public commentators worry that intersectionality licenses (or has been mistakenly taken to license) intolerance of differences of perspective and excessive deference to the experiential authority of the marginalized.[66]

We say more about how we can engage in accountable CSA responsibly in the next two chapters, but for now, it is worth noting that some activism labeled intersectional does seem to usefully attend to otherwise neglected forms of heterogeneity. One example is the AIWA (Asian Immigrant Women Advocates), which is a community organization that organizes and provides training for Asian women in low-paid industries. As part of its work, it identifies shared problems common to other identities, such as women, workers, and immigrants, and works to establish programs to address these problems. One program is a health clinic created to treat chronic pain and injury among garment workers, which also sought to connect workers with medical professionals and public policy officials to establish collaborative relationships for the future.[67]

However, this does not mean that all forms of intersectional activism are free of concerns about boxing in.[68] Intersectional activists can deploy overly tight scripts about political association and action. Asad Haider recalls his frustration when, as a student activist

COLLECTIVE SELF-AUTHORSHIP PROCESSES   139

taking part in an occupation protest against tuition hikes, a group of fellow activists split off to form a distinct POC (people of color) caucus with accusations that the primary organization had become a "white space," despite objections from a multiracial opposition.[69] Haider notes that a group of core organizers argued that the claim that the student-activist occupation was a white space "rendered the activists of color who organized the occupation completely invisible" and benefited the administration at the expense of the occupation.[70] By declaring their opposition and then walking out of a meeting, the POC caucus seem to have refused communicative accountability with their fellow activists. By claiming to speak on behalf of POC in general, they failed to be attentive to, and make visible, the differences in perspectives among their fellow activists.

Just as it is possible to raise concerns about boxing in resulting from some intersectional political practices, intersectionality advocates might also raise concerns about our own perspective on group heterogeneity. Some might worry that in broadening the scope of accountability in CSA processes beyond matters of oppression, as we discussed in the previous section, our political practices might fail to alleviate, and perhaps even license, asymmetric burdens between members of groups or coalitions. Recall our example of the AFL-CIO's increase in accountability to its growing immigrant constituency with multilingual meetings and immigration reform advocacy. We could imagine that these efforts might have been made more difficult because of the organization's attentiveness to other kinds of heterogeneity that are not as closely tied to immigration status, such as the different industries that its member unions represent or the different geographic areas where their members reside. While immigrant union members might have made an intersectional claim about being disempowered as workers and as immigrants, this might not have been sufficient to enact change within the AFL-CIO without also working to persuade, and form compromises with, representatives of member unions with different perspectives on immigration policy.

140   WHAT DO WE NEED TO BREAK FREE?

Immigrant AFL-CIO members in this hypothetical scenario might reasonably object that a more intersectionally minded and structured organization would be better positioned to respond to the challenges of being an immigrant and a worker in the United States.

While we agree that undue burdens are a problem for CSA processes to take up, knowing that fellow group members face a burden is insufficient for addressing the "now what" question that we encounter with Rustin's dilemma. That is, when we find that a particular form of group difference challenges our coordinated pursuit of projects, we need to know more about the context and the other kinds of heterogeneity at work to determine how best to respond. And it will often be the case that addressing concerns about oppression or (dis)empowerment will also require attentiveness to other kinds of heterogeneity within the overburdened group. Imagine that those pushing for a greater role for immigrant members and immigration policy advocacy in the AFL-CIO formed an immigrant rights caucus. Despite their agreement on this basic set of projects, the members would surely exhibit other kinds of heterogeneity: different backgrounds with non-immigrant members and immigrants from different parts of the world, and differences of perspective about how best to agitate for change within the organization. The members of this caucus would also need accountability mechanisms to manage these forms of heterogeneity to make progress on their core concerns about the oppression of immigrants and workers.

Our view is not, however, that asymmetric burdens should always be accepted for the sake of a broader group or coalition. Like Patricia Hill Collins argues with her notion of flexible solidarity, we agree that it is important to guard against the entrenchment of hierarchies as part of coalition-building. As we have noted in this chapter, the threat of exit is an important mechanism of accountability and it can be usefully deployed when some group members' needs are not met. But knowledge of a particular asymmetric burden will not be enough to decide whether to exit a group

COLLECTIVE SELF-AUTHORSHIP PROCESSES   141

or a coalition. Imagine that the members of an immigrant rights caucus of the AFL-CIO have to consider not only the accountability of the organization to their projects, but also their own accountability to immigrants who are not yet in a union, but which could be organized were the caucus to be successful in the future. A premature exit might fail to advance the projects of even more vulnerable constituencies who could contribute to the CSA process in the future.

Finally, we also cannot assume that claims of asymmetric burdens will be uncontroversial, even among allies. Consider the tensions between narratives about graduate student employees as precarious workers versus professors-in-training during the 2015 strike at the University of Toronto. In a push for better funding packages from the university, graduate student workers called attention to the rising cost of living in Toronto and uncertainty about post-graduation employment prospects.[71] In so doing, they challenged the narrative that their conditions were justified because they were professors-in-training with appeal to conditions of precarity. But this shift in narrative was accepted to different degrees by other university stakeholders that served as useful sources of support.

Faculty were one important source of support for the graduate students' campaign. This support came in the form of solidarity statements from individual departments and attendance at faculty association rallies in support of the strike and its demands. However, the faculty differed with respect to how much they agreed with the challenge to the professors-in-training narrative. Some noted the value of course teaching assignments for graduate students' dossiers to prepare them for the job market, arguing that these arrangements were less exploitative than they would be for someone who had graduated from a doctoral program.[72] In light of this disagreement, graduate students could not rely exclusively on their precarity claim in securing support from the faculty association and other individual departments. They would also need additional strategies for building support that took this disagreement

142   WHAT DO WE NEED TO BREAK FREE?

into consideration and attempted to persuade stakeholders in ways that would resonate with them.

Ultimately, we recognize the value of intersectionality not only as a theoretical framework, but also as a guide to political practice that attends to heterogeneity, as we saw with the AIWA case. But we should also remain vigilant about the risk of boxing in that comes with the growth of "intersectional" as an identity label for some contemporary activists and recognize the importance of accountability to a wide range of heterogeneity, even to address differences of power, which have been the focus of intersectional activism.

How to Break Free

Like Charlie Parker, who felt caged by the traditional jazz musician script, those of us who have been boxed in by tight scripts would like to break free. And for those of us committed to democracy, we also seek a way to break free from identity trouble that fosters an ethos of boxing in. To do this, we cannot simply abandon the role of identity in our lives or in our politics, nor can we double down on our usual identity scripts no matter how restrictive they are. Naive skepticism and naive optimism are not the solution. To really break free from tight scripts, we have to recognize the power that we have to change how restrictive or flexible our identities are and make sure that they are working for us and our projects. Like the members of a community garden, each of us has to engage in some form of coordination of our projects with others around us to break free. Without attending to the needs of different plants, and differences in sunlight and moisture in different parts of the garden, we may not be as successful in growing what we set out to grow. But if we coordinate with others, we can take advantage of the different information, expertise, and collective impact that only a larger group can provide.

Similarly, we can respond to the threat of tight scripts by working with others to take control of them through the CSA processes presented in this chapter. Yet the threat of boxing in is ever-looming. To avoid boxing others in, and breaking down the coalitions on which we rely, we need to remain attentive to the heterogeneity within and between our groups. To do so, we must hold one another accountable to be responsive to these differences, all while creating space for the coordination of our life-shaping projects. In Part III, to which we now turn, we discuss our civic responsibilities to do so and how we can approach them with respect to micro- and macro-politics.

PART III
HOW DO WE BREAK FREE?

5

Micropolitics

Responsibilities of Collective Self-Authorship

Groups of people with different collective identities living in the same neighborhood may engage in collective self-authorship (CSA) projects that bind them with ingroup members—with whom they share racial, ethnic, or religious identities—while putting them at odds with neighbors who do not share these specific identities. When this happens, neighborhood residents can find themselves divided over education, jobs, housing, policing, and other matters. These differences may materialize and may be magnified in the groups and organizations that they join to pursue their goals. But this situation can change dramatically if they engage in CSA that involves cooperation with their diverse group of neighbors to pursue a common goal.

This happened in a Brooklyn, New York, neighborhood, Williamsburg/Greenpoint, in the mid-1990s when two of its largest minority groups, Hasidic Jews and Latinos, who had been at odds over many matters including affordable public housing throughout the 1970s and 1980s, formed an environmental justice organization to address disproportionately high pollution rates in their community—a common goal.[1] Neighborhood activists from each group joined with other racial and ethnic groups to organize a Community Alliance for the Environment (CAFE). Bringing this alliance together, giving it direction, and sustaining it, by using the diverse collective identities represented within the alliance to their advantage, required work. It also required activist leaders, as well as rank-and-file alliance members, to assume certain responsibilities

Boxed In. Derrick Darby and Eduardo J. Martinez, Oxford University Press. © Oxford University Press 2024.
DOI: 10.1093/9780197620236.003.0006

148   HOW DO WE BREAK FREE?

to ensure that their collective identities remained flexible enough—
not boxing themselves or others in—to facilitate their CSA goals.
This chapter identifies some of the work required to manage group
heterogeneity to delineate the civic responsibilities of CSA.

Collective self-authorship, in virtue of being collective, always
involves managing group heterogeneity. And identity scripts are
tools for this purpose. However, as we show in Chapters 1 and 2,
collective identities can cause trouble when scripted too tightly
such that they carry the risk of boxing in ourselves and others.
So, when we deploy them in CSA, we have an overarching civic
responsibility to mitigate this risk. In other words, we have a responsibility to make sure that CSA is accountable to group heterogeneity. By "civic" we mean being a citizen of a particular
community, organization, group, alliance, or some other network.
There are certain things that we must do, in our various roles as
citizens, to discharge this overarching responsibility. We must
search for heterogeneity. We must amplify or make it visible. And
we must act in ways that are responsive to it. These are the component civic responsibilities of ensuring that CSA is accountable to
group heterogeneity.

In whatever network individuals participate, be it an organization fighting for civil rights, a fan club supporting a *fútbol* team,
or a community garden group, all members have an overarching
civic responsibility, as well as component civic responsibilities, to
help advance the collective life-shaping projects facilitated by participation in these networks. And this is true for formal or informal
representatives of these groups, for rank-and-file members, and for
all of them as citizens of a larger society with a basic structure that
specifies the background regulations, laws, and policies that bear
on achieving their goals. Likewise, it is true for all of them insofar
as they may be citizens of smaller organizations with analogous
background norms that play a similar role.[2] There must be a division of labor to do the work of ensuring that CSA is accountable to
group heterogeneity. And discharging these civic responsibilities is

MICROPOLITICS 149

particularly vital for successful CSA in the political realm, where the kind of identity trouble we discussed in Chapter 2 can be especially counterproductive.

Relying upon micropolitics case studies, paying special attention to ones pertaining to environmental matters, we identify and illustrate three component civic responsibilities that must be undertaken to make sure that our collective identities work for us and not against us in forming and sustaining small-scale networks vital to CSA.[3] These networks need not be permanent or long-lasting. For however long they are needed, we must take up these crucial responsibilities to keep them intact. The work we do in this chapter, and in the next one, will complete our argument for why we must, and what it takes to, make our collective identities safe for democracy.

Environmentalists and Wyoming Ranchers

Chloe loves birds. And she is active in the National Audubon Society. But as a birder, who cares deeply about preserving the natural habitats of birds, she isn't that crazy about being called an environmentalist. This term has a bad rap, especially among conservatives. Saddling someone with this collective identity can hinder efforts to encourage environmentalists and conservative ranchers in Wyoming to pursue their common goal of environmental conservation. Based on how these ranchers see things, says Chloe, "an environmentalist is this person who is just misguided and doesn't understand. Or is completely off their rocker."[4] To avoid this reaction being directed her way, Chloe calls herself a centrist, not an environmentalist, when she shows up on the ranch. She works to get ranchers and environmentalists to see that they care about the same thing—environmental conservation—and that they have reason to work together. However, unlike the CAFE activists in Brooklyn, Chloe, in her activist work, did not try to

150 HOW DO WE BREAK FREE?

get potential alliance partners to rally around a shared environmental identity. Instead, she sought to rally environmentalists and Wyoming ranchers around a shared goal.

The problem here is not environmentalist identity as such. Rather, the problem is that this identity is scripted too tightly. One study of perceptions that people hold about environmentalism found that three themes loomed large when participants were asked what it means to be an environmentalist.[5]

1. Environmentalists value nature, its preservation, and want to protect it from harmful human activity.[6]
2. Environmentalists are actively involved in protecting and conserving nature, and this shows up in how they live and in everything they do.[7]
3. Environmentalists are altruistic and self-sacrificing as devoted stewards of the Earth and are concerned for the welfare of future generations.[8]

Alongside these positive associations, researchers also found more negative ones. And it is a short step from viewing environmentalists as passionate about nature to worrying about environmental extremism. "An environmentalist in my mind," said one participant in the study, "is someone . . . who is green in everything that they say and do, drives a Prius, recycles, things that Captain Planet would endorse."[9] Other participants worried about environmentalists being too green, or as a conservative Wyoming rancher might say, they worried that environmentalists can be "off their rocker." Some study participants described them as "zealots" who are aggressive, stubborn, and unrealistic. "The environmentalists I see talk of unrealistic goals," said one participant, "zero net carbon emissions (we'd basically have to go to a pre-industrial age), non-pesticide food (which means less food and more hunger), and a widespread conversion to solar power (ignoring the fact that few areas are suitable for it)."[10]

MICROPOLITICS 151

When this collective identity gets a negative spin, labels that are initially neutral, such as "greenie," "tree-hugger," and "conservationist," can easily become slurs that serve to tighten the environmentalist script. This worry motivated Chloe—clearly concerned about protecting birds and their habitats—to eschew being called an environmentalist. She understood that she would be boxed in by conservative Wyoming ranchers, which would make it more challenging for her to get them to see the value of pursuing CSA with environmentalists who shared a similar goal of environmental conservation. Although Chloe did not use this label herself, she did not throw up her hands and walk away. Instead, she took responsibility for ensuring that environmentalists and Wyoming ranchers could work together in CSA. Before we discuss the work she did to discharge this civic responsibility, comparing and contrasting it with the work done by CAFE activists, let us reflect on how we got to this point in the book's argument.

The worry about being boxed in by an overly restrictive environmentalist script is a real one. Recall from Chapter 1 that when this happens there are mechanisms—identity-shaping and identity-policing tools—at work that make particular identities hard to combine into a unified life plan. And these mechanisms can operate formally and institutionally or informally and interpersonally. The rancher case is an instance of the latter. Imagine that there were individuals in their group who considered themselves conservative ranchers but were also serious about advocating for and practicing environmentally friendly ranching. Fellow conservative ranchers might employ these mechanisms in ways that make combining conservative and environmentalist identities into a unified life plan difficult. If this happens, the boxed in ranchers can feel pressure to take specific actions (e.g., employing non-environmentally-friendly waste disposal practices on their ranches), or can be primed to have particular thoughts or feelings (e.g., thinking that environmentalists are aggressive and stubborn), or they can be prodded to reject associations with environmentalist individuals and organizations.

152   HOW DO WE BREAK FREE?

The worry here is that tightly scripted identities that box in—due to insufficient regard for intragroup heterogeneity—can inhibit a person's ability to engage in collective life-shaping projects with others who do not share the relevant identity. We have an overarching civic responsibility to mitigate this risk by working to ensure that CSA is accountable to heterogeneity.

At some point, all of us have felt that particular identities we embrace are too tightly scripted. Not much may ride on this, at times. However, on other occasions, such as when we wish to work with others to pursue common political projects, being boxed in can cause considerable trouble. For example, our natural tendency to sort fellow citizens into ingroups and outgroups, based on collective identities we share with some but not with others, can lead to adopting a friends-and-enemies mindset, which breeds animosity, distrust, and limited communication—all of which make engaging in CSA across identity divisions difficult.

In Chapter 2, we distinguished responses to the troubles associated with being boxed in by tight identity scripts into two main camps—the skeptics and the optimists. Skeptics highlight the drawbacks of identity-driven politics for democracy, while optimists emphasize the democratic benefits of identities. We think that both camps must be taken seriously, so we defend a form of qualified optimism, whereby identities can facilitate democratic problem-solving if citizens take up the responsibility to ensure that CSA is accountable to heterogeneity.

In Chapter 3, we described how collective identities function, in part, to underscore their dynamic nature and the need to take heterogeneity within and between groups seriously.[11] Just as heterogeneity must be managed for CSA when working within an ingroup, where there may be more homogeneity relatively speaking, it must also be managed when coalitions or other networks form between more or less homogenous groups that come together to coordinate pursuit of their life-shaping projects. Tightly scripted identities will raise the same kinds of identity trouble. Optimists must account

MICROPOLITICS 153

for the challenges raised by reliance on our dynamic collective identities. And, for their part, skeptics must accept that identities are much too central to our personal and collective lives to be set aside or diminished.

Identity trouble is especially concerning given the stakes of political activity in a democracy, where crucial outcomes can depend on our being able to work together and engage in collective problem-solving across differences. Climate change is arguably our most pressing problem—if we destroy the planet, we destroy ourselves. Clearly, we need to work together to address it. In the case at hand, overly restrictive conservative rancher identities, which box people in with ideologies, can pose an obstacle to addressing climate change collectively with those who embrace more pro-environment identities.

The divide on this issue can be captured in more explicitly partisan terms. For example, an empirical study in psychology noted differences in the beliefs of right-leaning and left-leaning political elites about the causes of climate change.[12] The former elites are more skeptical than the latter about human-caused explanations. Their skepticism was, in some instances, also directed at challenging the scientific consensus and even denying that climate change is happening at all. Right-leaning ingroup members sometimes use threatening terms such as "Environmental Taliban" and "Communists" to represent left-leaning outgroup individuals and organizations supporting environmental causes as enemies to be defeated.[13] Portraying environmentalists as threats and associating the ingroup conservative identity with believing that the environment should be utilized for human purposes were found to correlate with prioritizing economic matters such as industrial growth. Whatever the target of skepticism, the labeling tactics, and underlying motivating factors, the problem is not with being a conservative but with scripting this identity in ways that are inflexible and do not allow for collective self-authorship to address problems of common concern.

154 HOW DO WE BREAK FREE?

Attending to climate change and its impacts—on a small or large scale—is a clear-cut case where working together is as essential as dealing with deadly pandemics such as COVID-19. And we must acknowledge that our collective identities can create challenges as well as opportunities. It is tempting to think that the sharp right-left political differences on climate change are merely about differences in ideology or beliefs concerning the value of nature or the importance of economic matters. But this study finds that right-wing beliefs about environmentalists as a threat to the status quo loom larger in accounting for political polarization.[14] We are particularly interested in an implication drawn from this study. If right-wing denial of climate change, or rejection of the scientific consensus on its causes, can be mainly accounted for by ideological concerns about environmentalists' threats, and not by lack of education or knowledge, then gaining their cooperation in collective self-authorship projects may require interventions that are less threatening to conservative beliefs. For instance, environmentalists may seem less threatening to the conversative belief that growing the economy and creating jobs are preeminent values, if environmentalists push for creating green jobs. Indeed, we agree that "[m]essages to take action on climate change are unlikely to be effective, for instance, if the messenger is perceived as wanting to negatively alter society, and may instigate pushback."[15]

So, outgroup environmental activists who are aware of this, but want to forge coalitions with conservatives, will put less emphasis on trying to educate them about the man-made causes of climate change and instead emphasize building bridges to work with them on creating jobs for green industries. This is a way to act responsively to heterogeneity after recognizing it, which is another component civic responsibility of ensuring that CSA processes are accountable to heterogeneity. Likewise, pro-environment conservatives, who feel boxed in by the restrictive script, may work to loosen it by using the kind of accountability mechanisms that we discussed in Chapter 4 to compel ingroup members to be more

MICROPOLITICS   155

receptive to fellow members who see value in supporting efforts to create green jobs and to support green industries. To be sure, "a Republican leading figure with pro-environmental concerns might come across as an outgroup member, or at least not a full ingroup member, which may hinder any attitude change."[16] But this is precisely why accountability mechanisms are such a powerful tool; this Republican can threaten to exit the group, possibly taking others along, if the party identity is not made more flexible to account for the kind of heterogeneity that green Republicans represent.[17]

The interventions suggested by this study underscore the importance of framing work that can contribute to making identities safe for democracy. In this case, the argument is that the most effective way to gain right-wing support is to frame climate change mitigation in a non-threatening manner, and to stress the value of intergroup cooperation to deal with a common "enemy"—climate crisis. And this is work that can be done within groups, where individuals are trying to break free from tight scripts, as well as between groups, where individuals are trying to build larger networks to tackle the problem more effectively. Chloe's work with environmentalists and Wyoming ranchers was about building a larger network to tackle environmental conservation. The work of Hasidic and Latino CAFE activists in Brooklyn was about building a larger network to tackle neighborhood pollution. But as we shall discuss in more detail later, the framing work used in both cases was strikingly different. Yet both strategies constitute ways of discharging the component civic responsibility to act in ways that are responsive to heterogeneity.

Toxic Avengers Need Allies

The mayor of New York City resides in Gracie Mansion. So, Williamsburg resident Victor Torres quips: "If you want to build incinerators, how's the yard at Gracie?"[18] And putting words in

156 HOW DO WE BREAK FREE?

the mayor's mouth, Torres imagines that "the Mayor would have choice words, including, you're crazy."[19] Torres and his Brooklyn neighbors recognized that they suffered from a disproportionate share of environmental pollution. And they believed that this was due to their status as racial and ethnic minorities of modest means. Rich white people, in other parts of the city, would not stand for such pollution in their backyards and political elites would be loath to support industries that targeted these neighborhoods. Torres and his neighbors were certainly not crazy for believing this.

CAFE Alliance founders knew that securing environmental justice, which in this case would involve a more equitable distribution of toxic pollutants, was going to be difficult, especially in a city where the wealthy and big businesses wield lots of power and have the ear of political elites. To have any chance for success, they would have to grow their numbers to strengthen the movement. And they would have to do this, in part, by getting a heterogenous group of neighborhood residents to join the cause. While they were all Williamsburg/Greenpoint residents, and shared this neighborhood identity, they were also black, Latino, and Hasidic. The CAFE activists needed their diverse group of neighbors, including those that formed separate environmental action groups, such as the Toxic Avengers, to understand that it was imperative to form a broader coalition to fight environmental injustice. And this was the pitch: "What brings us together is that we have the same interests, we're living in the same place, the air is polluted just as well and we're afraid of the same environmental pollutants."[20]

The CAFE Alliance was formed because a group of neighbors wanted to secure the benefits of collective action in pursuit of a common goal. Working together politically for some period of time, while managing the risk associated with neglecting their differences in background, perspectives, and empowerment, would allow these Brooklynites to share insights and expand their influence.[21] Before offering our prescriptions for how to manage this risk—by spelling out the component civic responsibilities of

MICROPOLITICS 157

making CSA accountable to group heterogeneity—we will offer a few insights about coalitions and highlight some benefits and challenges of working within them.

Coalitions are networks that form when smaller groups come together in pursuit of a common objective.[22] They can take many different forms. Coalitions can bring together organizations from within the same social movement or they can draw from organizations across different movements.[23] They can operate with different intended durations, forming to stage a specific event or operating indefinitely to address an enduring threat. And they can operate at different scales, as local, national, or even transnational.[24] For example, the CAFE Alliance is a within-movement coalition, bringing together groups and organizations from the environmental justice movement. Its duration was determined by specific threats to the neighborhood, such as the toxic incinerator, and it operated at a local scale.

We should also not assume that coalitions presuppose consensus or that what binds them together does not change over time.[25] Different processes of collective action can lead to, and sustain, coalitions.[26] The CAFE Alliance could be viewed as a *conflictual coalitional process*, according to which, "collective actors are densely connected to each other in terms of alliances, and may identify opponents explicitly, but those alliances are not backed by strong identity links. The networks among actors mobilizing on a common goal take a purely contingent and instrumental nature."[27] Viewed this way, we would put less stress on efforts to mobilize neighborhood residents around a shared collective identity (e.g., vulnerable minorities). The groups and organizations to which they belong would remain the primary source of identification. However, in the course of a campaign, alliance partners may form identity links where none had existed previously, and this may lead to solidarities and collective action projects that outlast the campaign that first brought them together. So, what starts as a conflictual coalitional process may become a consensus one, where

158   HOW DO WE BREAK FREE?

members see themselves as sharing an identity-based solidarity that gives purpose and direction to their CSA projects.

Researchers identify various factors that account for the formation, longevity, and success of coalitions. These factors include resources, organizational goals and structure, ideological, cultural, and identity congruence, and characteristics of the broader environment such as political opportunities, threats, and institutional structures.[28] Another especially important factor—falling under the heading of social ties—is the presence and influence of "coalition brokers" or "bridge builders."[29] These individuals, who typically have social ties to different organizations, communities, and groups, play a crucial role in helping members of distinct networks come together in pursuit of CSA projects. Chloe was a bridge builder. She worked to bring together environmentalists and conservative Wyoming ranchers to pursue conservation efforts to protect birds and their natural habitat. To do this work, bridge builders must search for group heterogeneity, they must make it visible to potential coalition partners, and they must act (and encourage action) to mitigate the risk of identity trouble that stems from failures to respond appropriately to inter- and intragroup differences. Carrying out these civic responsibilities, which we will say more about shortly, contributes to bringing coalitions into existence, sustaining them, and making them successful.

The CAFE Alliance was a diverse coalition. Researchers who study social movements and civil resistance have found that diverse coalitions are valuable because they bring more resources to the table, including knowledge and networks.[30] And the broader-based mobilization that they make possible not only increases their size, making a more powerful statement than less diverse coalitions, it can also contribute to a higher success rate in achieving coalitional goals. When coalitions make a more powerful statement, by engaging a diverse group of individuals and networks in CSA to achieve a common goal, this can garner more media attention, it can enhance the coalition's public visibility, and it can

MICROPOLITICS   159

pressure political elites to be responsive to the coalition's demands. The CAFE founders hoped to secure these and other benefits by forming a diverse alliance of neighborhood residents.

But with benefits also come serious challenges.[31] Coalitions need to find the right balance between satisfying members of groups and organizations that join the coalition while being flexible enough to get these diverse groups to cooperate long enough to achieve common goals. This will require, among other things, that they are on the same page about the problems they face collectively, the goals they wish to achieve collectively, and the means they will pursue to achieve them. However, all of this is difficult to achieve in relatively homogenous coalitions, and the difficulty can increase with the diversity of a coalition. Overly restrictive identity scripts may impose expectations on ingroup members about what to think, how to act, and with whom to associate, which box them in and stand in tension with their projects, and inhibit the pursuit of CSA.

Coalition-building is hard for the same reasons that managing ingroup differences in background, empowerment, and perspective is challenging. Identity trouble can threaten or break down coalitions, or even prevent them from forming, thus serving as an impediment to CSA. Whatever form our networks take—groups, organizations, alliances, social movements—we have to worry about the dangers posed by tight identity scripts. Bridge builders like Chloe are mindful of these dangers and try to make diversity a coalitional strength by tapping into it to advance accountable CSA processes. Managing the risks associated with ignoring heterogeneity takes work. Maintaining coalitions that are instrumental to realizing our CSA goals also requires work.

We need effective tools that help with managing heterogeneity, whether we are pursuing CSA within a small ingroup or within a larger coalition. We also need to assume certain civic responsibilities. Earlier, in Chapter 4, we argued that accountability mechanisms such as communication, threat of exit, and selection of representatives give us the tools to manage how flexible

160 HOW DO WE BREAK FREE?

or restrictive our identities are, and to make sure that they work for us and not against us. These mechanisms provide hope for making identity heterogeneity a coalitional strength. But we must also attend to the interpersonal work done by individuals as representatives of groups, as constituents, and as contributors to background conditions that affect our efforts. In the sections that follow we consider some of this work to distinguish three component civic responsibilities of collective self-authorship.

Searching for Mules and Honeybees

A researcher wanted to understand why more people did not engage in pro-environmental behavior to mitigate climate change.[32] He believed that psychological barriers, or what he called "dragons of inaction," impede green behavior. One example of such a dragon is the limited cognitive ability of humans to seriously entertain what might happen in a distant future. So getting humans to think about the impact of what we do now on the climate two hundred years from today is difficult. Other dragons include our propensity to underestimate the risks of climate change, as well as underestimating our ability to take action that will be effective in dealing with it— falsely thinking that no small things we do can have any impact. But these psychological dragons do not have a hold on everyone. Some people, called "mules," already bear considerable responsibility in working to mitigate climate change. Other people, called "honeybees," do not act with the same motivations as mules, but nevertheless help the environment without it being an intended goal. Knowing whether we are dealing with mules or honeybees, and knowing what makes each type of person tick, can be useful for determining the best policy interventions or pro-environmental practices to pursue. It can also affect the kind of responsiveness to heterogeneity that is required. Should a coalition broker frame the goal of a prospective alliance between a group of mules and a group

MICROPOLITICS 161

of honeybees as a push for "go green" stickers on energy-efficient products or "save $$" stickers on them? Or should they adopt some other frame?

Understanding the various dragons that impede green behavior is vital for getting more people to be like mules or honeybees. It is an example of group heterogeneity that we should factor into our participation in CSA processes to improve their efficacy and accountability to heterogeneity. In Chapter 4, we identified accountability mechanisms that we can use to break free from tight scripts. These mechanisms include communication, the selection of representatives, and the threat of exit. But just knowing about these mechanisms or having them in place in an organization is not enough; we also need to make use of these mechanisms responsibly. This is the work marked out by the component civic responsibilities of CSA.

When thinking about the additional work to be done to ensure that CSA is accountable to heterogeneity, and the component civic responsibilities marked by this work, we start with the search for heterogeneity within our groups and networks. Whether we are working to mitigate climate change, to conserve the environment, or to fight environmental injustice, when we do this by engaging in CSA with others in some sort of network, be it a small community group or a larger alliance of multiple groups, it is imperative that we discern the kind of group heterogeneity we are dealing with, especially as it pertains to what might cause identity trouble for us. Searching for heterogeneity is about realizing that we attach different meaning to labels, that we identify with them in different ways (some aspects may be more or less salient), and that we are treated in different ways. It is, of course, also about realizing that these are related to differences in our backgrounds, perspectives, and empowerment.

In an effort to build a pro-environmental alliance, a bridge builder like Chloe might ask, are we dealing with mules or honeybees? Mules are willing to assume responsibility for climate

162   HOW DO WE BREAK FREE?

change, environmental conservation, or environmental justice, purposefully pursue these goals, and are more likely to call themselves "environmentalists." Honeybees, on the other hand, are people who positively impact the environment without aiming to do so. They may choose walking or biking over polluting cars for health reasons. They may consume fewer polluting resources because of being thrifty or preferring a simple way of life. They may object to putting toxic incinerators in minority urban neighborhoods because they believe that citizens should have greater autonomy in such matters. While serving their narrow ends without explicit concern for the environment or for justice, honeybees unwittingly have a positive impact on the environment or on realizing environmental justice. Understanding these differences will dictate the kind of action in response to heterogeneity that might be needed to make CSA successful.

A bridge builder like Chloe, seeking to form or sustain a broader pro-environmental alliance that includes people who are more strongly affected by dragons of inaction than mules or honeybees, must also ask which dragons are affecting different ingroup or outgroup coalition partners. Assuming that people are risk-averse, and that risk comes in different species including functional risk ("Will this Tesla leave me stranded?"), physical risk ("Will this Tesla blow up in my garage?"), financial risk ("Is the price of this Tesla worth the marginal environmental benefit?"), and social risk ("What will my friends in Texas who drive pickups say when I pull up in a Tesla?") to guard against identity trouble we must also look for these differences between potential coalition partners.[33] Searching for such differences will inform the kind of responsiveness needed to expand the group of mules or honeybees or, perhaps, to bring members of both groups together within a broader coalition. The mule-honeybee case is general. Some imagination is required to envision the collective identities at issue and how heterogeneity appears. So let us consider another, more concrete, case that requires less imagination.

MICROPOLITICS 163

Research on three environmental movement organizations in the United Kingdom also illustrates the importance of searching for identity heterogeneity, especially when trying to form a pro-environment coalition of groups with distinctive collective identities.[34] Chiswick Wildlife Group (CWG) is a local conservation organization. Environmental Direct Action Group (EDAG) is radical organization fighting climate change. Friends of the Earth (FoE) pursues pro-environmental action by working with willing government and corporate partners. CWG has a conservationist identity. Its members share an interest in protecting natural sites and habitats. EDAG has a radical identity. Its members share an interest in taking aggressive action against bad environmental actors and making pro-environment behavioral changes in how we live—from what we eat, what we wear, and how we travel—to bring about systemic change. FoE has a reformist identity. Its members share an interest in working within the system to change laws, policies, and practices that are detrimental to the planet. To fully understand their dynamics and complexity, we would need even more information about the substance of these respective collective identities. We would need to consider the meanings assigned to these labels, patterns of identification, and treatment of group members. In other words, we would need to consider how these identities work, following our discussion in Chapter 3.

Regardless of how these details are filled in, we must also beware of how scripting these identities too tightly can box people in. Collective identities do not only serve to unite coalitions. In light of the heterogeneity within social movements, collective identities have "the potential to create conflicts between organizations that define themselves differently, have clashing ideologies, and engage in different styles of protest, even if they, as part of the same movement, share a broad concern."[35] Our goal need not be the creation of an overarching collective identity that binds groups or organization and fuels collective action. It could be, more modestly, to make sure that we are fully cognizant of identity heterogeneity and

164   HOW DO WE BREAK FREE?

making sure that our pursuit of collective action through CSA is accountable to heterogeneity. To do this, we have a responsibility to be on the lookout for heterogeneity. We have a responsibility to search for it.

Imagine that Chloe took her bridge-building talents on the road to the United Kingdom. Imagine that she heard about these three environmental movement organizations and hoped to bring members of each together to engage in CSA in pursuit of a pro-environment cause. Searching for heterogeneity would be a crucial first step. Members of these organizations share a broad concern with the environment, but there will be differences at the broader organizational level, as well as between group members within each organization. Conservationists like CWG members want to protect the land and natural habitats from inappropriate and unnecessary development and want to manage them for maximal biodiversity. Reformers like FoE members want a sustainable global community where protection of the environment and meeting people's needs are not in conflict. And they want to focus on influencing elite decision makers, for example, by political lobbying and by working with corporate partners. Radicals like EDAG members want to use grassroots direct action to address and undo the root causes of climate change, which for them is tied to the action and inaction of governments and large corporations and to people who make anti-environment lifestyle choices.

Failure to acknowledge such differences could be an obstacle to forming alliances, which makes CSA unattainable, or it may render existing alliances fragile, which makes CSA unsustainable. And the same is true when we fail to search for heterogeneity between group members within organizations. Group members from different socioeconomic backgrounds may have different reasons for caring about environmental issues. Members with low socioeconomic status (SES) may place more weight on concerns pertaining to health and well-being, such as pollution, while those with high SES may be more concerned with habitat conservation and species

MICROPOLITICS   165

preservation.[36] These differences may also explain group variation in perceptions about who is "really" concerned about the environment.[37] And they can explain why group members can also have different views about what counts as an environmental issue.[38] Searching for heterogeneity is one component civic responsibility of CSA. Educating others about it—amplifying or making it visible—is another.

Educating Vegans and Carnivores

Plant-based diets are promoted as being beneficial for the environment. Although few people (less than 5% of the population in the UK/USA) follow vegetarian or vegan diets, some who do embrace collective identities that derive content from what some researchers describe as "moralized minority practices."[39] As with other collective identities we have discussed in this book, being a vegan can be understood using the taxonomy we introduced in Chapter 3 which includes the elements of meaning, identification, and treatment-as. Individuals can vary in how strongly or weakly they identify with a vegan identity. And there could be cases in which we are treated as vegans, based on our eating practices or travel habits, even when we do not wish to be so identified. For instance, as some researchers note, "although one could abstain from animal products while not wanting to necessarily be socially categorized in terms of the social identity of 'vegan,' in many shared eating contexts this is practically difficult to do. The social world often involves a risk that others read us as members of social groups, regardless of whether we see ourselves as such."[40] Some people may want to avoid being identified as vegans altogether, while others may accept the label but reject ways of filling in the identity script that leave them feeling boxed in.

Intragroup heterogeneity emerges with variations in these elements and this includes variation in the meaning assigned to collective identities. Ignoring this gives rise to the phenomenon at

166   HOW DO WE BREAK FREE?

the heart of this book: boxing in. Recall that we can box ourselves in and be boxed in by others. Suppose that Vince is a vegan but not for moral reasons. He thinks that veganism is good for his health and for the environment. He is also very accepting of meat-eaters. The vegan script can be restrictive if others who embrace this identity believe that expressing moral condemnation of carnivores is generally required based on a shared understanding of what it means to be a vegan. Some members of this group might also discourage Vince from associating with meat-eaters. And this can be an obstacle to Vince engaging in CSA with meat-eaters to pursue common pro-environmental projects. The same result might follow if meat-eaters wrongly perceived, in Vince's case, that all vegans are apt to look upon meat-eaters with moral contempt and are disinclined to associate with them.

Not surprisingly, non-vegans might construe those who engage in vegan practices as a threat to their sense of themselves as moral beings. Similarly, those who strongly identify with a green environmental identity, and shame those who fly rather than train or sail, can appear to threaten the moral self-concept of those who do not share this identity.[41] Some researchers, examining the impact of moralizing identity on intergroup interaction, find that shaming majority outgroup members can weaken the commitment of minority ingroup members to group practices as they seek to avoid outgroup majority derogation.[42] These researchers also find that minority ingroup members who strongly identify with tight scripts make it more difficult for the group to grow its numbers and inspire societal change.[43] For vegans who want more people to adopt sustainable diets and environmentally friendly modes of travel, both of these consequences are undesirable.

Imagine that Vince's passionate concern for the environment makes him open to working on pro-environmental causes with potential allies. Suppose that some of these potential allies do not embrace vegan dietary practices, yet they work to reduce wasteful material consumption practices; they also support clean

MICROPOLITICS 167

air, sustainable farming, and other initiatives that Vince supports. Although these allies will classify Vince as vegan, he is eager to make sure that the attribution of this collective identity to him does not pose an obstacle to pursuing pro-environment life-shaping projects with potential meat-eating allies. While some of Vince's fellow vegans may question whether meat-eaters can ever be "real" allies if they are unwilling to change their dietary habits, Vince, rejecting this view, may work to amplify heterogeneity among vegans and to educate both ingroup and outgroup members about important intragroup differences.

One way to do this is by distinguishing different ways of understanding the meaning of the script. Suppose we assume that the vegan script does have a moral component and that it can be more or less demanding.[44] What would a less demanding script look like? A less demanding understanding might set an ideal for the perfect vegan world, in which meat-eating would cease to be a practice, but would allow that any change in current practices that approaches this ideal is morally laudable. So, for example, meat-eating allies might be willing to support making vegan dining options more widespread without giving up their preferences for meat options. This would be morally laudable. In contrast, a more demanding understanding may hold that this is not enough, requiring that at a minimum meat-eating be denounced as immoral, and that anyone engaged in the practice be subject to moral condemnation. From this hardline perspective, the consumption of animals and animal products is strictly forbidden. Rejecting this view, Vince may adopt the less demanding understanding and take up the responsibility of educating others about this difference among vegans. He could do so with a view toward creating or sustaining CSA projects with potential outgroup allies who eat meat, but who also want to pursue pro-environment causes.

Educating potential allies about intragroup heterogeneity—or amplifying it—can create opportunities for cross-group coalition-building to pursue CSA projects. Potential allies who may have

168 HOW DO WE BREAK FREE?

been working with an understanding of a collective identity that boxed themselves or others in, creating an obstacle to intergroup coalition-building, may come to see the problem with that understanding. Taking up this responsibility to make heterogeneity visible, as Vince did, may also support the formation of networks with a fairly diverse set of members who then become—by virtue of the diversity of their network—better positioned to take advantage of political opportunities to pursue their CSA projects.

This is precisely what happened in the CAFE case. The alliance sought to bring attention to a cause and to garner support from the mayor's office for stopping industrial pollution in their neighborhood. At the time, New York City leadership was emphasizing diversity and this created a political opportunity to leverage the diversity of the CAFE alliance—made up of a diverse set of racial, ethnic, and religious group members—to get the attention of City Hall.[45] One activist recalled the impact of bringing such a diverse multiethnic coalition before the mayor: "We sat down with Mayor Dinkins. And I can tell you it was the first time Latinos, Hasidim, African American, Polish people all came together before him. He'd never seen anything like that before."[46] But leveraging their diversity to seize this political opportunity for influence meant that work was needed to educate members of the alliance about their differences rather than ignoring them. Toward this end, alliance leaders and group members had to assume responsibility for making their many differences visible, and for educating others about harmful stereotypes that could undermine their pursuit of CSA.

While highlighting diversity can enable an alliance to leverage a political opportunity to advance CSA, lumping different groups together under a larger diversity umbrella may mask important differences, such as differences in power—real or perceived—between groups. And this can have an adverse impact on building and sustaining diverse environmental coalitions.[47] Another aspect of the education relevant for CSA is amplifying differences in power

MICROPOLITICS 169

between group members, which are often rooted in racial, ethnic, and religious differences, as well as differences in SES. Before CAFE formed, there were concerns among Latino and African American residents of Williamsburg that the city was giving preferential treatment to Hasidim by targeting sections of the neighborhood where they lived for accelerated development, by affording them a greater share of choice affordable housing, and by using a more lenient standard for them in confrontational interactions with police.[48] All of this could be cited as evidence of differences in power or social standing (or at least perceived differences) between these groups, and failure to address such concerns—in part by making them visible—can undermine CSA. Power differences, as this case illustrates, can show up in differences in how group members are treated by other persons and by societal institutions. Educating group members about such differences may, in turn, involve educating them about the role that pernicious ideologies play in sustaining differences in power and treatment.

Philosophers have examined the relationship between race and ideology. Some have argued that racial identity is ideological to the extent that it contains illusory elements, for example, false assumptions about a racial group's inferiority, and these assumptions are used to create, sustain, or to justify oppressive practices or social relations.[49] Taking responsibility for educating group members about heterogeneity may also involve disabusing people of these illusory beliefs that sustain oppressive social relations.[50] And when we fail to do this, or when our attempts are unsuccessful, our efforts to engage in CSA with those who harbor such beliefs can be compromised in some cases, leading us to exit coalitions, and in other cases preventing them from forming.

One instance of exit of this kind happened when black (and non-white) British activists left a London-area environmental group whose white members harbored ideological beliefs about Nigerians and Africans to explain the cause of extreme and destructive flooding that they endured—chalking it upto their

170   HOW DO WE BREAK FREE?

alleged dysfunction, negligence, and greed.[51] Interviews with white members of this group revealed a similar pattern when discussing other non-Europeans, including Indians: "Varied racialized responses to environmental disaster were read as evidence of essential, basic differences in various groups' very nature, a state of being that could only be articulated in distinction from other groups' supposed traits and characteristics."[52] The cumulative frustrations tied to unsuccessful efforts to disabuse white members of oppressive stereotypes and being valued (as group members) more for their potential contributions to physical tasks like planting trees for the groups' environmental projects, rather than for their intellectual contributions, proved too much to bear for the few non-white members, who exited the group.[53]

Pernicious ideological beliefs can also prevent alliances from forming—including alliances between groups that appear to be natural allies, as was the case in the aftermath of an industrial accident affecting a Laotian immigrant community in California. There was an explosion at a Chevron refinery in Richmond, California, on March 25, 1999.[54] Some Laotian residents in this community could not benefit from the county's "shelter-in-place" warning system because it was not multilingual. A San Francisco, California, environmental justice group, the Asian Pacific Environmental Network (APEN), used this event to mobilize the Laotian community to fight for environmental justice. It also used it to create broader alliances between second-generation Laotian and other communities of color, including African American communities, to address environmental and other injustices. This seems like a natural alliance given evidence that Laotians are situated closer to black in the US racial order.[55] APEN, which focused on issue-target coalitions, hoped that shared experiences of environmental pollution and neglect could be a basis for solidarity between Laotians and African Americans.

But for some members of the Laotian community, particularly young, middle- and high-school-age Laotian women, who had

MICROPOLITICS 171

spent less time in the group, their acceptance of stereotypes about African Americans and internalization of the view that Laotians are model minorities, because of their work ethic and the like, created more distance rather than cooperation with potential African American allies. APEN had an admirable goal: "a basic principle that guides APEN's organizing is that their work should not create a wedge between Laotians and other communities of color. Rather, the goal should be to identify linkages and produce alliances across race."[56] Educating about heterogeneity needed to be an element of producing such alliances, in particular, education about differences in how groups are treated, and the role that racial ideology and xenophobia play in understanding injustice and oppression. Although this was part of APEN's youth campaigns and activities, in this case, education about power and ideology (specifically anti-black stereotypes) did not fully set in. And this created a serious obstacle to CSA. Some teenage Laotians were unable to view blacks as potential coalition partners.

Our collective identities as Hasidim, Latinos, Laotians, or African Americans can create obstacles to working together on environmental pollution and other projects, unless we take certain actions. And, as we argued in the previous chapter, in democratic contexts where action on climate and other issues involves reliance on formal and informal representatives to take certain actions on behalf of heterogenous groups engaged in CSA we must rely upon accountability mechanisms to make sure that our collective identities are not too tightly scripted. Making them overly restrictive can box us in and make it difficult to coordinate the collective pursuit of life-shaping projects, which we share in common with others, such as reducing wasteful consumption practices or stopping the construction of industrial incinerators in an urban neighborhood.

Social activists and organizers are keenly aware of the considerable challenges raised by holding diverse coalitions together to address problems of common concern. Attending to the identity

172　HOW DO WE BREAK FREE?

work they do supplies rich case studies that we have used to illuminate the nature and value of civic responsibilities we must take up to form and sustain networks instrumental to pursuing our life-shaping projects. So far we have considered the work of searching for heterogeneity and amplifying it through education. We now take up ways of acting responsively to heterogeneity—the final component civic responsibility of CSA we shall consider—paying special attention to what social movement theorists refer to as "framing" processes.

Finding the Right Frame

A study we referenced earlier, which draws a distinction between mules and honeybees, supports the point that when dealing with conservative ranchers or right-leaning conservative elites, it may be more effective to get them to be more like honeybees than mules.[57] Doing the latter, which may involve trying to persuade them to embrace a superordinate environmentalist identity, is likely to elicit strong pushback and probably even hostility in some instances. With this in mind, we can appreciate the significance of the following observation: "conservatives are as likely as liberals to buy energy efficient lightbulbs advertised as money-saving technologies, but less likely than liberals when 'environmentally friendly' stickers are displayed on the bulbs."[58]

Suppose that this is true. Suppose further that Chloe, our Audubon Society activist hoping to forge an alliance between environmentalists and conservative ranchers, wanted to issue a call to action that could engage both groups, not only to conserve bird habitats, but also to act in other ways conducive to sustaining the environment. Assuming that there are significantly more honeybees in the latter group while mules dominant the former, Chloe might select a pro-environment frame urging them to save money by supporting energy-efficient products and technologies.

MICROPOLITICS   173

As a bridge builder, Chloe recognizes that this motivational frame is likely to have more resonance with honeybees than a frame that centers on going green to save the Earth.

The work of finding the right frame to account for intra- and inter-identity group heterogeneity is an example of the third civic responsibility of collective self-authorship, to act according to heterogeneity. Attending to this responsibility, along with the responsibilities of searching for heterogeneity and amplifying it, is vital to mitigating the risk of neglecting heterogeneity in ways that contribute to the identity troubles that can subvert democracy. Taken together, these component responsibilities comprise the ethics of making identity safe for democracy.

Social movement activists rely on framing to facilitate shared understanding within coalitions and foster collective action. They help activists to develop and understand the meaning of their work and the identities that unify or divide them.[59] Researchers who study social movements distinguish three essential framing tasks.[60] *Diagnostic framing* lays out an understanding of a problem or issue that needs to be addressed. This could be a concrete problem, such as an industrial incinerator spewing out toxic pollutants in an urban community, or it could be a more general problem, such as the environmental injustice of burdening neighborhoods that have certain demographic profiles with a disproportionately higher share of polluting incinerators. *Prognostic framing* presents a way to address the problem or issue. *Motivational framing* offers a rationale for taking action to address the problem, as well as for maintaining participation. With each of these tasks, framing helps those taking part in collective action to make sense of the projects they pursue and their reasons for pursuing them.

By coordinating social movement activists' self-understanding and sense of purpose, different frames can hinder or advance accountability to group heterogeneity. And as with identities themselves, framing is not a static matter. It is a dynamic process; frames—whether diagnostic, prognostic, or motivational—are

174 HOW DO WE BREAK FREE?

constantly being constituted, contested, reproduced, and replaced as networks form, endure, and disband.[61] So the right frame for a given life-shaping project can change as the group or movement, or its circumstances, change.

Within social movements or other smaller networks seeking to unify a diverse set of individuals, groups, or organizations, framing processes are vital. They are widely regarded, "alongside resource mobilization and political opportunity processes, as a central dynamic in understanding the character and course of social movements."[62] And framing can impact a network or movement's conception of its identity. As one article notes: "Framing processes that occur within the context of social movements constitute perhaps the most important mechanism facilitating identity construction processes, largely because identity constructions are an inherent feature of framing activities."[63] However, framing is not always directed at promoting a shared identity. The work of linking individuals to networks can be rooted in collective action frames that variably stress a shared identity, a shared issue, or even a sense of sympathy brought on by a shared experience, such as a bystander identifying with anti-police-brutality protestors because they too were a victim of police assault at a peaceful protest rally.[64]

Recall the Williamsburg/Greenpoint, Brooklyn, CAFE case with which we began this chapter. There are at least two ways to read this case. We can interpret the work of finding the right frame as a matter of forging a common collective identity around which the different individuals and groups could bond. For instance, the researcher who studied this organization contends: "By laying aside their differences, CAFE members constructed a collective identity that emphasized their commonalities and enabled them effectively to challenge the incinerator."[65] But the findings present little evidence that forging a common identity was crucial to creating and sustaining the alliance. It is true that the residents understood that they were all part of the same neighborhood community. It is true

MICROPOLITICS   175

that they believed that the incinerator would expose them to environmental poison. And is certainly true that there were efforts to frame the struggle to stop the incinerator as a struggle for justice, insofar as their status as a majority-minority community suggested that discrimination was at work in the decision to locate it in their neighborhood.[66] But the thrust of the case study supports an alternative diagnostic framing, which we can interpret primarily as a matter of getting residents to rally around a shared issue. And the issue is potential exposure to toxic pollutants. An alliance activist organizer put the point this way: "We trust each other now. We've sustained all kinds of problems. If we have that kind of faith and trust in each other, it's because this is cancer country now. Because studies coming up are showing we're cancer country."[67]

So another way to proceed is not by forging a new collective identity but by highlighting a common problem or core issue of concern that can serve as a source of unity for groups with diverse collective identities. CAFE activists in Williamsburg/Greenpoint did this kind of work by focusing neighborhood residents' attention on their collective vulnerability to bad air or toxic pollutants, which they all experienced in virtue of where they lived. "It's in the air. . . . You know, I think the environment effects [sic] everyone," said one activist who worked to unify members of this multiethnic community, "no one could turn a blind eye to it."[68] Getting neighborhood residents to see that what was "in the air"—and what more would be in the air if the incinerator project went forward—was a dire threat to everyone in the community provided a powerful reason for them to undertake CSA.

Given the history of disagreement between some groups within the alliance, this issue-framing made sense. Identity-framing can be more contentious than issue-framing.[69] Of course, as group members within the alliance become more understanding and trusting of one another, in part due to carrying out the civic responsibilities of collective self-authorship, it is possible that bonds of solidarity or efforts to create a more encompassing

176 HOW DO WE BREAK FREE?

collective identity could provide new social glue to hold them together for future shared life-shaping projects.

There are at least two ways of reading the Williamsburg case: identity or issue. However we read it, what's clear is the importance of finding the right frame—one that is properly responsive to heterogeneity. Finding the right frame need not be about finding a way to reach consensus or to ensure that each group gets what it most wants. The frame that gets adopted may be skewed to a particular point of view but, in some cases, this might be what is needed to sustain a fragile alliance or coalition.[70] It is also important to note that there can be significant variation in collective action frames. There can be variation between the frames adopted by rank-and-file group members and group leadership.[71] And there can be variation in framing tasks; for example, members of a network may adopt very different prognostic framing, which is something we certainly see in environmental movements.[72]

Chloe, Vince, and CAFE activists are compelling examples of the significance of finding the right frame. And working to find the right frame is one example of how democratic citizens can take up the third component responsibility, to act according to heterogeneity. Of course, there are other kinds of actions that can serve this role as well; for example, in the context of community engagement, taking action to make meetings more accessible to immigrant workers with translation services, different meeting times, and targeted outreach efforts;[73] or in the context of interfaith engagement, engaging in prayer exchanges where participants teach one another about the prayer practices in their respective traditions.[74] While the right frame or the right action will differ across contexts, the more general lesson to draw is that by acting in ways that are responsive to the heterogeneity in our midst, we can promote accountability in the CSA processes that we are a part of.

The responsive actions of activists like Chloe and CAFE are also made possible by their own work, and that of others, to take up the other component responsibilities of identifying, and communicating about, heterogeneity. The work of finding the right frame, and of other actions in CSA processes, is made easier through communication with others who are knowledgeable about the relevant differences in perspective, background, and empowerment in their midst. For this reason, successful uptake of our civic responsibilities will often require successful cooperation with others who are also taking up these responsibilities. In the next section, we consider how demanding these responsibilities are and how developing an ethos of collective self-authorship can enhance cooperation and improve our capacity to take up these responsibilities.

A New Ethos

The work of organizers like CAFE in Brooklyn and Chloe in Wyoming, who take care to respond to heterogeneity in cooperation with others, bears some similarities to the life-shaping projects of the figure that started Chapter 1: Charlie Parker, also known as Bird. Recall that Bird chose a life plan as a jazz musician and a true artist, fighting to break free from the prevailing tight scripts for black jazz musicians as entertainers for predominantly white audiences. Bird broke free through his participation in a community of likeminded musicians, centered around Minton's jazz club in Harlem. At Minton's, musicians like Bird could experiment, improvising with others to develop new sounds, new techniques, and new forms of mastery over their instruments without having to worry about the prevailing norms and expectations for black musicians. We can now understand this community centered around Minton's as an example of CSA.

Both jazz musicians and community organizers contribute to CSA processes through deliberate practice, but also must develop ways of being responsive to others they cooperate with. In the case of jazz musicians like Bird, they can hone their craft by

178   HOW DO WE BREAK FREE?

practicing scales, training their ears, and learning jazz standards. When they deploy skills developed through practice by playing with others, they have certain responsibilities to keep the collective performance going, such as keeping time, staying in key, playing impressive solos but not overplaying, and so on. And to carry out these responsibilities effectively, they must develop habits that enable them to be responsive to other musicians, such as nonverbal cues to decide who will solo next, listening for tempo changes, and identifying parts of another musician's solo to echo in their own. To contribute to performances with technical mastery and dazzling improvisation that complemented the whole ensemble, musicians like Bird could not simply focus on deploying their own skills as individual musicians; they had to develop the right mindset and habits to deploy those skills while effectively collaborating with others. Their life-shaping projects as jazz musicians and true artists were advanced by cultivating the right *ethos* to collaborate effectively.

Community organizers like Chloe and CAFE activists are in an analogous position when contributing to their CSA processes. It is useful to be skilled in communicating with others, as Chloe demonstrates in her engagement with Wyoming ranchers, by taking up the component responsibilities of identifying and communicating about heterogeneity. And this skill may not come naturally; it is something that can be cultivated with practice over time, much like Bird's mastery of the alto saxophone. But taking up these civic responsibilities is not just a matter of deliberate practice and action; it is also about developing an *ethos of collective self-authorship*, much like an ethos of collaboration for jazz improvisers.

Chloe had to develop the habit to deploy her communication skills in ways that would not only help her discharge these responsibilities but make it easier for others to do the same. This included conservative Wyoming ranchers, and others interested in environmental causes, who also needed to search for heterogeneity in their midst, to make it visible to others, and who needed

MICROPOLITICS   179

to find the right frame. Instead of being concerned with signaling her group affiliations or winning a zero-sum political battle, Chloe prioritized taking up her responsibility to respond to heterogeneity with others. Instead of acting according to the ethos of boxing that we encountered in Chapter 2, she cultivated an ethos of CSA. We should not expect uptake of the civic responsibilities discussed in this chapter to involve a series of isolated calculations. Instead, it will be more like playing jazz; it will depend on deliberate practice to develop skills, which are deployed regularly through the right habits and with the right mindset over time.

Does replacing an ethos of boxing in with an ethos of CSA require that each person engaged in CSA take up all three component responsibilities? And does each person need to do so in all three roles: constituents, representatives, and contributors to background conditions? If the answer to both questions is "no," the ethics of making identity safe for democracy may not seem demanding enough. We might worry that the view is not demanding enough if it is possible to fulfill one's responsibilities with just one of the three roles, such as someone who is responsive to heterogeneity as a representative in the workplace (e.g., a boss or union representative), but avoids addressing any background conditions related to workplace or union policy. And we might worry that the view is not demanding enough if it is possible to merely search for heterogeneity but not to amplify it or act on it. If the answer to both questions is "yes," it seems that the view is too demanding. The general concern is that the ethics of making identity safe for democracy may be too easy to satisfy or too difficult.

To be sure, one may indeed worry that it is too demanding to expect a single person to discharge all of these responsibilities. And it is clear that the demands only increase if we expect each person to take up these distinct responsibilities in their roles as constituents of a group engaged in CSA, as representatives, and as contributors to the background conditions that affect the success or failure of their efforts. People like Chloe and Vince, as well as people who

180 HOW DO WE BREAK FREE?

are mules, working to save the planet and willing to forge coalitions with others who hold different identities, may be eager to search for heterogeneity, amplify it, and act on it. Furthermore, they may be eager to do so as rank-and-file members of a pro-environment group, as group leaders, and as members of a society where background rules, policies, norms, and the like need to be adjusted for CSA success. But not everyone is a mule. Can we expect—or more to the point—can we ethically demand the same of non-mules?

We believe that it is not too difficult to discharge these responsibilities in our everyday lives. Whenever we find ourselves working with others to pursue life-shaping projects, we inevitably have conversations where we learn about one another. We learn about our similarities and differences and take note of them. We educate others about what we learn. And if we are truly committed to cooperation to achieve a common goal, we act in ways that are responsive to these differences. Part of the appeal of our view is that it identifies things that happen quite naturally, in our quotidian interactions, as component responsibilities of CSA. Reflective engagement in these interactions will be conducive to replacing an ethos of boxing in with an ethos of CSA. This will, in turn, facilitate future uptake of civic responsibilities and make them less demanding.

Of course, not everyone wants to be a group leader or to engage in the work needed to transform societal or organizational background conditions that bear on the success or failure of CSA, but these things are not expected of everyone. So long as some people within a network are willing to do these things, there is hope. The truth is that carrying out any one of the component responsibilities is a vital part of a collective effort to make sure that our identities work for, and not against, the pursuit of CSA. And the truth is that all members of a group need not assume every role. What's important is that some members of a network—whether it be a small group, a coalition, an organization, or a social movement—are taking up one or more of these component civic responsibilities

MICROPOLITICS 181

and that some members are doing so in each of the three essential roles. This kind of deliberate uptake in a broader, committed network will foster the right environment for an ethos of CSA to take hold, much like Minton's was the right environment for Bird and other musicians to perform while developing a new ethos of CSA to break free from their tight scripts.

Be an Organizer, Not a Hobbyist

One challenge democratic citizens face is that their current political environment, especially at the level of macropolitics (to be discussed in Chapter 6), inhibits uptake of their civic responsibilities. As we established in Chapter 2, many democracies feature some form of identity trouble, which can make both micro- and macropolitical efforts to resist boxing in more challenging. We face ingrained tendencies and incentives toward familiar, troubling forms of political engagement: us-versus-them thinking, a winners-and-losers mindset, identity signaling instead of problem-solving, and homogenous conceptions of "the people." Each of these tendencies makes it more difficult for us to identify, amplify, and act according to heterogeneity that is neglected by, or cuts across, the most salient forms of social division.

One pitfall that is especially prevalent in light of identity trouble is the tendency to approach politics as, what political scientist Eitan Hersh has coined, a political hobbyist. Hersh describes the term as "a catchall phrase for consuming and participating in politics by obsessive news-following and online 'slacktivism,' by feeling the need to offer a hot take for each daily political flare-up, by emoting and arguing and debating, almost all of this from behind screens or with earphones on."[75] When we approach collective self-authorship as hobbyists, we tend to be motivated to satisfy our own emotional needs and curiosities, at the expense of organizing with others to advance our collective life-shaping projects.[76]

182 HOW DO WE BREAK FREE?

Hobbyism is not a totally new phenomenon—Hersh recounts civil rights activist Ella Baker's frustration upon visiting a meeting of the Albany, New York, NAACP branch, when she found that the attendees only wanted to talk about the Deep South and had not identified, nor acted against, problems with racial segregation in schools in Albany.[77] But it might be especially easy to fall into this trap in our current context given the ubiquity of online political content and discussion opportunities presented by social media. It can be fun to join in the online political discussions of the day, often focused on national, partisan politics, but the time and effort devoted to commenting on these discussions can come at the expense of work that might better advance the CSA processes we are part of and that might better enable us to take up our civic responsibilities.[78]

Online tools can be useful for political projects within CSA processes. But to avoid the hobbyist pitfall, such engagement should proceed with an ethos of CSA. It should be oriented toward particular projects with an eye toward contributing to the organizational infrastructure on which CSA processes rely. One example is the Right to Information movement in India, which mobilizes in support of citizens' rights to request and obtain information from public authorities, and combat corruption.[79] The movement has made use of in-person and online activities in complementary ways to advance its life-shaping projects. For example, it utilized public social media posts to amass large crowds to jointly make requests for information about hospital records to investigate concerns about understaffing and performance irregularities.[80]

One challenge the movement faced is activists being killed or assaulted in attempts to silence them after discoveries of corruption. In response, the movement organized a hybrid online/offline network to report acts of violence. When concerns are raised, the movement can mobilize groups of activists to all file the same request for information (so that one person cannot be singled out). When activists receive threats of violence, they can report them via

MICROPOLITICS   183

a civil society organization-run helpline, which can then share information about the threats with the media, police, and the broader public online.[81] As the movement has used online means in its CSA, they have been attentive to heterogeneity in their constituency with respect to access. They have used different media, such as WhatsApp and Facebook, to reach constituencies without access to Gmail and have also used in-person communication to reach those who do not have reliable internet access at all.[82]

The Right to Information movement has used both online and in-person means to mobilize support for their core projects, while also building a broader organizational infrastructure to sustain their efforts over time. This is a key difference between participants in this movement, who have engaged in politics as organizers like Ella Baker did, and political hobbyists, who do not contribute to organization-building to develop collective power. Hobbyists tend toward a mode of political engagement mostly as spectators with occasional commentary to join in on collective, online forms of discussion. They seek out information for personal enjoyment or for the feeling of being up-to-date, but without a specific project to contribute to or organizational infrastructure to develop. By contrast, the members of this social movement use online engagement to advance their collective projects and forge mechanisms of accountability for their constituencies to utilize.

It is as organizers, whose political engagement is aimed at advancing specific projects and contributing to CSA, that we can avoid the pitfall of hobbyism. This chapter offers a blueprint for how to do so. We have analyzed our responsibility to respond to heterogeneity in terms of three component responsibilities to search for, amplify, and act according to heterogeneity. We must take up these responsibilities in our roles as constituents, representatives, and contributors to background conditions. And we have noted how our uptake of these responsibilities can be facilitated by supplanting an ethos of boxing in with an ethos of CSA. Following this blueprint allows us to advance our respective CSA

184   HOW DO WE BREAK FREE?

processes and resist boxing in. But as we discuss in the next chapter, micropolitics does not always suffice to advance our life-shaping projects. We often need to operate at much larger scales, working with greater numbers and pursuing more ambitious projects. This requires additional strategies and tools to facilitate and maintain uptake-at-scale of our civic responsibilities.

6

Macropolitics

Scaling Up

Millions joined the seven-day Global Climate Strike that began on September 20, 2019. People from all walks of life—with different nationalities, religions, races, ethnicities, ideologies, and class backgrounds—called for action to fight climate change and its deleterious effects, especially on the world's most disadvantaged populations. During this historic week, in an address to the United Nations Climate Action Summit in New York City, climate activist Greta Thunberg said: "You have stolen my dreams and my childhood with your empty words. And yet I'm one of the lucky ones. People are suffering. People are dying. Entire ecosystems are collapsing. We are in the beginning of a mass extinction, and all you can talk about is money and fairy tales of external economic growth. How dare you!"[1] Thunberg is certainly not alone in viewing climate change as an existential crisis.

We can tackle climate change on a more modest, and manageable, scale, as did the Brooklyn residents who formed the CAFE alliance to fight for environmental justice in their local community. But a problem this substantial will require much more work and will involve many more actors. Our collective self-authorship will require scaling up to engage in macropolitics. We cannot rely solely on local, environmental, collective life-shaping projects. To address it on a larger scale we must unite people and organizations nationally and internationally. This chapter addresses the challenge of scaling up, which requires uptake of our component civic

Boxed In. Derrick Darby and Eduardo J. Martinez, Oxford University Press. © Oxford University Press 2024.
DOI: 10.1093/9780197620236.003.0007

186 HOW DO WE BREAK FREE?

responsibilities at scale. And it completes our argument for why we must, and what it takes to, make our identities safe for democracy.

Climate Divisions

When taking up the macropolitical work that Thunberg and other climate activists carry out, discharging our civic responsibilities to account for heterogeneity can be especially challenging. Consider the different perspectives taken by developed and developing nations on international policy responses to climate change. On the one hand, national governments of developed countries such as the United States (under the Biden administration), Germany, and Sweden have pushed for changes to international institutions, including the International Monetary Fund (IMF) and World Bank, to mitigate climate change. They call for restricting investments in natural gas projects and for making financial support contingent on recipient countries' plans to decrease emissions.[2]

Some advocates have criticized these policies from the perspective of developing and the least developed countries (LDCs). For instance, the economist Vijaya Ramachandran has argued that these policy changes are "unjust, ineffective, and disastrous for the world's poor."[3] She writes:

It's unjust because rich countries are forcing the World Bank and IMF to deprioritize poverty reduction despite this mission being vital to protect developing countries from the climate shocks caused by rich countries' emissions. It's ineffective because poor countries make up only a tiny fraction of global emissions—and their share will remain small even if they were to grow rapidly using fossil fuels. And it will be a disaster for the 3 billion people struggling to escape misery because every dollar spent on the new carbon-reduction mission is a dollar that could instead go into education, medical services, food security, and critical infrastructure.[4]

Ramachandran also worries that developed countries conflate the tasks of mitigation and adaptation. Mitigating climate change by decreasing emissions, on her view, is primarily a task for developed nations who have historically produced the most emissions. But adaptation is especially urgent for those in the least developed nations owing to the unequal burden that results.

The urgency of adaptation in response to the climate crisis has been a priority for some public officials from LDCs. For example, in a 2021 op-ed, Lazarus Chakwera, the president of Malawi, called for financial support for adaptation as an obligation owed to LDCs:

> Africa has done little to create the climate crisis. Yet the locust plagues in the Horn of Africa, the first climate change famine in Madagascar and the water crises in southern Africa are all evidence that my continent is already paying the price of others' emissions. The fund that some would like diminished is not charity, but a cleaning fee that must be paid.[5]

While some environmentalists from developed countries see international policy as an important lever to reduce emissions and alleviate a shared burden, many from developing countries and the LDCs see such proposals as another unfair burden and misunderstanding of their situation. If not properly considered by advocates and decision-makers, these differences in perspective can pose a threat to the kind of coordinated global environmental action that Thunberg and other climate activists champion. As we see, there is a great deal of potential disagreement underlying a shared concern with addressing climate change. And these climate divisions—amounting, in this case, to differences of perspective—illustrate the challenge of taking up our civic responsibilities once we scale up to the international level.

188   HOW DO WE BREAK FREE?

Disagreements are also pervasive among environmentalists working in social movement organizations. Consider ongoing disagreements about the importance of international climate agreements and the United Nations Climate Change Conference (UNCCC). UNCCC meetings are often the site of protests pushing for policy changes.[6] And some environmentalists see these protests as an opportunity to influence international climate policy by applying pressure on the parties to international agreements to make more demanding contributions. But others see a reliance on the UNCCC as misguided, believing that such institutions are unlikely to take the necessary actions to address climate change. So these activists and organizations use protests around major climate meetings as opportunities to change public interpretations of these agreements and to mobilize others into a longer-term climate movement.

Both kinds of disagreements about international environmental policy and activism arise from different perspectives internal to environmentalism. The diverging perspectives proceed from concerns about climate change and how to respond to it. So scaling up climate action to the international level, which is necessary given the global scale of the problem, requires, among other things, political decision-making that can be responsive to these different perspectives and to other kinds of intra- and intergroup heterogeneity. But unlike many examples in the previous chapter, potential contributors to this collective life-shaping project do not all fit in the same room, garden, or neighborhood. They are a massive, heterogeneous, group strewn across the globe with different backgrounds, perspectives, and forms of empowerment. Still, environmental collective action at the broadest level requires at least some coordination and outreach that are responsive to the kinds of group heterogeneity we have discussed. And this is the difficult work of macropolitics.

We described the content of our component civic responsibilities, and how we can take them up when engaging in micropolitics, in the previous chapter. These responsibilities still apply at the macropolitical scale: to mitigate the costs of being boxed in by tight scripts, we have to identify, amplify, and be responsive to forms of heterogeneity in our midst. But as we have seen in the case of environmental action in response to climate change, sometimes scaling up to macropolitical action is necessary for our collective self-authorship (CSA) processes. Given the diversity of perspectives on environmentalism, as well as other kinds of group heterogeneity, it can be difficult to maintain our uptake of these responsibilities while scaling up. Fortunately, there are concrete steps that we can take as citizens, representatives, and contributors to background conditions to attenuate this challenge. Most importantly, we can aim to participate in, and structure, our organizations and institutions to facilitate the uptake of our civic responsibilities to account for group heterogeneity. This enables us to meet the challenge of scaling up.

The Challenge of Scaling Up

There is a great deal of intragroup heterogeneity among environmentalists at the international scale. And this makes scaling up to take global climate action challenging. When those engaging in CSA aim to operate at a larger scale, they often have to coordinate with a more diverse population. And this introduces new forms of heterogeneity to account for as they take up their civic responsibilities. We can see this dynamic at work, even at a relatively small scale, when building up a movement from a neighborhood to play a bigger role in citywide politics. In the 1970s, residents of Birmingham, a neighborhood in East Toledo (in the city of Toledo, Ohio) felt that their life-shaping projects were threatened for a few reasons. Public institutions, such as their local library branch, were threatened by budget cuts. Neighborhood institutions, such as local Catholic churches and local restaurants, were threatened by plans

190   HOW DO WE BREAK FREE?

for street-widening projects and a new railroad overpass.[7] Some residents felt that the pillars of their neighborhood were under threat, in favor of priorities coming from other parts of the city.

Identity work was part of neighborhood residents' response to these threats. For some residents of Birmingham, their local identity as "East-siders" was salient given their sense of abandonment by the rest of the city. Local representatives utilized this identity to mobilize others to contest these proposals through collective action like mass checkouts of library books and protests against street widening. This East-sider identity was shared across Birmingham's ethnic and racial groups, including Hungarians, Slovaks, Latinos, and African Americans. Crucially, it was reinforced by the prominent population of first- and second-generation Hungarian Americans, who connected their local and ethnic identities to local cultural institutions that could join into a broader coalition, such as a local Hungarian club. The prevalence of Hungarian identity also provided identity-related resources with which to mobilize, such as wearing Old World dress during protests and presenting local government officials with traditional Hungarian food.[8]

However, as the East Toledo neighborhood movement that started in Birmingham attempted to scale up to other neighborhoods, it encountered challenges. Other neighborhoods in East Toledo did not have as salient or cohesive a set of ethnic and local identities to serve as a basis for interpreting shared problems and mobilizing collective action. Organizers would try to interpret slumlords' buildings in terms of neighborhood safety frames or railroad crossings in terms of children's safety frames, but they did not have the same shared identity resources with which to promote shared interpretations as they did in Birmingham.[9] Different levels of investment in the movement across neighborhoods also created unstable relationships: Birmingham residents contributed more resources to organizing efforts and their neighborhood received the most attention, which created feelings of resentment from others in East Toledo.[10] Some residents of East Toledo also took issue with

MACROPOLITICS 191

the use of confrontational tactics and paid organizers.[11] While aspiring to scale up to work with all of East Toledo, this movement had not properly taken account of the differences of perspectives and forms of identification in other neighborhoods outside of Birmingham. Ultimately, the social movement organizations that started and grew in Birmingham, and which were responsive to salient forms of heterogeneity within that one neighborhood, were mostly unsuccessful in expanding collective action to a broader set of East Toledo residents.

This East Toledo case study demonstrates the challenge of scaling up, even at the relatively small scale of a region within a small city. Our CSA processes and engagement in politics can emerge and prove useful for our immediate context, but they may not apply seamlessly to new contexts, even with others who share an identity or set of projects with us. We can describe these difficulties as a particular kind of challenge.

The Challenge of Scaling Up: Given a tendency for more heterogeneity at larger scales, as well as less familiarity with that heterogeneity among constituents and representatives, uptake of our civic responsibilities—to search for heterogeneity, to make it visible, and to account for it—tends to be more difficult to maintain.

As we expand the scope of our collective self-authorship—from tending to neighborhood-related life-shaping projects to taking on more ambitious ones requiring coordination with citywide, statewide, nationwide, or even international partners and networks—we encounter new forms and distributions of intra- and intergroup heterogeneity. But we must still take up our civic responsibilities to identify, amplify, and act according to the heterogeneity present at this broader scale. And this leads to the challenge of maintaining uptake (of our responsibilities) at larger scales.

While it is difficult to assess counterfactuals in any one case study, it seems like the challenge of scaling up impeded attempts

192 HOW DO WE BREAK FREE?

to organize the broader group of East-siders in Toledo. The identity frames, approaches to organizing, and strategies for protest that worked well in the neighborhood of Birmingham did not transfer seamlessly to the residents of other neighborhoods. With a greater ability to identify and communicate about these forms of heterogeneity, organizations working on these efforts would have been in a better position to be responsive to that heterogeneity from the start, and to set up mechanisms of accountability in light of them.

The challenge of scaling up is not just a roadblock to collective action; it also presents risks of boxing in. This is especially true when trying to engage in macropolitics at the national level when a nation is in the throes of identity trouble and an ethos of boxing in. Recall our discussion of environmentalism that began this chapter. Given differences in backgrounds, perspectives, and empowerment, there is a risk of new members of the environmentalist movement boxing in themselves and others as they engage in CSA processes. When we consider prominent misconceptions of the relationship between identifying as an environmentalist and one's racial and class background, US survey research suggests that Americans tend to overestimate the degree to which environmentalists are whiter, wealthier, and have higher levels of educational attainment than the general population. This mistaken perception leads respondents to underestimate the diversity of those who identify as environmentalists and who identify with environmental organizations. Furthermore, this misperception extends to different American demographic groups—it is not confined to one specific subgroup.[12]

In this case, many Americans seem to be operating with scripts that connect racial and class-based characteristics with being (and not being) an environmentalist, which could in turn affect treatment-as environmentalists for both those who do and do not conform to these expectations. For example, environmental groups might not devote enough resources to recruiting members

MACROPOLITICS 193

who do not conform to these scripts about the demographics of environmentalists as white, wealthy, and highly educated, and those who do not conform to these scripts may not see these organizations as appropriate for them to join. In this situation, both environmentalists and potential environmentalists would box themselves and others in with overly tight scripts about the kind of people who can, or are likely to, be environmentalists and work with environmental organizations.

Greater attentiveness to the heterogeneity among people who identify as environmentalists would mitigate this form of boxing in. And as it turns out, there is some experimental evidence to suggest that exposure to images of racially diverse environmentalists increases associations between non-whites and environmentalists among non-white respondents.[13] This highlights the importance of taking up our civic responsibilities to identify, amplify, and act on heterogeneity. Doing this would drive environmentalists to seek out these forms of diversity in their ranks and act in ways that are attentive to it. Instead, due to misconceptions, born out of tight scripts and unfamiliarity, boxing in can continue unabated and prevent outreach that would advance the CSA of environmentalists. This is another manifestation of the challenge of scaling up.

Three Strategies for Scaling Up

We have established the challenge of scaling up—a challenge that becomes pressing as we extend CSA beyond our community gardens to the globe, moving from small-scale local life-shaping projects like creating space in our garden for peaceful reflection to organizing a global climate strike to pressure industrial polluters. To scale up, we must secure uptake of our component civic responsibilities at scale. But first we need strategies for scaling up. In this section we consider three strategies for scaling up through

194   HOW DO WE BREAK FREE?

coalition-building processes. When successfully deployed, these approaches help us overcome the challenge.

The first strategy is what we call a *linked-struggle* approach. On this view, there is rarely, if ever, a truly single-issue struggle. Often we will find that trying to combat one form of oppression or one shared problem will be unsuccessful without also combating others. Consider the National Sexual Violence Resource Center's (NSVRC) statement on racism:

> As an organization committed to the mission of ending sexual harassment, assault, and abuse, we recognize it will take ending all forms of racism to accomplish this. Racism, specifically anti-Black racism, is a root cause of sexual violence. Harmful beliefs that view other groups as lesser—like sexism, heterosexism, transphobia, ableism, and racism—feed into the inequity and abuse that underscore all forms of sexual violence. In order to prevent sexual violence, we must acknowledge and take steps to undo the systemic ways anti-Black racism shows up in our communities and our work.[14]

The NSVRC, in pursuit of its project of combating sexual violence, identifies multiple forms of hierarchical beliefs based on different axes of identity, and sees them all as contributing to sexual violence. On this view, individuals and organizations working to combat sexual violence should also work to combat heterosexism, transphobia, ableism, and racism.

More broadly, those who advocate a linked-struggle approach typically appeal to shared membership between different groups and the relationship between different mechanisms of oppression to demonstrate the importance of linking struggles. Given how the social world is structured, social movements can scale up by making these connections explicit. For example, following the US Supreme Court's *Obergefell* decision requiring states to issue same-sex marriage licenses, Brandon Patterson published a magazine article entitled "Why You Can't Be Pro-Black and Homophobic at the Same Time." He notes shared membership in the LGBT and black communities, while arguing that homophobia among black Americans is "problematic because blackness and LGBT identities are not mutually exclusive. There are lesbian black women, gay black men, bisexual black people, transgender black men and women, 'genderqueer' black people—identifying as neither gender or both—and black people who are any combination of any of the above."[15]

Patterson also notes shared and overlapping mechanisms of oppression:

> You do not mean "black lives matter" if you protest when an unarmed straight black man is killed by the police because they are black, but don't care about the many transgender black women who have been murdered this year because they were trans. If we are to liberate black people as a whole, then we must combat all forms of discrimination against black people, including anti-LGBT discrimination and that which we inflict upon them from within our own communities. The struggle must be multilayered, just like the identities of black people. Every chain must be broken.[16]

Much like the NSVRC, Patterson sees the project of black liberation from oppression as incomplete without an accompanying form of LGBT liberation. Following the linked-struggle approach, he proceeds by mobilizing other black people to link the struggle against racism with the struggle against homophobia, thereby providing a means of scaling up the movement against homophobia.

In contrast to the linked-struggle approach, others pursue a scaling up strategy that focuses on one core issue or set of issues. Some advocates turn to a *single-issue* approach because they are dissatisfied with the broad scope of the linked-struggle strategy. One example is the United Kingdom advocacy group 50:50 Parliament,

196 HOW DO WE BREAK FREE?

which, as its name indicates, works to promote gender parity in the parliament of the United Kingdom. Zoe Hunter Gordon, who works with the group, notes her dissatisfaction with the Women's March, which sought to be an umbrella for a broad variety of women's and other progressive causes:

> I personally found that depressing, the lack of a clear goal. I am aware that different women are at different stages, but I'm at a point with my own activism where I need to hear from women moving towards goals. I would be really interested to know how many women from that march followed up their actions in the next week.

Gordon calls attention to one potential shortcoming of a linked-struggle approach; namely, the absence of a tangible, short-term goal on which everyone in the movement can focus.[17] She adds: "If you can stick to one thing and give people a website or a petition, for me I hope that's something they can follow up on more easily than telling them to google lots of different things. There's just too much."[18] Furthermore, this focus on one issue allows 50:50 Parliament to work with a variety of stakeholders, including multiple parties represented in parliament, rather than being associated with just one partisan group or issue lineup.

The single-issue approach is also visible in some forms of coalition-building between established, more cohesive groups. Alicia Garza, a community organizer and co-creator of #BlackLivesMatter and the Black Lives Matter Global Network, whom we discussed in Chapter 4, describes a useful example from her time as an organizer in California. Garza describes deploying a single-issue approach to bring together different community organizations to support an affordable housing ballot initiative in a San Francisco neighborhood. The coalition included local churches, environmental justice advocacy organizations, and a more challenging partner for Garza at the time, the Nation of Islam.[19]

MACROPOLITICS 197

She describes the challenge posed by the differences between her home organization and the Nation of Islam:

At times our membership was hostile to the idea of building a popular front with the Nation of Islam in particular. While our organization was nondenominational, our base was largely Christian. Similarly, our organization was pro-queer, anti-capitalist, intentionally multiracial, and feminist. We were advocates and practitioners of nonviolent direct action. The Nation of Islam differed from us on many of the political pillars that were the bedrock of our organization. The Nation was not anti-capitalist and in fact was pro-Black capitalism. They were not pro-queer organizationally and they were not multiracial. Our stances on patriarchy differed substantially.[20]

Given these differences of perspective, the single-issue approach provided a way for these different constituencies to scale up to advance a shared project.

Garza notes how the focus on one issue bound the coalition together and also made their campaign more persuasive to those outside of it:

What allowed us to be dangerous together was that we were indivisible on the issue of the initiative. We demonstrated a respect for one another and our differences in ways that allowed us to appreciate the strengths that we brought to the table. And, more important, the community respected our unity: If two organizations that couldn't be more different politically could work together, surely this was a fight worth getting involved in.[21]

While it is possible to deploy a single-issue approach in a way that simply ignores heterogeneity within one's group or coalition, that was not how this coalition operated, according to Garza. She recalls learning from the Nation of Islam's approach to organization

198   HOW DO WE BREAK FREE?

and mobilization and ultimately describes their approach to working on those shared initiative as follows: "We didn't look past our differences—we found the courage to look into them."[22] By identifying coalition partners who shared this particular project, these local churches, environmental justice organizations, and the Nation of Islam were all able to advance their influence in politics beyond what would have been possible working on their own.

There is a third approach to scaling up that neither makes a claim to a necessarily linked struggle nor calls for focusing on a single issue. Instead, this approach to scaling up emphasizes the *bonds of solidarity* between different groups. Consider the activism and rhetoric from activist groups that primarily organize among Latinos in the United States, who mobilized to protest the Trump administration's suspension of immigration from several Muslim-majority countries. One activist, Polo Morales, in Los Angeles, explained his participation in these protests as follows: "We stand in solidarity with Muslims because they are our brothers and sisters ... Angelenos, our friends. . . . They come to work, they contribute to the value of this country. When they are attacked we stand up with them."[23]

Morales cites existing relationships, as friends, neighbors, and coworkers, with Muslims in Los Angeles targeted by this federal policy change as a motivation for acting. While there are, of course, Latino Muslims, the approach in this case does not emphasize overlapping membership or interlocking mechanisms of oppression in the style of the linked-struggle approach. Instead, these existing relationships serve as the motivation for contributing to collective action, expressing a commitment to defend and support one's friends and neighbors who have been targeted, with an implicit recognition that they will do the same when the roles are reversed.

One illustration of how the bonds of solidarity approach has been utilized for scaling up is the phenomenon of sympathy (or solidarity) strikes, where members of other unions, who are not directly party to a dispute, strike alongside another union that is on strike against their common employer.[24] As a result, one local union's dispute with management can be influential, even if most employees belong to another union, since the dispute has the potential to shut down the whole company through solidarity actions. Solidarity strikes can even be initiated due to political activity outside of the labor movement. For example, multiple labor unions in Iran have taken part in strikes in solidarity with the women's rights movement in the country. Petrochemical workers, healthcare workers, and sugar cane workers have all gone on strike in support of the movement. This has, in turn, influenced some unions' platforms with the inclusion of demands about the freedom to choose one's attire.[25] Through these bonds of solidarity, the women's rights movement scales up to incorporate the influence of organizations that do not necessarily take women's collective self-authorship to be their core mission.

Shifting Strategies

Scaling up requires attentiveness to heterogeneity, all kinds, including differences in perspective about which strategies for scaling up to adopt. Critical readers will wonder how we address this point. Do we endorse a linked-struggle, single issue, or bonds of solidarity approach? In short, we propose that each one be considered a tool rather than a prescription for handling the challenge of scaling up. While each tool can be successful depending upon context, activists, organizations, and social movements can certainly disagree on which one is best.

Consider ongoing debates about the relationship between the labor movement and reproductive rights activism, especially in light of the US Supreme Court's 2022 *Dobbs* decision reversing *Roe v. Wade*. Some activists, following a linked-struggle approach, have highlighted how reproductive rights are labor issues. Here is Emma

200 HOW DO WE BREAK FREE?

Mahony, a New York City–based activist, writing in *Jacobin*, a left-wing political magazine:

> Women have the right to decide whether and when to take these risks and manage the burdens that pregnancy and child-rearing have on their working life and financial future. Taking away that decision is a violation of their rights as workers. In the labor movement, we are only as strong as our weakest members. When women have less bargaining power—when they are forced into positions where they must take whatever employers offer them—it impacts the bargaining power of all workers.[26]

Some unions seemed to act in accordance with this linked-struggle call to action. For example, the president of the SEIU (Service Employees International Union) stated: "We're going to make sure that everybody running for the U.S. Senate and the Congress makes a commitment to standing for pro-choice position, just as we insist on them being pro-union."[27]

But some unions and union members reject this perspective. For instance, some national unions, such as the Teamsters, United Autoworkers, and Communications Workers of America, eschew the linked-struggle approach, probably because their membership is seriously divided on the abortion question. Some pro-life activists objected to linking these struggles with a single-issue approach response: "The union was not formed to promote abortion. . . . You got rank-and-file union members who had their dues being taken, and their leadership is speaking out for abortion," argued David O'Steen, the National Right to Life Committee executive director.[28] And some regional union bodies continued to endorse pro-life political candidates, even when leaders from their national-level organizations publicly expressed pro-choice positions.[29] We see, therefore, that organizations engaging in macropolitics can encounter disagreements about these

MACROPOLITICS 201

approaches to scaling up, alongside disagreements about public policy and other matters.

Moreover, adopting a single-issue approach is not a neutral or uncontroversial response to differences of perspective within one's group. Some activists cite the following quote from prominent black feminist Audre Lorde to object to single-issue approaches in the political projects they are part of: "There is no such thing as a single-issue struggle because we do not live single-issue lives."[30] Lorde made this claim in a 1982 speech at Harvard University, at an event celebrating Malcolm X, where she articulated a rationale for the linked-struggle approach:

> If we are to keep the enormity of the forces aligned against us from establishing a false hierarchy of oppression, we must school ourselves to recognize that any attack against Blacks, any attack against women, is an attack against all of us who recognize that our interests are not being served by the systems we support. Each one of us here is a link in the connection between anti-poor legislation, gay shootings, the burning of synagogues, street harassment, attacks against women, and resurgent violence against Black people.

Those following Lorde's perspective might argue that adopting a single-issue approach is ineffective and unaccountable: ineffective because a single-issue approach fails to address the relationship between different forms of oppression targeting different groups; and unaccountable because it fails to respond to the forms of heterogeneity within different groups, such as poor, queer women targeted by many of the threats Lorde lists. Furthermore, insisting on a single-issue approach might be unduly restrictive by forcing those who take part in different CSA processes to partition different parts of their lives, such as by marginalizing queer people in racial CSA processes.[31] Similarly, those who endorse a bonds of solidarity

202 HOW DO WE BREAK FREE?

approach might see the adoption of a single-issue approach as a betrayal of these bonds.

In particular contexts, organizations aiming to scale up, as part of their CSA, must often choose between one of these approaches. But it would be a mistake to see this an invariable moral commitment. Moreover, it would be wrongheaded to think that we need a knockdown argument for using one approach rather than another. Instead, we suggest that it would be more fruitful to think of them as complementary tools that we can toggle between to respond to the challenge of scaling up. One reason to adopt this point of view is that the conditions of CSA can change over time, which can mean that a new approach will be most useful for maintaining uptake of our civic responsibilities. For instance, a single-issue approach might be useful for framing a shared problem to unite disparate groups before bonds of solidarity form or a shared understanding of a linked struggle emerges. But as CSA processes unfold over time, robust bonds of solidarity or a stronger sense of linked fate might develop, making one of the other two approaches a better fit for constituents' self-understanding and priorities.

The Fight for $15 movement in the United States is an illustrative example. In 2012, US workers at fast food franchises, such as McDonald's, KFC, and Papa John's, came together, with the support of the Service Employees International Union (SEIU), to discuss their shared work conditions. Workers across major franchises were being paid stagnant, low wages while facing wage theft, off-the-clock work demands, and unsafe working conditions. The movement eventually coalesced around a core set of demands, much like the aforementioned 50:50 campaign in the United Kingdom. In this case, workers advocated for a $15 minimum wage and a union.[32] As the movement grew in size and public salience, it drew the attention of elected officials, and through this influence, inverted the standard model of labor organizing. Typically, workers form a union and once it achieves formal recognition, the union

MACROPOLITICS 203

bargains for higher wages and other improvements to working conditions. Instead, the Fight for $15 movement directly interacted with other voters, elected officials, and corporations, pushing for changes to working conditions and local minimum wage laws despite the fact that most of the movement was not unionized.[33]

While the movement has not succeeded in raising the federal minimum wage, or in getting franchisees recognized as joint employers, which would facilitate unionization, it has been successful in raising wages for many low-wage workers, in part through increases in state- and county-level minimum wage levels.[34] Adriana Alvarez, a McDonald's employee from Chicago, helpfully describes the success of the movement both on a macro and micro scale. In addition to being able to provide a better life for her son with her higher wages, her experience of increased accountability in the workplace is described in *The Guardian*:

> Before the Fight for $15, she said managers regularly asked workers to work off the clock to finish jobs they hadn't completed on their shift for no pay. There was more shouting, more hostility. That has stopped now. "They know we can show up with 50 people in a store," she laughed.[35]

Furthermore, Alvarez has directly engaged in macropolitics through the movement and seeing its success changed her perspective on what was possible:

> Along the way, she has met senators, she has a picture with [Bernie] Sanders, been on a call with [Joe] Biden, welcomed the pope to the US and met workers from different industries, from teachers to airport and healthcare workers, who are also fighting for a better deal. She too has been surprised that the fight has been so successful. When people first started telling her they wanted $15 an hour, she said she told them they were "crazy."[36]

204 HOW DO WE BREAK FREE?

As Alvarez's experience indicates, the Fight for $15 successfully scaled up and facilitated the CSA of a certain class of workers, while empowering them on the macropolitical scale. The single-issue approach arguably provided a useful frame for workers in disparate workplaces and with different employers to notice a shared set of circumstances, as well as a target for their life-shaping projects.

But as it grew in size and prominence, as it scaled up, the movement faced a new set of circumstances. It had already been established as a potent macropolitical force, and participants viewed themselves as workers with a particular shared set of projects. Now some of those who had been mobilized by the movement started to take on roles as representatives in other domains of politics, such as by running for local elected office.[37] In addition, organizers who gained experience through, and were mobilized by, the Fight for $15 have taken on a prominent role in organizing around other issues. For example, Fight for $15 organizers have highlighted the connections between racial justice initiatives and workers' rights, using some of the rhetoric of the linked-struggle approach.

Here is Rasheen Aldridge, a former employee at Jimmy John's and organizer in the Fight for $15 movement, who was elected to the Missouri State Assembly:

> You can't really talk racial injustice without talking economic injustice.... You can't forget that those same black workers still live in the same community that is oppressed, that is over-policed. Those workers were the same workers that also went to the streets of Ferguson, have protested, because they feel like Mike Brown could have been them, regardless if they was working at McDonald's or if they was working at a healthcare facility.... It's all connected.[38]

Participants in the Fight for $15 movement, like Aldridge, carried over lessons and recruitment from their experience in that

MACROPOLITICS 205

CSA process to other forms of CSA and vice versa. The linked-struggle approach is a way to connect their work across different contexts and to reflect the connections that constituents themselves are making about their experiences. In so doing, they may also be taking another step in scaling up the different movements they are part of in a way that may not have been as feasible at the outset of the Fight for $15, when a single-issue approach helped the movement to grow. In this way, the capacity to toggle between these different approaches, rather than endorsing and acting on one as a matter of principle, is more conducive to accounting for the different backgrounds, perspectives, and forms of empowerment within a given CSA process. And this is precisely what we should expect wherever an ethos of collective self-authorship supplants an ethos of boxing in.

Unsavory Partners

The foregoing strategies are tools that we can toggle between, depending on context, to address the challenge of scaling up. Some participants in the Fight for $15 movement, such as Rasheen Aldridge, found the linked-struggle approach useful as CSA processes unfolded over time. But we need not always aim to pursue a linked-struggle approach for scaling up. Alicia Garza, as we noted, found the single-issue approach a better tool in her campaign for affordable housing. Given limited time and resources, organizations inevitably face some trade-offs with respect to the projects they can take on and prioritize. Reaching agreement on the nature of our linked struggles and establishing robust bonds of solidarity can be costly endeavors. And this can come at the expense of progress on issues where there is already alignment between constituents and representatives. Imagine a labor union that aimed to take a stand on every salient public issue of the time and to organize a solidarity strike for each one. Some unions members are

206 HOW DO WE BREAK FREE?

likely to grow weary and exit out of frustration, making the union less effective at realizing its core mission of representing workers' interests in a particular workplace.

Activists, organizations, and movements may also face trade-offs with respect to the partners they select for engaging in CSA. And a refusal to work with certain partners, perhaps out of a concern with ideological purity, or as a matter of principle, can also be costly. The prospect of working with unsavory partners becomes more likely as we scale up and extend CSA processes beyond our ingroups to pursue life-shaping projects at a macropolitical level (though it can certainly happen at the micro level too).[39] Working with such partners, as we deploy any of the above strategies for scaling up, may induce discomfort. Consider Alicia Garza's reflections on her experience working with the Nation of Islam in a coalition to advance shared interests in affordable housing in San Francisco. Here there was discomfort as some members of her organization undoubtedly viewed them as unsavory partners. In this case, Garza's group faced the question of what to do next, or as we described it earlier in the book, they had to ask: now what?

Should they reject these partners and pursue their shared project separately or should they engage in CSA with them? This is always a difficult choice. And it can be all the more difficult when the differences between us and those whom we take to be unsavory partners run deep—cutting into our core moral and political principles. Garza notes that despite her discomfort with the partnership, and the many differences between her own organization and the Nation, she came to appreciate them as partners, and learned about organizational structure and strategies of mobilization through this partnership. She also saw value in the single-issue approach in this context. More generally, she reasons, single-issue, temporary, coalition-building initiatives provide opportunities to learn about how to engage constituencies beyond one's own and counteract the tendency to signal commitment to one's group with an interest in ideological purity.[40]

MACROPOLITICS 207

However, in other cases, bucking Garza's example, activists and organizations may be unwilling to move forward with unsavory coalition partners, especially when more than mere discomfort is clearly at stake. Suppose that we believe in the equal moral worth and dignity of all persons regardless of race, ethnicity, gender, or nationality. This is a core moral commitment. Also suppose that we believe in democracy—that all persons eligible to vote should have an equal opportunity to select governing principles and political representatives in free and fair elections—and in democratic governance in which no one should be prevented from running for office and assume lawmaking authority on the basis of morally arbitrary facts about them such as their race, gender, or sexuality. This is a core political commitment. Should we engage in CSA with unsavory coalition partners when fidelity to these or other core moral and political commitments is at stake? More specifically, do we work with antidemocratic and morally perverse partners who support racism in politics or who harbor racial and ethnic animus toward individuals and groups in our organizations or movements?

The 1964 Democratic National Convention in Atlantic City, New Jersey, followed less than one year after the historic March on Washington organized by Bayard Rustin. At the time, although African Americans exerted considerable influence working at the grassroots level, they were virtual outsiders within the American political system of democratic governance—nationally and statewide. During this convention they sought to gain an equal voice within the national Democratic Party. Although more liberal than the Republican Party at the time, members of the Old South in the national Democratic Party still exercised great power and wielded it to uphold America's long-standing racial divide. Despite this, Rustin and others sought to form a broad coalition of liberals, labor, and minorities in the party with the hope of winning a simple majority to push a more egalitarian national agenda working within the political system. However, in the rural South, in places like Mississippi, where the grip of old-fashioned racism was still strong, some black Democrats rejected coalition-building with white racists at the national level in favor of gaining majority control over statewide institutions.

A significant moment leading up to the 1964 convention came when the Mississippi Freedom Democratic Party (MFDP), which formed because of racial exclusionary state practices and which petitioned the Democratic National Convention (DNC) to seat their party in place of the all-white Democratic Party delegation from Mississippi, rejected a compromise agreement proposed by President Lyndon B. Johnson, who sought to unite the two groups for the greater benefit of the national Democratic Party. The compromise was for the MFDP to accept two at-large seats and to accept the seating alongside racist white delegates who would vow support for DNC candidates in the election, and who would agree to bar racially segregated delegations from the 1968 DNC convention. The MFDP rejected this compromise and the opportunity to engage in CSA with unsavory partners. Rustin believed that this was a tactical mistake. And he thought that the cost of purity, in this case, was simply too high. "The most important thing in our minds at Atlantic City," said Rustin, "was to feel that we were making headway even if in realistic terms our gains were largely token."[41] But Fannie Lou Hamer, an MFDP delegate, who said, "We didn't come all this way for no two seats,"[42] and other MFDP delegates chose fidelity to democratic political commitments over CSA with racist and antidemocratic Mississippi delegates.

Although moral evaluation of prospective CSA coalition partners may be a factor—and an important one at that—it is certainly not the only deciding factor in answering the question, now what? As Rustin intimated in his assessment of the MFDP's decision to reject CSA with rival Mississippi delegates, we must also attend to other considerations, which is something that pragmatically oriented politicians have also noted. In 2023, as Germany experienced a rise in far-right politics with the ascendancy of the Alternative for Germany (AfD) party, it found itself at a crossroads.

MACROPOLITICS 209

Having previously pledged to never cooperate with the AfD, designated as a "suspected" extremist organization by Germany's domestic intelligence agency, the leader of the Christian Democratic Party, Friedrich Merz, signaled a willingness to work with the AfD in local governments in the aftermath of the group having success in local elections. Defending Merz against intra-party critics, one of his deputies remarked: "If it's about a new day care center in the local Parliament, for example, we can't vote against it just because the AfD is voting along."[43]

The point here is that it is one thing to stand on purity, but another to let the right be the enemy of the good. In this case, the value of an issue, on which we can agree, may be a deciding factor in a decision to engage in CSA with an unsavory partner. We may not be able to muster enough support—due to our smaller or their greater numbers—to realize a good initiative without cooperating, which gives us a pragmatic reason to cooperate. The moral stakes of not cooperating might be too costly which gives us a moral reason to cooperate (think about putting single mothers without childcare at a further disadvantage in the labor market and in the income inequality distribution if we do not provide for day care). Uncertainty about what happens if we do not cooperate may give us an epistemic reason to cooperate (think about recurring partisan battles in the United States over whether to raise the debt ceiling or let the federal government default on its debts).

Ultimately, addressing the challenge of scaling up requires the capacity to learn about and reach out to new collaborators and potential constituencies, while continuing to identify, amplify, and act according to the heterogeneity among one's pre-existing collaborators. It also requires calculations about when, and to what extent, we should pursue CSA with unsavory partners. As with the challenge posed by boxing in more generally, responding to the challenge of scaling up requires flexibility to deploy different strategies and tools in different contexts as well as the flexibility to work with different partners who, in some

210   HOW DO WE BREAK FREE?

cases, may be deemed unsavory. Rather than endorsing one approach for scaling up, or an absolute prohibition against working with unsavory partners, we can take up our component civic responsibilities by preserving the flexibility to advance different life-shaping projects with different partners at different points in time in varying circumstances.

Tools for Uptake

At the end of Chapter 5, we noted that an ethos of boxing in and being a hobbyist can get in the way of growing a social movement. Organizers, unlike hobbyists, aim to contribute to CSA processes and the organizations that facilitate them. At the macropolitical scale, where not everyone we are working with will fit in one room, individual resolve and commitment are not enough to overcome the entrenched effects of tight scripts. At a larger scale, there can be many more identity labels and scripts to contend with, along with a greater variety of accompanying differences of background, empowerment, and perspective. Under these circumstances, the degree to which organizations are structured in better (or worse ways) to facilitate (or hinder) our uptake of our civic responsibilities is crucial. We can think of the structure of the organizations and social movements in which individuals operate as providing better or worse tools for the uptake of our civic responsibilities to identify, amplify, and act according to heterogeneity.

One basic, yet useful, starting point is the importance of the formal recognition of representatives. It can be tempting, in the context of some social movements, to strive for a looser, more spontaneous, form of organization. Yet despite its attractiveness at the outset of some social movements, the absence of a more formal organizational structure can hinder uptake of civic responsibilities and engagement with the broader macropolitical system. One such instance is the Occupy Wall Street (OWS) movement, a 2011 wave

MACROPOLITICS 211

of political actions protesting economic inequality. The movement started in 2011 with activists occupying Zuccotti Park in downtown Manhattan. Activists continuously camped in the park, including overnight, and took part in other actions such as marches across the nearby Brooklyn Bridge. The strategy soon spread to other cities across the country.

The movement was notable in its tendency toward horizontalism.[44] The main decision-making body at each site was a general assembly: anyone could speak and make proposals using a call-and-response technique known as the "people's mic" during these assemblies, and decisions were made with a modified consensus procedure.[45] This decision-making process aligned with the movement's broader egalitarian self-understanding, highlighted by its signature chant of "We are the 99%," as contrasted with the wealthiest 1% of the population. These identity scripts were part of the movement's initial success. And its rapid rise in size and public salience is indicative of the broad set of constituencies that resonated with this call to action.

But the movement's horizontalism and consensus procedures brought with them an uneasiness with political representation, and a refusal among some of its members to establish an official platform or set of demands.[46] OWS scaled up swiftly and brought economic inequality to the public consciousness. However, it also faded rapidly, as occupation camps were cleared by police within a few months, without any concrete policy achievements. As political scientist John Ehrenberg argued:

> The problem is that process is not the same as politics, and OWS often acted as if it really believed that the future could be created by proclamation. Long after it became clear that "structurelessness" often created the conditions for hierarchy and that effective action requires authority and decision, OWS continued to pretend that putting forth noble ideas could substitute for the hard, prosaic work of organizing.[47]

212 HOW DO WE BREAK FREE?

While OWS participants were not political hobbyists, their unease with structures of representation made their swift scale-up unsustainable. It made the uptake of civic responsibilities more challenging, as attending to heterogeneity was very costly due to the reliance on general assemblies and consensus decision-making. It also made accountability mechanisms less accessible. The primary mechanisms in operation were informal, such as the threat of exiting the movement, or quite crude, such as communicating in cumbersome general assembly meetings.[48] Greater comfort with formal organization and representation could have facilitated responsiveness to intragroup heterogeneity, and utilization of CSA processes with which to negotiate and deliberate about articulatable demands.[49]

To facilitate uptake of our responsibilities and sustainable collective action, we should embrace representation and formal organization as useful tools for macropolitics. Representatives can take advantage of existing political opportunities to identify, amplify, and encourage action according to forms of intra- and intergroup heterogeneity.[50] For a useful example of how this role can be carried out, consider the role of interest group coalition advocacy directed at federal administrative agencies in the United States.

Administrative agencies, such as the Department of Transportation or the Equal Employment Opportunity Commission, are important, though perhaps overlooked, sites of political representation in the United States. Agency rulemaking is an influential source of policymaking, and agencies seek out public input, often through notice-and-comment periods where they share proposed rules with the public for comment, and respond to significant comments. Interest groups representing broader constituencies, such as the Asian American Justice Center or Immigration Voice, can take part in the process by submitting comments on proposed rules. However, it can be difficult for smaller groups to do so given the resources and expertise required to identify relevant rules and provide the more substantive comments that are more likely to influence agency rulemaking.[51] To overcome these challenges, interest groups can work in coalitions with others to pool their knowledge and resources to submit joint comments that are more likely to successfully persuade policymakers. Furthermore, coalitions that are organizationally diverse, by including some combination of charitable organizations, unions, businesses, trade associations, and citizen groups, tend to be more successful in influencing agency rulemaking.[52] Organizations working in coalitions with others are also more likely to advocate on behalf of multiply marginalized constituencies, thereby taking up responsibilities to respond to intragroup heterogeneity.[53]

By embracing representation via interest groups, those taking part in CSA can take advantage of the opportunities in the existing political system to advance their life-shaping projects. Representatives can work within organizations to take up their civic responsibilities by aggregating information, collaborating with others in coalitions, and taking advantage of existing political opportunities to advocate for their constituents. And the organizations and social movements that they are a part of can also facilitate their ability to enact these responsibilities, as well as their constituents' ability to hold them accountable for doing so.

Another useful means of facilitating uptake is to empower local representatives and organizations to engage in autonomous decision-making while nested in larger organizations and social movements. Empowering local organizations to engage in identity work can facilitate cooperation across lines of social division in response to the challenge of scaling up. For example, sociologist Joanna Robinson describes the bridging work of local social justice organizations in her research on environmental-labor coalitions in British Columbia and California.[54] Despite converging collective projects related to green jobs and sustainability, these coalitions were formed in the context of a background of distrust: some members of labor unions were reticent to join coalitions with environmentalists because they saw them

214 HOW DO WE BREAK FREE?

as insufficiently concerned with making sure green jobs were unionized, while environmentalists distrusted labor unions as insufficiently concerned with the environmental impact of their jobs.[55] In other words, there were disagreements about the degree to which their struggles were linked, and the bonds of solidarity between these groups were frayed. Despite this background of distrust, these coalitions have succeeded in shifting state-level policy related to shared interests, as in the case of the defeat of Proposition 23 in California, which would have overturned the state's clean energy bill. National- and state-level organizations struggled in their initial mobilization efforts but fared better when local partner organizations were able to convene different constituencies using interpretive frames for the issue that were more locally resonant.[56] However, the work of local organizations alone was also insufficient without the resources and broader network provided by national- and state-level organizations.[57]

Mary Brewer, one local organizer involved in the campaign against Proposition 23, described the shift in mindset among environmental organizations:

> And there is a level of empathy that had to occur for people to actually see the value of these people, who may not be as educated, who may not perfectly understand policies, but who actually do understand environmental impacts and unemployment on a day-to-day basis. And our work on this really helped shift the minds of mainstream environmental organizations to the point where they said "wait, we need you, let's be friends!"[58]

As Brewer's statement indicates, the development and maintenance of these coalitions helped to make the importance of a broader, and more diverse, set of constituencies visible to mainstream environmental organizations. Once these additional constituencies were enmeshed in particular campaigns, they now had access to more accountability mechanisms to drive macropolitical organizations, making them responsive to their projects. And the same is true with respect to accountability between environmental and labor organizations—they could use mechanisms within coalitions to hold one another accountable. In this way, the nesting of empowered local organizations within a broader movement facilitated accountability to a wider array of heterogeneity in the advancement of shared projects.

Keeping the Background in View

Our examples of how to facilitate uptake of civic responsibilities have focused, thus far, on how the structure of organizations can provide opportunities for representative and constituent action. But we should not lose sight of the third part of our division of labor from Chapter 5: contributions to background conditions, which are also crucial to combating identity trouble and facilitating uptake. At the large scales of macropolitics, background conditions can structure opportunities to create and maintain accountability to diverse constituencies. But they can also create incentives to deploy tight scripts and avoid cross-cutting coalitions. We all have some influence on these conditions and should work to change them. So when we take up our civic responsibilities, we should utilize the opportunities that background conditions provide, when necessary, to combat identity trouble and tight scripts.

An especially salient approach to accountability at the macro scale is the role of opposition parties in representative government. Just because a political party or coalition has secured enough votes in an election to form a government or populate the executive branch does not mean that they should not be accountable to the perspectives of other parties and representatives in opposition. For example, the parliaments of member states of the European Union (EU) have various institutional tools for opposition parties

216 HOW DO WE BREAK FREE?

to oversee and scrutinize the government's contributions to EU policymaking.[59] In Denmark, the government is required to secure a mandate from the parliament for its negotiating position.[60] In Germany, the government is required to provide documentation at the early stages of EU proposals, as well as information about the positions of different European institutions and other national parliaments that are party to the negotiations.[61] Depending on the balance of representation in parliament, ruling parties may require support from opposition parties to secure mandates for their own proposals, which also gives the opposition power to influence the content of these proposals.[62] These are all features of the structure of national governments and their relationship with the EU that facilitate the accountability of ruling parties to their political opposition.

It is perhaps less salient, but also important, to be attentive to the intragroup heterogeneity among those in power, which can in turn facilitate accountability to those in opposition when there are cross-cutting shared perspectives. It can be useful, then, to make use of, and sustain, institutional background conditions that facilitate the process of identifying, amplifying, and acting according to intra-party and intra-coalition differences. In parliamentary systems, where it is common for multiple parties to form a coalition government, members of different parties may occupy the different ministerial leadership positions, such as the minister of defense or minister for the environment. This presents a set of challenges: the different members of a coalition have to agree on a policy platform despite their different perspectives and hold each other accountable to their agreements despite their different ministerial domains of authority.[63] Luckily, parliamentary democracies such as Germany and the Netherlands do have institutional means, as part of their background conditions, to facilitate intra-coalitional accountability, for example, standing committees of legislators, who can hold hearings, develop expertise in their corresponding policy domain, and use that expertise to scrutinize proposed legislation.[64]

MACROPOLITICS 217

Political science research suggests that coalition partners use these committees as a means of intra-coalition accountability and not just as a source of opposition. One result is that proposed legislation that divides the ruling coalition tends to face delays to being put to a vote.[65]

In addition to keeping the background in view to take advantage of less-salient accountability mechanisms, it can also be valuable to reform background conditions to combat identity trouble. For example, in the United States, some commentators have raised concerns about the role of geographic districts in state and federal elections.[66] In particular, many commentators and citizens worry about partisan gerrymandering, whereby legislative districts are drawn by state legislatures to create or preserve partisan advantage. In addition to considerations of electoral fairness, gerrymandering is concerning because when legislative districts are consistently dominated by one party, the perspectives of non- and opposing-partisan voters may be neglected and less visible in other parts of the country. As a result, it is more difficult to identify, amplify, and act according to the full range of heterogeneity within each constituency.

Recall, from Chapter 2, Silas House's concerns about the boxing in of (especially rural) Democratic voters in Kentucky. He describes being boxed in by scripts deployed by Democrats from other parts of the United States that saw Kentucky as intrinsically aligned with salient Republican political representatives.[67] The people that House encountered, who deployed such tight scripts, neglected the political heterogeneity in other states. Given trends of increasing partisan residential segregation that we discussed in Chapter 2, uneven distributions of partisan alignment and political perspectives may become increasingly common, which would amplify these concerns about limited exposure and tight political scripts. This might also be concerning if, in less-competitive districts, candidates for public office face incentives to reinforce, rather than challenge, tight scripts related to partisanship.

218 HOW DO WE BREAK FREE?

Insofar as district-based representation contributes to identity trouble and reinforces tight scripts, this warrants changing this feature of the background conditions.[68] There are a few potential means of doing so. One strategy would be to incorporate other forms of electoral representation that are not tied to geographic districts or which do not feature a one-to-one correspondence between districts and representatives. For example, in other countries, some or all members of parliament are elected via proportional representation based on party list voting.[69] In this system, parties with voters who are dispersed throughout the country, but without a plurality of voters in any one jurisdiction, can still gain representation in the parliament. For example, a party with only 10% of nationwide voters could gain representation in the parliament despite not winning the majority of the votes in any one constituency. Proportional election of, at least some, representatives might combat concerns about tight scripts by incentivizing attentiveness to differences of perspective distributed across different geographic constituencies, including political minorities within a given geographic area.

Another means of changing the background conditions would be to change how districts are drawn. Some advocates have proposed greater restrictions on the redistricting process or the use of nonpartisan redistricting commissions to combat partisan gerrymandering.[70] However, attempts at adopting such reforms have produced mixed results. Some commissions' decision-making has resulted in gridlock between their Democrat and Republican members, while others have been overridden by their state legislatures. In addition, some commentators argue that the adoption of these commissions in some states, while others remain partisan-controlled, is unwise, as it would involve ceding ground in partisan competition if Democrat-controlled state governments adopt nonpartisan procedures while Republican-controlled state governments retain partisan-based gerrymandering.[71] Such drawbacks may result from imperfect applications of these reforms.

MACROPOLITICS 219

There are potential fixes, such as populating commissions with nonpartisan members alongside procedures to discourage gridlock, and empowering commissions, all while organizing for nationally coordinated reforms of redistricting processes. Given the importance of national coordination, organizing to change the background conditions in these ways clearly requires an ambitious form of scaling up. Nevertheless, given the impact this could have on many different CSA processes, it is a challenge that we, as contributors to background conditions, should take up.

In addition to leveraging the opportunities afforded by background conditions and working to change those that contribute to identity trouble, we can also work to create new institutional opportunities to take up our civic responsibilities. One way of doing so would be to embrace new consultative institutions to political background conditions, as they might serve as especially useful sites of identifying heterogeneity that is neglected by existing accountability mechanisms.[72] Mini-publics, which are assemblies composed of a randomly selected group of citizens, provide a feasible way to engage with citizens directly to consult on policymaking.[73] Mini-publics typically focus on a particular topic, such as electoral reforms or municipal urban planning policy. Participants usually develop knowledge on the subject through briefing materials and/or discussion with experts. They then express judgments either through polling before and after participation or through the production of a policy proposal document.

Mini-publics can, at their best, provide a valuable form of popular consultation by serving as an indication of what the broader public would think about a topic were they to have the time to learn about it and discuss it with others. They could be especially useful to guide policymakers and hold them accountable to the public on issues of lower public knowledge and/or salience.[74] They could also be used within particular political parties as a source of input about partisan constituents' perspectives on the potential policy platform of the party.[75] These mini-publics could identify forms of

220 HOW DO WE BREAK FREE?

heterogeneity not captured by other indicators of public opinion, which select for the most engaged members of the public or might be indicative of reasoning based on tight scripts. Incorporating new forms of public consultation into the background institutional conditions of democracy could provide additional tools for identification, amplification, and action pertaining to forms of heterogeneity present among constituents.

We should keep background conditions in view whether we are operating as representatives or constituents because we all contribute to the political environment in which we operate. Much like the content of our identity scripts, this environment is not static and it can be shaped by our collective action. In sum, our reasons for keeping the background in view are threefold. We should utilize the existing opportunities and accountability mechanisms that it provides for CSA. We should organize to reform background conditions when they contribute to identity trouble. And, finally, we should create new institutions to shape these conditions when they can better facilitate the uptake of our civic responsibilities.

Embracing the Challenge

Our social movements must be equipped to organize those with a variety of backgrounds, perspectives, and forms of (dis)empowerment to address the global challenge of climate change. We must attend to disagreements about the contributions of the most and least developed countries to climate mitigation and adaptation, misconceptions about the race and class demographics of environmentalists, existing forms of distrust between labor unions and environmentalist organizations, and even those who are skeptical about the prospect of climate mitigation altogether. We must preserve the flexibility to consider different tactics, including street

MACROPOLITICS 221

protests, entrepreneurship and technological innovation, electoral contestation, and filing legal challenges. Additionally, we must preserve the compatibility between climate action and a vast array of identity labels from eco-feminist to Christian conservative.

We have identified tools for attending to group heterogeneity even at the macro scale. We can deploy all three strategies for scaling up—highlighting linked struggles, formulating single-issue alliances, and strengthening bonds of solidarity—depending on context and coalition partners. We can make strategic calculations about when and how to cooperate with unsavory partners when the cost of purity is too high. Following the lead of labor-environmental coalitions, we can organize others to take climate action through the full range of CSA processes, rather than sticking to the sidelines as a hobbyist. We can structure our organizations and movements to embrace the power of representation, empower local representatives to make decisions, and utilize tools to identify, amplify, and act according to the heterogeneity in our midst. We should embrace the fact that climate initiatives in different neighborhoods, regions, and countries may have different foci, despite being nested in a broader, international movement. And, lastly, we should not passively accept the background conditions we inherit, especially if they are not serving our CSA projects. As part of our macropolitical engagement, we can strive to change these conditions, such as by changing electoral rules to better facilitate the accountability and oversight of national governments' contributions to international climate agreements.

Contrary to the conclusions of ardent identity politics skeptics, the use of identities in macropolitics does not inevitably lead to a failure of democratic accountability. We can utilize macropolitical tools and tactics to overcome the challenge of scaling up and make our identities work for us to advance our climate change projects, rather than boxing us in as tight scripts. This is important not just for the success of our contemporary collective self-authorship

222 HOW DO WE BREAK FREE?

projects, but also to preserve opportunities for the CSA of future generations, as Greta Thunberg has argued:

> If I live to be 100, I will be alive in the year 2103. When you think about the future today, you don't think beyond the year 2050. By then, I will in the best case, not even have lived half of my life. What happens next? The year 2078 I will celebrate my 75th birthday. If I have children or grandchildren, maybe they will spend that day with me. Maybe they will ask me about you, the people who were around back in 2018. Maybe they will ask why you didn't do anything while there still was time to act? What we do or don't do right now will affect my entire life and the lives of my children and grandchildren. What we do or don't do right now, me and my generation can't undo in the future.[76]

We started this discussion of macropolitics by noting the difficulty of scaling up to address major challenges such as climate change. When faced with this fact, one could fall back on only taking responsibility for one's local community at the micro scale. But this chapter shows that retreat is not required because we can meet the challenge of scaling up. This completes our argument for why we must, and what is involved in, making our identities safe for democracy.

Conclusion

No matter the identities we incorporate into our life plans, the international coordination required to address climate change is a major challenge we all face. Given its urgency, we cannot let identity trouble impede our efforts to respond. And we must leverage democracy's problem-solving capacity to do so effectively. Despite operating at a much larger scale, responding to climate change is yet another instance of Rustin's dilemma—coordinating the collective pursuit of projects in a manner that is attentive to intra- and intergroup heterogeneity. Much like Rustin needed to attend to the heterogeneity among activists with different conceptions of black identity as well as the different identities and political perspectives among those he hoped to recruit in the fight for economic justice, contemporary organizers need to attend to the heterogeneity of potential partners in the pursuit of environmental sustainability and climate justice. No matter what instance of Rustin's dilemma we face, we must guard against the risks associated with being boxed in by tight scripts. The framework we provide in this book enables us to mitigate these risks by taking up the overarching responsibility to make collective self-authorship (CSA) accountable to group heterogeneity.

Given the depth of democracy's challenges, and how entrenched tight scripts are in our norms, practices, and institutions, we should not expect quick fixes, even when most stakeholders earnestly take up their civic responsibilities. But this should not be too discouraging. The democratic landscape can change over time and new opportunities for collective action can emerge. For example, at the time of completing this book, in the summer of 2023, there

Boxed In. Derrick Darby and Eduardo J. Martinez, Oxford University Press. © Oxford University Press 2024.
DOI: 10.1093/9780197620236.003.0008

224 CONCLUSION

are hopeful signs of newly emerging opportunities for macro-level policy changes to address economic inequality in the United States. Relevant signs include support from some high-profile Republican senators for collective bargaining and federal legislation to restrict non-compete agreements. They also include a co-sponsored bill by Josh Hawley, a Republican senator from Missouri, and Elizabeth Warren, a Democratic senator from Massachusetts, to claw back executive pay from failed banks and hold banks accountable for excessive risk-taking.[1]

Progressive activists and legislators interested in such policy initiatives to tackle economic inequality have an opening to engage in coalition-building. And seizing these opportunities will involve collaboration between representatives and groups that are not typically seen as moderate. For example, neither Hawley nor Warren is portrayed as a moderate within their parties, yet they have collaborated on this shared economic priority. This kind of partnership requires maintaining flexibility about whom to associate with. It also requires concerted efforts by activists to hold elected officials and national organizations accountable for following through on the relevant priorities. This is the hard work of collective self-authorship that takes center stage in our book.

Economic inequality is a common and enduring problem for democracies. It was a problem that Rustin sought to address in his organizing work. And it motivated him to embrace a broader set of coalition partners than other veterans of the Civil Rights movement, such as Stokely Carmichael, were willing to accept. Perhaps, then, Rustin would have welcomed these current opportunities for diverse coalition-building to tackle economic inequality. While his career as an organizer is now over, his work, including efforts to respond to the dilemma posed by group heterogeneity, created greater opportunities for organizers that followed him to engage in new forms of collective action in service of CSA. The kinds of multi-racial coalition-building that are possible today were made possible, yes by the work of representatives like Rustin, but also

CONCLUSION   225

by the work of many other activists including Ella Baker, as well as some not remembered in history books. Creating opportunities for future generations—who will be no less diverse than we are today— to take up our enduring challenges via CSA processes might be all that we can hope for in the face of especially entrenched forms of identity trouble.

Much like we owe it to fellow self-authors to take up our civic responsibilities, we owe it to the organizers of the past to continue to chip away at the challenges that stand in the way of democratic problem-solving and accountable collective self-authorship today. We do not have to take up, nor solve, every societal challenge that we currently face for this approach to prove useful; we just have to pass the baton.

Acknowledgments

This book would not have been possible without support and thoughtful engagement with our ideas from our colleagues, friends, and family. We have benefited immensely from the feedback we received and we would like to thank everyone who took the time to engage with our ideas.

We are very grateful to Will Umphres and Sahar Heydari Fard for taking the time to read and provide detailed comments on a draft of the entire manuscript. Thanks to Christian Davenport for helpful comments and advice at many stages of this project, including at its early stages as an article and later stages as we revised the manuscript. We are also grateful to Mercy Corredor, Randall Harp, Kayla Jackson, Mayaki Kimba, Filipa Melo Lopes, Temi Ogunye, Sarah Soule, and two anonymous referees for comments on draft chapters of the book. We appreciate your generous and insightful comments. They certainly helped to make this a better book.

We also benefited greatly from the opportunity to present parts of the book to audiences at Princeton University, Fordham University, Rutgers University, the University of Cincinnati, Nuffield College at Oxford, the London School of Economics, the University of Zurich, the Free University of Berlin, Ludwig Maximilian University of Munich, the Massachusetts Institute of Technology, and the 2023 PPE Society Annual Meeting in New Orleans. Thank you to everyone who took the time to attend these presentations, ask insightful questions, and make helpful comments.

Thank you to Peter Ohlin, executive editor, for helpful feedback and supporting this project and to the editorial team at Oxford University Press. The origin of this book project was an article that we coauthored and published in the *Journal of Political Philosophy*

228 ACKNOWLEDGMENTS

in 2022. Thank you to Christopher Achen, Darren Davis, Maxime Lepoutre, Stephen Macedo, Mara Ostfeld, Larry Temkin, and three anonymous referees for their feedback on that paper. It helped us develop our ideas for this book as well.

We are grateful for the support of the Charles P. Taft Research Center at the University of Cincinnati, the School of Arts and Sciences at Rutgers University, and our colleagues. We also owe a special thanks to the Rutgers University Press for allowing us to use a wonderful conference room for several days to edit our manuscript in light of all the great feedback that we received, and to the employees at the New Brunswick, New Jersey, location of Jersey Mike's for keeping us well-fed during our marathon sessions.

Book writing demands significant attention, time, and commitment. We have spent countless hours working on this project, at times in solitude and at times collaboratively. And more often than not, when we were not actually working, we were thinking about our project and work yet to be done. This undoubtedly made us less than ideal partners at times. So our greatest debts are to Angela and Annabelle—our spouses—to whom we dedicate this book. Without their love, support, and patience we would not have been able to invest so much of ourselves into this book.

Notes

Introduction

1. Bayard Rustin, *Fear, Frustration, Backlash: The New Crisis in Civil Rights* (New York: Jewish Labor Committee, 1966), 5.
2. Bayard Rustin, *The Failure of Black Separatism* (New York: Harper & Brothers, 1970), 3.
3. While we will contribute to the aforementioned debate about the role of democracy in identity and provide a pathway forward for democratic cooperation in the face of tight scripts, this book will not provide a novel defense of democracy, nor will it endorse a particular view about its ultimate justification. Instead, we proceed with a fairly minimal conception of democracy's importance for advancing shared goals in Chapter 2, which defenders of many particular views of democracy's proper function and value can endorse. This book is also focused on the contributions of identity to democracy, rather than a comprehensive account of democracy in general. Existing accounts in democratic theory highlight multiple functions of democracy, including its deliberative and aggregative functions. Democratic theorists have also identified many values that democracy might realize, such as equality and freedom. Regardless of one's preferred view about the function or value of democracy, as long as advancing shared goals is part of that view, and identities are politically impactful, our framework should be applicable. For a useful starting point on democratic theory and different accounts of democracy's value, see Tom Christiano and Sameer Bajaj, "Democracy," in *Stanford Encyclopedia of Philosophy*, March 3, 2022, https://plato.stanford.edu/entries/democracy/.
4. We call attention to the dynamic and complex nature of collective identities, which makes the heterogeneity they exhibit difficult, but important, to account for. Of course, other features of the social world are also dynamic and complex, such as political ideologies and cultural practices. And these other features of the social world can interact with identity. For example, collective identities can be defined by ideologies and cultural practices, but also ideologies and practices can be sustained because individuals have come to associate them with identity scripts. Ultimately, our focus in this book is on the role of identity in democracy, and we discuss other features of the social world insofar as they are relevant to our focus. This allows us to contribute to the debate between identity politics optimists and skeptics while providing action guidance that takes seriously our collective agency over the identities that shape our lives. That said, it would be useful for future work to take up the dynamics and complexity of identity and other features of the social world in an even broader framework. Research at the intersection of social theory and complexity theory might be one promising way to do so. For examples of this work, see Sylvia Walby, "Complexity Theory, Systems Theory, and Multiple Intersecting Social inequalities," *Philosophy of the Social Sciences* 37 (2007): 449–470; Sahar Heydari Fard, "Diversity, Polarization, and Dynamic Structures: A Structural Turn in Social Contract Theory," in *New Approaches to Social Contract Theory: Liberty,*

230 NOTES

Equality, Diversity, and the Open Society, ed. Michael Moehler and John Thrasher (New York: Oxford University Press, forthcoming).

5. The action-guidance we are interested in does not require identifying the precise nature and boundaries of social categories. This has been the focus of others working in the subfield of philosophy called social ontology, which examines the nature and properties of the social world. Some social ontologists, for example, are concerned with identifying the nature and boundaries of social categories like gender and race. We grant that the nature and boundaries of identities can be ambiguous and contested. But social scripts can continue to operate despite this ambiguity. We can make sense of different perspectives on the nature and boundaries of social identities with our account of collective self-authorship in Chapter 4. For useful starting points for the social ontology of race and gender, see, respectively: Joshua Glasgow, Sally Haslanger, Chike Jeffers, and Quayshawn Spencer, *What Is Race? Four Philosophical Views* (New York: Oxford University Press, 2019); and Sally Haslanger and Ásta, "Feminist Metaphysics," in *Stanford Encyclopedia of Philosophy*, August 11, 2017, https://plato.stanford.edu/entries/feminism-metaphysics/.

6. Rustin, *The Failure of Black Separatism*, 2.

7. Bayard Rustin, *Strategies for Freedom: The Changing Patterns of Black Protest* (New York: Columbia University Press, 1976), 78.

8. Ibid., 79.

9. Ibid., 80.

10. Ibid.

11. Ibid., 49.

12. *The Reminiscences of Bayard Rustin, no. 8: Interview of Bayard Rustin by Ed Edwin, November 6, 1985* (Alexandria, VA: Alexander Street Press, 2003): 1–42.

13. Just as citizens with different preferred policy platforms can endorse and apply our framework to combat tight scripts, so can citizens with different moral commitments. Our framework does not assume the truth of, and is compatible with, different moral theories such as consequentialism, deontology, contractualism, and virtue ethics. We also do not assume a particular priority ranking between moral and political values such as equality and freedom. As long as those who endorse these views can recognize the value of pursuing a life plan, which we discuss in Chapter 3, and the value of democracy as a means of advancing shared goals, which we discuss in Chapter 2, they should be concerned about the problem of being boxed in by tight scripts. It is also open to those with different normative commitments to conclude that the civic responsibilities we outline in Chapter 5 can be outweighed by other normative considerations, whether moral, aesthetic, or epistemic, in cases of trade-offs. We do not provide guidance about how to handle trade-offs with responsibilities that follow from normative theories that are more general than, or external to, the civic domain that is our focus. For a useful summary of the aims and functions of moral theories, see Julia Driver, "Moral Theory," in *Stanford Encyclopedia of Philosophy*, June 27, 2022, https://plato.stanford.edu/entries/moral-theory/.

14. For this and subsequent references to "group" heterogeneity we will mean both intragroup and intergroup heterogeneity.

Chapter 1

1. Ralph Ellison, "On Bird, Bird-Watching and Jazz," in *The Collected Essays of Ralph Ellison*, ed. John F. Callahan (New York: The Modern Library, 2003), 260.

2. Ibid., 247.

3. Ibid.

NOTES 231

4. Stanley Crouch, *Kansas City Lightning: The Rise and Time of Charlie Parker* (New York: HarperCollins, 2013), 98.
5. Jay-Z, *Decoded* (New York: Spiegel & Grau, 2010), epilogue.
6. Later in this chapter, in the section "Boxed In: A Taxonomy," we provide a taxonomy of different ways of being boxed in according to how we think and feel, how we act, and whom we associate with. In Chapter 3, we provide a taxonomy of different components of identity: label, identification, and treatment-as. Both taxonomies are relevant to this example. Oprah treats Jay-Z as a rapper, according to a script about how rappers act, which excludes reading books about karma. In so doing, she boxes him in, making it more difficult for him to engage in discussion with her as a fellow reader, and also reinforcing this tight script about how rappers act.
7. Paola Ramos, *Finding Latinx: In Search of the Voices Redefining Latino Identity* (New York: Vintage Books, 2020), 269.
8. Jill McCorkel and Jason Rodriguez, "'Are You an African?' The Politics of Self-Construction in Status-Based Social Movements," *Social Problems* 56 (2009): 357–384, 373. We also discuss this example in Derrick Darby and Eduardo J. Martinez, "Making Identities Safe for Democracy," *Journal of Political Philosophy* 30 (2022): 273–297, 291–292.
9. Katherine E. Wadkins, "Freakin' Out: Remaking Masculinity through Punk Rock in Detroit," *Women & Performance: A Journal of Feminist Theory* 22 (2012): 239–260.
10. Ibid., 244.
11. This is referring back to a quote from Paola Ramos describing the reaction of middle school students to a performance by Browns Crew. She notes: "In their songs, they rap about immigration, but they also talk about identity in the Midwest and segregation in Milwaukee. They sing in English but also in Spanish and Spanglish. They make those schoolkids feel they can break out of *any* box they want." Ramos, *Finding Latinx*, 269.
12. Tightly scripted identities restrict us because of the operation of particular mechanisms, which we discuss in the section "Trans Soldiers and Black Writers" of this chapter. We also provide a taxonomy of different ways of being boxed in by tight scripts in the section "Boxed In: A Taxonomy."
13. This example and those that follow in this chapter are thought experiments inspired by research and reporting on the experiences of people with the relevant identities and projects. We have incorporated these inputs into characters within a narrative to increase readability and the accessibility of the explanations that follow from them. Interested readers can look to the endnotes for references that explain the details that inspire each thought experiment.
14. Eduardo Herrera, "Masculinity, Violence, and Deindividuation in Argentine Soccer Chants: The Sonic Potentials of Participatory Sounding-in-Synchrony," *Ethnomusicology* 62 (2018): 470–499, 486.
15. James Baldwin, "Freaks and the American Ideal of Manhood," in *James Baldwin: Collected Essays* (New York: The Library of America, 1998), 815.
16. Rory Magrath, "'To Try and Gain an Advantage for My Team': Homophobic and Homosexually Themed Chanting among English Football Fans," *Sociology* 52 (2018): 709–726, 716.
17. "As Biden Lifts a Ban, Transgender People Get a Long-Sought Chance to Enlist," *New York Times*, January 25, 2021, https://www.nytimes.com/2021/01/25/us/biden-transgender-ban-military.html?action=click&module=Spotlight&pgtype=Homepage.
18. Like Jimmy and Juan in the *fútbol* fans case study, Ron is not an actual person, but one whose profile combines various aspects of transgender and military identity

232 NOTES

drawn from actual persons, and from a plausible set of characteristics associated with bearers of these identities.

19. Adam F. Yerke and Valory Mitchell, "Transgender People in the Military: Don't Ask? Don't Tell? Don't Enlist!" *Journal of Homosexuality* 60 (2013): 436–457, 438.

20. Ibid.

21. Bobbi J. Van Gilder, "Sexual Orientation Stigmatization and Identity Work for Gays, Lesbians, and Bisexuals in the U. S. Military," *Journal of Homosexuality* 66 (2019): 1949–1973, 1956.

22. Ibid.

23. Ralph Ellison, "The World and the Jug," in *The Collected Essays of Ralph Ellison*, ed. John F. Callahan (New York: The Modern Library, 2003), 185.

24. Ibid., 160.

25. Ibid., 167.

26. Ibid., 163.

27. This section relies upon the account of Christian conservativism and its relationship to criminal justice found in David Dagan and Steven Teles, *Prison Break: Why Conservatives Turned against Mass Incarceration* (New York: Oxford University Press, 2016).

28. Jack Schneider, "Escape from Los Angeles: White Flight from Los Angeles and Its Schools, 1960–1980," *Journal of Urban History* 34 (2008): 995–1012.

29. Dagan and Teles, *Prison Break*, 29.

30. Arab American Institute, "Demographics" (2021), https://www.aaiusa.org/demog raphics.

31. Hansi Lo Wang, "Next U.S. Census Will Have New Boxes for 'Middle Eastern or North African,' 'Latino,'" *NPR*, March 28, 2024, https://www.npr.org/2024/03/28/1237218459/census-race-categories-ethnicity-middle-east-north-africa.

32. This character is based on Farah Eltohamy, "The Census Says I'm White, but I'm Not," *The State Press*, last updated October 6, 2019, https://www.statepress.com/article/2019/10/specho-census-says-im-white#.

33. This character is based on Sarah Parvini and Ellis Simani, "Are Arabs and Iranians White? Census Says Yes, But Many Disagree," *Los Angeles Times*, https://www.lati mes.com/projects/la-me-census-middle-east-north-africa-race/.

34. This character is based on Leslie Berestein Rojas, "'Are We White?': SoCal's Arab-Americans Debate Which Box to Check on the Census," *LAist*, last updated February 25, 2019, https://laist.com/news/are-we-white-socals-arab-americans-debate-which-box-to-check-on-the-census.

35. This quote appears in Rojas, "'Are We White?'"

36. Parvini and Simani, "Are Arabs and Iranians White?"

37. Kristine J. Ajrouch and Amaney Jamel, "Assimilating to a White Identity: The Case of Arab Americans," *The International Migration Review* 41 (2007): 860–879.

38. This quote appears in Eltohamy, "The Census Says I'm White, but I'm Not."

39. This quote appears in Parvini and Simani, "Are Arabs and Iranians White?"

40. Khaled A. Beydoun, "A Demographic Threat? Proposed Reclassification of Arab Americans on the 2020 Census," *Michigan Law Review First Impressions* 114 (2015): 1–8.

41. This quote appears in Parvini and Simani, "Are Arabs and Iranians White?"

42. This quote appears in Rojas, "'Are We White?'"

43. Michel Foucault is an especially prominent social theorist who analyzes the role of institutions and norms in the exercise of power. For especially influential examples of his work, see his *Discipline and Punish: Birth of the Prison*, trans. Alan Sheridan (New York: Vintage Books, 1995) and *The History of Sexuality*, Volume 1: *An Introduction*, trans. Robert Hurley (New York: Vintage Books, 1990). For an

NOTES 233

overview of Foucault's work and its relevance to the study of political institutions, see Mark Bevir, "Foucault, Power, and Institutions," *Political Studies* 47 (1999): 345–359.

44. Ted Gioia, *The History of Jazz*, 2nd edition (New York: Oxford University Press, 2011), 190.

45. David H. Rosenthal, *Hard Bop: Jazz and Black Music 1955–1965* (Oxford: Oxford University Press, 1992), 13.

46. Crouch, *Kansas City Lightning*, 19.

47. Miles Davis with Quincy Troupe, *Miles: The Autobiography* (New York: Simon and Schuster, 1989), 53.

48. Ibid., 9.

49. Imanu Amiri Baraka [LeRoi Jones], *Blues People: Negro Music in White America* (New York: William Morrow, 1963).

50. Gene Santoro, *Myself When I Am Real: The Life and Music of Charles Mingus* (New York: Oxford University Press, 2000), 78.

Chapter 2

1. A 2014 analysis of data from a baby name app found that Maya was significantly more popular with Democratic parents than Republicans, and that Bailey was significantly more popular with Republican parents than Democrats. See Mark Edmond, "The Politics of Baby Names," *Verdant Labs*, November 13, 2014, http://verdantlabs.com/blog/2014/11/13/political-names/.

2. Political scientists have measured increases in these sorts of attitudes toward opposing partisans in the United States under the conceptual header of "affective polarization," which focuses on feelings toward opposing partisans rather than differences in issue positions. For an overview, see Shanto Iyengar, Yphtach Lelkes, Matthew Levendusky, Neil Malhotra, and Sean J. Westwood, "The Origins and Consequences of Affective Polarization in the United States," *Annual Review of Political Science* 22 (2019): 129–146. Druckman and Levendusky find that American partisans tend to dislike opposing partisan elites more than opposing partisan voters, though they dislike both. See James N. Druckman and Matthew S. Levendusky, "What Do We Measure When We Measure Affective Polarization?," *Public Opinion Quarterly* 83 (2019): 114–122.

3. For evidence of discrimination based on partisan identity, see Shanto Iyengar and Sean J. Westwood, "Fear and Loathing across Party Lines: New Evidence on Group Polarization," *American Journal of Political Science* 59 (2015): 690–707; Sean J. Westwood, Shanto Iyengar, Stefaan Walgrave, Rafael Leonisio, Luis Miller, and Oliver Strijbis, "The Tie That Divides: Cross-National Evidence of the Primacy of Partyism," *European Journal of Political Research* 57 (2018): 333–354; Andrew M. Engelhardt and Stephen M. Utych, "Grand Old (Tailgate) Party? Partisan Discrimination in Apolitical Settings," *Political Behavior* 42 (2020): 769–789.

4. Jeffrey Lyons and Stephen M. Utych, "You're Not from Here!: The Consequences of Urban and Rural Identities," *Political Behavior* 45 (2023): 75–101. Lyons and Utych find that both urban and rural residents in the United States see individuals in their communities as more likely to share their values, and individuals from other communities as less likely to share their values. They also find that both urban and rural residents tend to see their respective kinds of communities as receiving less than their fair share of resources. Rural residents tend to see suburban and urban communities as getting more than their fair share, while urban residents tend to see suburban communities as getting more than their fair share.

5. Shanto Iyengar and Masha Krupenkin, "The Strengthening of Partisan Affect," *Political Psychology* 39 (2018): 201–218. Iyengar and Krupenkin find that hostility

234 NOTES

toward the political party one opposes has driven increases in affective polarization in the United States and has eclipsed enthusiasm for one's own party as a driver of political participation relative to the 1980s.

6. The political scientist Lilliana Mason distinguishes issue polarization, the increasing partisan alignment of positions along a range of policy issues, from what she calls *social polarization*, which refers to an increasing social distance between supporters of different parties. See Lilliana Mason, *Uncivil Agreement: How Politics Became Our Identity* (Chicago: University of Chicago Press, 2018), 21–23. There is some debate among researchers about the degree to which citizens, as opposed to political elites, have undergone ideological polarization over time. See Morris P. Fiorina and Samuel J. Abrams, "Political Polarization in the American Public," *Annual Review of Political Science* 11 (2008): 563–588. But it is less controversial that citizens have socially polarized with increasing alignment of racial, religious, geographic, and partisan identities.

7. Mason, *Uncivil Agreement*, 8.

8. Jacob R. Brown and Ryan D. Enos, "The Measurement of Partisan Sorting for 180 Million Voters," *Nature Human Behaviour* 5 (2021): 998–1008.

9. Michele F. Margolis, *From Politics to the Pews* (Chicago: University of Chicago Press, 2018).

10. Costas Panagopoulos, Donald P. Green, Jonathan Krasno, Michael Schwam-Baird, and Kyle Endres, "Partisan Consumerism: Experimental Tests of Consumer Reactions to Corporate Political Activity," *The Journal of Politics* 82 (2020): 996–1007.

11. Alexandra Samuel, "Dating Apps Are Intensifying Online Partisanship," *JSTOR Daily*, February 18, 2020, https://daily.jstor.org/dating-apps-are-intensifying-online-partisanship/.

12. Alan I. Abramowitz and Steven Webster, "The Rise of Negative Partisanship and the Nationalization of US Elections in the 21st Century," *Electoral Studies* 41 (2016): 12–22.

13. "Political Polarization in the American Public," *Pew Research Center*, June 12, 2014, https://www.pewresearch.org/politics/2014/06/12/political-polarization-in-the-american-public/.

14. Ibid.

15. Natalie Jomini Stroud, "Media Use and Political Predispositions: Revisiting the Concept of Selective Exposure," *Political Behavior* 30 (2008): 341–366.

16. Douglas J. Ahler and Gaurav Sood, "The Parties in Our Heads: Misperceptions about Party Composition and Their Consequences," *The Journal of Politics* 80 (2018): 964–981, 968.

17. Silas House, "A Warning from a Democrat in a Red State," *The Atlantic*, January 3, 2021, https://www.theatlantic.com/ideas/archive/2021/01/warning-democrat-red-state/617501/.

18. Ibid.

19. Ibid.

20. Andres Reiljan, "'Fear and Loathing across Party Lines' (Also) in Europe: Affective Polarisation in European Party Systems," *European Journal of Political Research* 59 (2020): 376–396; Markus Wagner, "Affective Polarization in Multiparty Systems," *Electoral Studies* 69 (2021): 102199.

21. Federico Vegetti, "The Political Nature of Ideological Polarization: The Case of Hungary," *The Annals of the American Academy of Political and Social Science* 681 (2019): 78–96, 84–85.

22. Ibid., 86–88.

23. Ibid., 92.

NOTES   235

24. Ibid.
25. Dalibor Rohac, "Hungary and Poland Aren't Democratic. They're Authoritarian," *Foreign Policy*, February 5, 2018, https://foreignpolicy.com/2018/02/05/hungary-and-poland-arent-democratic-theyre-authoritarian/.
26. These fan slogans are mentioned in Steven A. Lehr, Meghan L. Ferreira, and Mahzarin R. Banaji, "When Outgroup Negativity Trumps Ingroup Positivity: Fans of the Boston Red Sox and New York Yankees Place Greater Value on Rival Losses than Own-Team Gains," *Group Processes & Intergroup Relations* 22 (2019): 26–42, 29.
27. In a series of experiments on a sample of Red Sox and Yankees fans, Lehr, Ferreira, and Banaji, "When Outgroup Negativity Trumps Ingroup Positivity," 38, find that the magnitude of outgroup hostility toward their rivals exceeded the warmth for their own favored team, especially when their team was on the bottom of the competitive hierarchy.
28. Arlie Russell Hochschild, "The American Right: Its Deep Story," *Global Dialogue*, August 6, 2016, https://globaldialogue.isa-sociology.org/articles/the-american-right-its-deep-story. For an extended version and discussion of Hochschild's deep story, see Arlie Russell Hochschild, *Strangers in Their Own Land* (New York: New Press, 2016), chapter nine.
29. Hoschschild, *Strangers in Their Own Land*, 128.
30. Victoria Esses, John F. Dovidio, Lynne M. Jackson, and Tamara L. Armstrong, "The Immigration Dilemma: The Role of Perceived Group Competition, Ethnic Prejudice, and National Identity," *Journal of Social Issues* 57 (2002): 389–412.
31. Sandra Sequeira, Nathan Nunn, and Nancy Qian, "Immigrants and the Making of America," *The Review of Economic Studies* 87 (2020): 382–419.
32. Kai Arzheimer and Carl C. Berning, "How the Alternative for Germany (AfD) and Their Voters Veered to the Radical Right, 2013–2017," *Electoral Studies* 60 (2019): 102040; Jeffrey Gedmin, "How 'Populist' Is the AFD?" *Brookings Institute*, December 4, 2019, https://www.brookings.edu/articles/how-populist-is-the-afd/; L. Constantin Wurthmann, Stefan Marschall, Vasiliki Triga, and Vasilis Manavopoulos, "Many Losers—One Winner? An Examination of Vote Switching to the AfD in the 2017 German Federal Election Using VAA Data," *Party Politics* 27 (2021): 870–882.
33. Gedmin, "How 'Populist' Is the AFD?"; Damien McGuiness, "Hanau Shooting: Why Germany's Far-Right AfD Is Blamed over Racist Violence," *BBC*, February 22, 2020, https://www.bbc.com/news/world-europe-51588602.
34. In February 2021, the German Office for the Protection of the Constitution declared the AfD a "suspected case" of antidemocratic extremist activity, which is a designation that licenses surveillance. However, this decision was challenged in court and was suspended a few weeks later. See Emily Schultheis, "Germany Is Treating a Major Party as a Threat to Its Democracy," *New York Times*, February 19, 2021, https://www.nytimes.com/2021/02/19/opinion/afd-germany-ban.html; Melissa Eddy, "German Court Suspends Right to Surveil Far-Right AfD Party," *New York Times*, March 5, 2021, https://www.nytimes.com/2021/03/05/world/europe/afd-germany-extremism.html.
35. For example, economic debates about the effects of immigration on wages have centered around data from the influx of refugees from Cuba to South Florida during the Mariel boatlift. For opposing views on these effects, see David Card, "The Impact of the Mariel Boatlift on the Miami Labor Market," *ILR Review* 43 (1990): 245–257; George J. Borjas, "The Wage Impact of the Marielitos: A Reappraisal," *ILR Review* 70 (2017): 1077–1110. Borjas's analysis was prominently cited in 2017 by Stephen Miller, a Trump administration official, to justify the administration's efforts to lower immigration rates. Amita Kelly, "Fact Check: Have Immigrants Lowered Wage for Blue-Collar American Workers?" *NPR*, August 4, 2017, https://www.npr.org/2017/08/04/541321716/fact-check-have-low-skilled-immigrants-taken-american-jobs.

236 NOTES

36. Political preferences about international trade and economic inequality have also been shown to be influenced by zero-sum beliefs. See Diana C. Mutz and Eunji Kim, "The Impact of In-Group Favoritism on Trade Preferences," *International Organization* 71 (2017): 827–850; Shai Davidai and Martino Ongis, "The Politics of Zero-Sum Thinking: The Relationship between Political Ideology and the Belief That Life Is a Zero-Sum Game," *Science* Advances 5 (2019): eaay3761.

37. For an account of democratic institutions at risk under such circumstances, see Steven Levitsky and Daniel Ziblatt, *How Democracies Die* (New York: Crown Publishing Group, 2018).

38. The following description of the design of an experiment is based on Kabir Khanna and Gaurav Sood, "Motivated Responding in Studies of Factual Learning," *Political Behavior* 40 (2018): 79–101.

39. Ibid. Respondents were provided with ten cents per correct answer, and Khanna and Sood found that this incentive had a similar effect to the one dollar per correct answer incentive used in Markus Prior, Gaurav Sood, and Kabir Khanna, "You Cannot Be Serious: The Impact of Accuracy Incentives on Partisan Bias in Reports of Economic Perceptions," *Quarterly Journal of Political Science* 10 (2015): 489–518.

40. It is difficult to determine whether partisan differences in responses to factual questions are indicative of mere partisan cheerleading or reflect sincere differences in belief. Outside of experimental conditions, partisan differences in expressed beliefs are probably driven by both mechanisms. See D. J. Flynn, Brendan Nyhan, and Jason Reifler, "The Nature and Origins of Misperceptions: Understanding False and Unsupported Beliefs about Politics," *Political Psychology* 38 (2017): 127–150, 139. For our purposes here, we do not need to sort out the extent to which partisan differences are driven by partisan cheerleading or reflect sincerely held beliefs. As long as the motivation to signal one's group identity through reports of factual beliefs is operative, that contributes to the challenge posed by boxing in within the political domain. For an especially illustrative example that partisan cheerleading is influential in some cases, see Brian F. Schaffner and Samantha Luks, "Misinformation or Expressive Responding? What an Inauguration Crowd Can Tell Us about the Source of Political Misinformation in Surveys," *Public Opinion Quarterly* 82 (2018): 135–147. They deploy an experimental design to distinguish these two explanations by showing respondents pictures of Trump's and Obama's inauguration sizes (after their relative size became a partisan talking point) where the fact that Obama's crowd was larger is obvious. For an overview of this area of research, see John G. Bullock and Gabriel Lenz, "Partisan Bias in Surveys," *Annual Review of Political Science* 22 (2019): 325–342.

41. Dan M. Kahan, "Climate-Science Communication and the Measurement Problem," *Political Psychology* 36 (2015): 1–43, 2–7. However, Weisberg et al. find evidence to suggest that higher-order knowledge about the nature of science is associated with accepting scientific consensus on controversial topics such as evolution and climate change across religious identity and political orientations. See Deena Skolnick Weisberg, Asheley R. Landrum, Jesse Hamilton, and Michael Weisberg, "Knowledge about the Nature of Science Increases Public Acceptance of Science Regardless of Identity Factors," *Public Understanding of Science* 30 (2021): 120–138.

42. Schaffner and Luks, "Misinformation or Expressive Responding."

43. Dan M. Kahan, Hank Jenkins-Smith, and Donald Braman, "Cultural Cognition of Scientific Consensus," *Journal of Risk Research* 14 (2011): 147–174.

44. Kahan, "Climate-Science Communication and the Measurement Problem," 19.

45. Amy Gutmann and Dennis Thompson, "Deliberative Democracy beyond Process," *Journal of Political Philosophy* 10 (2002): 153–174; Elizabeth Anderson,

NOTES 237

"The Epistemology of Democracy," *Episteme* 3 (2006): 8–22; Hélène Landemore, *Democratic Reason: Politics, Collective Agency, and the Rule of the Many* (Princeton, NJ: Princeton University Press, 2012); Julian F. Müller, "Epistemic Democracy: Beyond Knowledge Exploitation," *Philosophical Studies* 175 (2018): 1267–1288.

46. Democratic theorists have developed various accounts of how citizens can contribute to collective problem-solving and the values that these contributions realize. One especially prominent account is the theory of deliberative democracy, and the most influential theorist in this domain is Jürgen Habermas. Habermas sees deliberation as essential for the legitimacy of democratic legal systems. See his *Between Facts and Norms: Contributions to a Discourse Theory of Law and Democracy*, translated by William Rehg (Cambridge, MA: MIT Press, 1996). For an overview of Habermas's view of democracy and its relationship to his view of citizens' deliberative powers, see Simon Susen, "Jürgen Habermas: Between Democratic Deliberation and Deliberative Democracy," in *The Routledge Handbook of Language and Politics*, ed. Ruth Wodak and Bernahrd Forchtner (Abingdon: Routledge, 2018), 43–66. In addition to legitimacy, democratic theorists have also appealed to the epistemic success of inclusive deliberation and majority-rule voting; see Hélène Landemore, *Democratic Reason: Politics, Collective Intelligence, and the Rule of the Many* (Princeton, NJ: Princeton University Press, 2013). Other theorists focus on civic engagement, often through local communities and organizations, as crucial for solving especially complex challenges, as well as to build civic trust to sustain democracy. See Peter Levine, *We Are the Ones We Have Been Waiting For: The Promise of Civic Renewal in America* (New York: Oxford University Press, 2013); Danielle S. Allen, *Talking to Strangers: Anxieties of Citizenship since Brown v. Board of Education* (Chicago: University of Chicago Press, 2004). A tendency toward signaling can come at the expense of earnest participation in deliberation, voting, and other forms of civic action, so all of these accounts are relevant to the aspect of identity trouble we discuss here.

47. Justin Tosi and Brandon Warmke, *Grandstanding: The Use and Abuse of Moral Talk* (New York: Oxford University Press, 2020), 6.

48. Ibid., 34.

49. Tosi and Warmke offer a largely critical assessment of moral grandstanding, while Neil Levy provides a defense of virtue signaling that responds to some of Tosi and Warmke's arguments. See Justin Tosi and Brandon Warmke, "Moral Grandstanding," *Philosophy & Public Affairs* 44 (2016): 197–217; Tosi and Warmke, *Grandstanding*; Neil Levy, "Virtue Signaling Is Virtuous," *Synthese* 198 (2021): 9545–9562.

50. Tosi and Warmke identify three problems posed by moral grandstanding in politics. They argue that grandstanding can undermine the conditions for compromise, it can lead politicians to support policies for the wrong reasons, and it can create perverse incentives for politicians to avoid solving problems if this means they cannot serve as a continued source of social status. See Tosi and Warmke, *Grandstanding*, 143–160. All of these concerns might also apply to identity-signaling in politics, but our focus here is on the concern that citizens will focus on identity-signaling *at the expense of* contributing to shared problem-solving.

51. Kirk A. Hawkins, "Is Chávez Populist? Measuring Populist Discourse in Comparative Perspective," *Comparative Political Studies* 42 (2009): 1040–1067, 1040–1041.

52. Roger Atwood, "Media Crackdown: Chavez and Censorship," *Georgetown Journal of International Affairs* (2006): 25–32.

53. Jane Mansbridge and Stephen Macedo, "Populism and Democratic Theory," *Annual Review of Law and Social Science* 15 (2019): 59–77, 60.

238 NOTES

54. Michael Kazin, *The Populist Persuasion: An American History* (Ithaca, NY: Cornell University Press, 1995), chapter 2.
55. Ibid., 28.
56. Mansbridge and Macedo argue that homogenous, exclusive conceptions of the people are not core elements of populism, but rather strongly suggested characteristics. See Mansbridge and Macedo, "Populism and Democratic Theory," 62. Other authors, such as Jan-Werner Müller and Albert Weale, treat homogenous conceptions of the people that misrepresent existing diversity and disagreement as more central to their conception of populism. See Jan-Werner Müller, *What Is Populism?* (Philadelphia: University of Pennsylvania Press, 2016), 111; Albert Weale, *The Will of the People: A Modern Myth* (Cambridge: Polity Press, 2018), 9.
57. Emily Schultheis, "Viktor Orbán: Europe Will Restore 'the Will of the People' on Migration in 2018," *Politico*, January 5, 2018, https://www.politico.eu/article/vik tor-orban-refugees-europe-will-restore-the-will-of-the-people-on-migration-in-2018/.
58. Nadia Urbinati describes how populist parties in power can humiliate "the political opposition and [propagate] the conviction that the opposition is morally illegitimate because it is not made of the 'right' people." Nadia Urbinati, "Political Theory of Populism," *Annual Review of Political Science* 22 (2019): 111–127, 119.
59. Hanna Love and Tracy Hadden Loh, "The 'Rural-Urban Divide' Furthers Myths about Race and Poverty—Concealing Effective Policy Solutions," *Brookings Institute*, December 8, 2020, https://www.brookings.edu/blog/the-avenue/2020/ 12/08/the-rural-urban-divide-furthers-myths-about-race-and-poverty-conceal ing-effective-policy-solutions/.
60. Christopher H. Achen and Larry M. Bartels, *Democracy for Realists: Why Elections Do Not Produce Responsive Government* (Princeton, NJ: Princeton University Press, 2016); Jason Brennan, *Against Democracy* (Princeton, NJ: Princeton University Press, 2016).
61. Amy Chua, *Political Tribes: Group Instinct and the Fate of Nations* (New York: Penguin Random House, 2018); Francis Fukuyama, "Against Identity Politics: the New Tribalism and the Crisis of Democracy," *Foreign Affairs* 97 (2018): 90–115; Francis Fukuyama, *Identity: The Demand for Dignity and the Politics of Resentment* (New York: Farrar, Straus, and Giroux, 2018).
62. Levitsky and Ziblatt, *How Democracies Die*, argue that extreme polarization and social sorting can undermine democratic institutions. Collins, Evans, Durant, and Weinel argue that populism can undermine citizens' commitments to conserving democracy. Harry Collins, Robert Evans, Darrin Durant, and Martin Weinel, *Experts and the Will of the People: Society, Populism, and Science* (Cham: Palgrave Macmillan, 2020).
63. Iris Marion Young, *Inclusion and Democracy* (New York: Oxford University, 2000); Maxime Lepoutre, "Democratic Group Cognition," *Philosophy & Public Affairs* 48 (2020): 40–78.
64. Andrea Benjamin, "Coethnic Endorsements, Out-Group Candidate Preferences, and Perceptions in Local Elections," *Urban Affairs Review* 53 (2017): 631–657. However, Benjamin finds that Latino leaders' endorsements did not have the same effect, so the persuasiveness of such endorsements can depend on the particular identity that is being deployed.
65. Kevin Arceneaux and Robin Kolodny, "Educating the Least Informed: Group Endorsements in a Grassroots Campaign," *American Journal of Political Science* 53 (2009): 755–770.
66. Arthur Lupia and Matthew D. McCubbins, *The Democratic Dilemma: Can Citizens Learn What They Need to Know?* (Cambridge: Cambridge University Press, 1998).

NOTES   239

67. Amir Shawn Fairdosi and Jon C. Rogowski, "Candidate Race, Partisanship, and Political Participation: When Do Black Candidates Increase Black Turnout?" *Political Research Quarterly* 68 (2015): 337–349.
68. Jane Mansbridge, "Rethinking Representation," *American Political Science Review* 97 (2003): 515–528, 523.
69. Kenneth Lowande, Melinda Ritchie, and Erinn Lauterbach, "Descriptive and Substantive Representation in Congress: Evidence from 80,000 Congressional Inquiries," *American Journal of Political Science* 63 (2019): 644–659.
70. Stacey Y. Abrams, "E Pluribus Unum: The Fight over Identity Politics," *Foreign Affairs* 98 (2019): 160–163.
71. Ilya Somin, *Democracy and Political Ignorance* (Stanford, CA: Stanford University Press, 2013); Brennan, *Against Democracy*.
72. Hunt Allcott, Levi Boxell, Jacob Conway, Matthew Gentzkow, Michael Thaler, and David Yang, "Polarization and Public Health: Partisan Differences in Social Distancing during the Coronavirus Pandemic," *Journal of Public Economics* 191 (2020): 104254; John Kerr, Costas Panagopoulos, and Sander van der Linden, "Political Polarization on COVID-19 Pandemic Response in the United States," *Personality and Individual Differences* 179 (2021): 110892; Damon C. Roberts and Stephen M. Utych, "Polarized Social Distancing: Residents of Republican-Majority Counties Spend More Time Away from Home during the COVID-19 Crisis," *Social Science Quarterly* 102 (2021): 2516–2527; John F. Camobreco and Zhaochen He, "The Party-Line Pandemic: A Closer Look at the Partisan Response to COVID-19," *PS: Political Science & Politics* 55 (2022): 13–21.
73. Nattavudh Powdthavee, Yohanes E. Riyanto, Erwin C. L. Wong, Jonathan X. W. Yeo, and Qi Yu Chan, "When Face Masks Signal Social Identity: Explaining the Deep Face-Mask Divide during the COVID-19 Pandemic," *PLoS One* 16 (2021): e0253195.
74. Jon Green, Jared Edgerton, Daniel Naftel, Kelsey Shoub, and Skyler J. Cranmer, "Elusive Consensus: Polarization in Elite Communication on the COVID-19 Pandemic," *Science Advances* 6 (2020): eabc2717; Alexandra Flores, Jennifer C. Cole, Stephan Dickert, Kimin Eom, Gabriela M. Jiga-Boy, Tehila Kogut, Riley Loria, et al., "Politicians Polarize and Experts Depolarize Public Support for COVID-19 Management Policies across Countries," *Proceedings of the National Academy of Sciences* 119 (2022): e2117543119.
75. Amy Erica Smith, "COVID vs. Democracy: Brazil's Populist Playbook," *Journal of Democracy* 31 (2020): 76–90, 82–83.
76. Pedro C. Hallal and Cesar G. Victora, "Overcoming Brazil's Monumental COVID-19 Failure: an Urgent Call to Action," *Nature Medicine* 27 (2021): 933–933.
77. Our argument proceeds with a minimal account of democracy's function, which is to advance citizens' shared goals. This is a minimal condition that those who endorse many more comprehensive accounts of democracy's function and/or value can endorse. For example, democratic theorists call attention to democracy's aggregative and deliberative functions. Some have argued that, at least under certain conditions, aggregation makes democratic decisions more accurate and responsive to a wider array of evidence. In addition, some democratic theorists have argued that deliberation can increase the legitimacy and rationality of democratic decision-making. If democracies successfully carry out either of these functions, they should be able to advance citizens' shared goals, especially as the extent to which the relevant goals are shared increases or the importance of those goals to citizens' life plans increases. Democratic theorists have also identified many moral values that democracy might realize, such as equality and freedom. Democracies' advancement of freedom and equality should also involve advancing citizens'

240 NOTES

shared goals. If citizens' goals are routinely frustrated rather than advanced despite their expression of them through political behavior, this would hinder their freedom, and could hinder equality if their goals are neglected in favor of the goals of others. In summary, our argument that identity trouble inhibits democracy's capacity to advance shared goals should be a cause for concern for those who endorse a variety of views in democratic theory. For more on the aggregation and deliberative functions of democracy, see Melissa Schwartzberg, "Epistemic Democracy and Its Challenges," *Annual Review of Political Science* 18 (2015): 187–203, and Anderson, "The Epistemology of Democracy." For particular accounts of the value of democracy that focus on equality and freedom, with an emphasis on each respectively, see Thomas Christiano, The *Constitution of Equality: Democratic Authority and Its Limits* (New York: Oxford University Press, 2008); Carol Gould, *Rethinking Democracy: Freedom and Social Co-operation in Politics, Economy, and Society* (Cambridge: Cambridge University Press, 1988). For a useful overview of democratic theory in general, see Tom Christiano and Sameer Bajaj, "Democracy," in *Stanford Encyclopedia of Philosophy*, March 3, 2022, https://plato.stanford.edu/entries/democracy/.

78. For example, Mark Lilla, *The Once and Future Liberal: After Identity Politics* (New York: HarperCollins, 2017).

79. Jane J. Mansbridge, *Beyond Adversary Democracy* (Chicago: University of Chicago Press, 1980).

80. Ibid., 60–65, 108.

81. Ibid., 97.

82. Ibid., 62–63.

83. Ibid., 118.

84. Jane Mansbridge, "Using Power/Fighting Power: The Polity," in *Democracy and Difference: Contesting the Boundaries of the Political*, ed. Seyla Benhabib (Princeton, NJ: Princeton University Press, 1996): 46–66, 57–58.

Chapter 3

1. Paola Ramos, *Finding Latinx: In Search of the Voices Redefining Latino Identity* (New York: Vintage Books, 2020), 3–4.

2. Ibid., 4.

3. Ashley Jardina, *White Identity Politics* (Cambridge: Cambridge University Press, 2019), 129–130, 149.

4. Jeremy W. Peters, "The Three Types of Republicans Donald Trump Created," *New York Times*, January 21, 2021, https://www.nytimes.com/2021/01/21/us/politics/trump-republican-party.html.

5. An extreme and chilling example of this contempt was evident in a political ad by a pro-Trump Senate candidate from Missouri toting a shotgun and asking voters to join the MAGA crew and to "get a RINO hunting permit." See Alan Feuer, "In Ad, Shotgun-Toting Greitens Asks Voters to Go 'RINO Hunting,'" *New York Times*, June 20, 2022, https://www.nytimes.com/2022/06/20/us/politics/eric-greit ens-rino-ad.html.

6. Kwame Anthony Appiah, *The Ethics of Identity* (Princeton, NJ: Princeton University Press, 2005). We also discuss Appiah's analysis of identity in Derrick Darby and Eduardo J. Martinez, "Making Identities Safe for Democracy," *Journal of Political Philosophy* 30 (2022): 273–297. Some of the illustrations of the analysis in this chapter are drawn from this essay.

7. Life plans, according to Appiah, integrate one's purposes or values over time. This integration takes place via the adoption of various identities to fashion a self. In the process of shaping the structure of our lives, we take on particular

NOTES 241

projects associated with these identities. To reflect this distinction between plans and projects, we use "life plans" to refer to over-arching frameworks of identities adopted by individuals or groups, and we use "life-shaping projects" to refer to particular pursuits that contribute to or realize those life plans. See Appiah, *The Ethics of Identity*, 13, 16–17, 22.

8. Appiah, *The Ethics of Identity*.
9. Ibid., 66–69.
10. Appiah stresses that identity scripts are vital to our agency to fashion an individual life plan. Identity scripts can also facilitate our collective agency by coordinating our pursuit of projects with others. But as we discuss in Chapter 4, the content of identity scripts is also under our collective agency and we can change them over time.
11. One way that we differ from other optimists is by being farther along the continuum in understanding just how dynamic identities are; we factor in considerable variation.
12. Amy Harmon, "BIPOC or POC? Equity or Equality? The Debate over Language on the Left, *New York Times*, November 1, 2021, https://www.nytimes.com/2021/11/01/us/terminology-language-politics.html.
13. Mike Madrid, "While Democrats Debate 'Latinx,' Latinos Head to the G.O.P.," *New York Times*, March 22, 2022, https://www.nytimes.com/2022/03/22/opinion/politics/latinos-democratic-party.html.
14. Ibid.
15. Geraldo L. Cadava, "Latino Voters Are Key to 2024, and They're Not Always Buying What Democrats Are Selling," *New York Times*, January 18, 2022, https://www.nytimes.com/2022/01/18/opinion/democratic-party-latino-voters.html; Jennifer Medina, "How Immigration Politics Drives Some Hispanic Voters to the G.O.P. in Texas," *New York Times*, February 28, 2022, https://www.nytimes.com/2022/02/28/us/politics/border-grievance-politics.html.
16. Jennifer Medina, "The Rise of the Far-Right Latina," *New York Times*, July 6, 2022, https://www.nytimes.com/2022/07/06/us/politics/mayra-flores-latina-republicans.html.
17. Miriam Jordan, "'I Don't Want to Be Called Russian Anymore': Anxious Soviet Diaspora Rethinks Identity," *New York Times*, March 4, 2022, https://www.nytimes.com/2022/03/04/us/immigrant-identity-russia-ukraine.html. This paragraph and the quotes within it draw from this article.
18. Though Ukrainian is a distinct language from Russian, many Ukrainians also speak Russian. Steven Erlanger, "Putin's War on Ukraine Is about Ethnicity and Empire," *New York Times*, March 16, 2022, https://www.nytimes.com/2022/03/16/world/europe/putin-war-ukraine-recolonization.html.
19. Ritchie Torres, "I'm Afro-Latino, but I Can't Join Both the Black and Hispanic Caucuses in Congress. That Must Change," *Washington Post*, July 19, 2020, https://www.washingtonpost.com/opinions/2020/07/19/im-afro-latino-i-cant-join-both-black-hispanic-caucuses-congress-that-must-change/.
20. It is interesting to note that Torres's opponent was a socially conservative Puerto Rican city councilman. The opponent and his supporters will likely have such concerns.
21. Kwame Anthony Appiah, *The Lies That Bind: Rethinking Identity* (New York: Liveright, 2018), 8.
22. For more on the fluidity of black nationalism, which highlights these two dimensions in African American public opinion, and the consequences that variations in the meaning of the label have for mobilizing different black constituencies, see Robert A. Brown and Todd C. Shaw, "Separate Nations: Two Attitudinal Dimensions of Black Nationalism," *The Journal of Politics* 64 (2002): 22–44.

242 NOTES

23. Appiah, *The Lies That Bind*, 9.
24. Lauren D. Davenport, "The Role of Gender, Class, and Religion in Biracial Americans' Racial Labeling Decisions," *American Sociological Review* 81 (2016): 57–84.
25. Ibid., 58.
26. Ibid., 58–59.
27. Paula D. McClain, Jessica D. Johnson Carew, Eugene Walton, Jr., and Candis S. Watts, "Group Membership, Group Identity, and Group Consciousness: Measures of Racial Identity in American Politics?," *Annual Review of Political Science* 12 (2009): 471–485, 473.
28. Ibid., 474.
29. Robert M. Sellers, Mia A. Smith, J. Nicole Shelton, Stephanie A. J. Rowley, and Tabbye M. Chavous, "Multidimensional Model of Racial Identity: A Reconceptualization of African American Racial Identity," *Personality and Social Psychology Review* 2 (1998): 18–39.
30. This example is an adaptation from ibid., 24–25.
31. Amanda Bittner and Elizabeth Goodyear-Grant, "Digging Deeper into the Gender Gap: Gender Salience as a Moderating Factor in Political Attitudes," *Canadian Journal of Political Science* 50 (2017): 559–578, 561.
32. Ibid., 571.
33. Lauren E. Duncan and Abigail J. Stewart, "Personal Political Salience: The Role of Personality in Collective Identity and Action," *Political Psychology* 28 (2007): 143–164.
34. Another factor that can influence identity salience—both in terms of affecting what identities become salient and in terms of the politicization of these identities—is manipulation by political elites, often with the aid of information technologies and institutions of the state such as media outlets. This kind of manipulation can be particularly effective in autocratic regimes that maintain tight control over the flows of information and use them to make national identity salient. See, for example, Gulnaz Sharafutdinova, "Public Opinion Formation and Group Identity: The Politics of National Identity Salience in Post-Crimea Russia," *Problems of Post-Communism* 69 (2022): 219–231.
35. Brown and Shaw, "Separate Nations: Two Attitudinal Dimensions of Black Nationalism."
36. Ibid.
37. Linda Martín Alcoff, "Is Latina/o Identity a Racial Identity?," in *Hispanics/Latinos in the United States: Ethnicity, Race, and Rights*, ed. Jorge J. E. Gracia and Pablo De Grieff (New York: Routledge, 2000), 23–44.
38. In fact, Ritchie Torres is not the only congressional representative to challenge prevailing conceptions of black and Latino identity in Congress. Adriano Espaillat, a representative from New York's 13th Congressional District, who is Dominican-American, has described himself as a "Latino of African descent" and has unsuccessfully pushed for membership in the Congressional Black Caucus. Heather Caygle, "Black Caucus Chafes at Latino Who Wants to Join," *Politico,* February 3, 2017, https://www.politico.com/story/2017/02/congressional-black-caucus-hispanic-adriano-espaillat-234575; Fadel Allassan, "Rep. Espaillat Pushing to Join Congressional Black Caucus," *Axios,* February 15, 2022, https://www.axios.com/2022/02/15/adriano-espaillat-black-caucus.
39. Natalie Masuoka, "Latino Identity and Political Participation," *American Politics Research* 36 (2008): 33–61.
40. Torres, "I'm Afro-Latino, but I Can't Join Both the Black and Hispanic Caucuses in Congress. That Must Change."

NOTES 243

41. Ibid.
42. Alice Walker, *In Search of Our Mothers' Gardens: Womanist Prose* (San Diego, CA: Harvest Books, 1983).
43. For a discussion of how colorism emerges in Latin America, specifically Puerto Rico, Mexico, and Brazil, and how it affects their sizable Afro-Latinx populations, see Jenneil Charles, "Colorism and the Afro-Latinx Experience: A Review of the Literature," *Hispanic Journal of Behavioral Sciences* 43 (2021): 8–31.
44. Ana Gonzalez-Barrera, "Hispanics with Darker Skin Are More Likely to Experience Discrimination than Those with Lighter Skin," *Pew Reports*, July 2, 2019, https://www.pewresearch.org/fact-tank/2019/07/02/hispanics-with-darker-skin-are-more-likely-to-experience-discrimination-than-those-with-lighter-skin/ (last accessed on August 11, 2020). For the full report, see https://www.pewsocialtrends.org/2019/04/09/race-in-america-2019/ (last accessed on August 11, 2020).
45. Maira Garcia, Sandra E. Garcia, Isabelia Herrera, Concepción de León, Maya Phillips, and A. O. Scott, "'In the Heights' and Colorism: What Is Lost When Afro-Latinos Are Erased," *New York Times*, June 21, 2021, https://www.nytimes.com/2021/06/21/movies/in-the-heights-colorism.html.
46. Ibid.
47. For a general discussion of the history of color caste in Latin America that provides support for this observation, see Charles, "Colorism and the Afro-Latinx Experience."
48. Ibid.
49. Ibid.
50. Mara Ostfeld and Nicole Yadon, "¿Mejorando La Raza?': The Political Undertones of Latinos' Skin Color in the U.S.," *Social Forces* 100 (2022): 1806–1832.
51. Ibid., 1821.
52. Garcia et al., "'In the Heights' and Colorism."
53. Nao Hagiwara, Deborah A. Kashy, and Joseph Cesario, "The Independent Effects of Skin Tone and Facial Features on Whites' Affective Reactions to Blacks," *Journal of Experimental Social Psychology* 48 (2012): 892–898.
54. Heather M. Kleider-Offutt, Alesha D. Bond, Sarah E. Williams, and Corey J. Bohil, "When a Face Type Is Perceived as Threatening: Using General Recognition Theory to Understand Biased Categorization of Afrocentric Faces," *Memory & Cognition* 46 (2018): 716–728.
55. Lance Hannon, Robert DeFina, and Sarah Bruch, "The Relationship between Skin Tone and School Suspension for African Americans," *Race and Social Problems* 5 (2013): 281–295.
56. Irene V. Blair, Charles M. Judd, and Kristine M. Chapleau, "The Influence of Afrocentric Facial Features in Criminal Sentencing," *Psychological Science* 15 (2004): 674–679; William T. Pizzi, Irene V. Blair, and Charles M. Judd, "Discrimination in Sentencing on the Basis of Afrocentric Features," *Michigan Journal of Race and Law* 10 (2005): 327–355; and Jill Viglione, Lance Hannon, and Robert DeFina, "The Impact of Light Skin on Prison Time for Black Female Offenders," *The Social Science Journal* 48 (2011): 250–258.
57. Jennifer L. Eberhardt, Paul G. Davies, Valerie J. Purdie-Vaughns, and Sheri Lynn Johnson, "Perceived Stereotypicality of Black Defendants Predicts Capital-Sentencing Outcomes," *Psychological Science* 17 (2006): 383–386.
58. Arthur H. Goldsmith, Darrick Hamilton, and William Darity, Jr., "Shades of Discrimination: Skin Tone and Wages," *The American Economic Review* 96 (2006): 242–245; Arthur H. Goldsmith, Darrick Hamilton, and William Darity, Jr., "From Dark to Light: Skin Color and Wages among African Americans," *The Journal of Human Resources* 42 (2007): 701–738; Joni Hersch, "The Persistence of Skin Color

244 NOTES

Discrimination for Immigrants," *Social Science Research* 40 (2011): 1337–1349; and Alexis Rosenblum, William Darity, Jr., and Tod G. Hamilton, "The Effect of Skin Color on Earnings by Region of Birth and Race for Immigrants to the United States," *Sociology of Race and Ethnicity* 2 (2016): 87–105.

59. Ekeoma E. Uzogara, Hedwig Lee, Cleopatra M. Abdou, and James S. Jackson, "A Comparison of Skin Tone Discrimination among African American Men: 1995 and 2003," *Psychology of Men & Masculinity* 15 (2014): 201–212.

60. Ekeoma E. Uzogara and James S. Jackson, "Perceived Skin Tone Discrimination across Contexts: African American Women's Reports," *Race and Social Problems* 8 (2016): 147–159.

61. Jennifer L. Hochschild and Vesla Weaver, "The Skin Color Paradox and the American Racial Order," *Social Forces* 86 (2007): 643–670.

62. Nikki Khanna, *Whiter: Asian American Women on Skin Color and Colorism* (New York: New York University Press, 2020), 9. For an earlier study, see Joanne L. Rondilla and Paul Spickard, *Is Lighter Better?: Skin-Tone Discrimination among Asian Americans* (Lanham, MD: Rowman & Littlefield, 2007).

63. Appiah, *The Lies That Bind*, 12.

64. Kenneth Lowande, Melinda Ritchie, and Erinn Lauterbach, "Descriptive and Substantive Representation in Congress: Evidence from 80,000 Congressional Inquiries," *American Journal of Political Science* 63(2019): 644–659.

65. Lowande et al., "Descriptive and Substantive Representation in Congress," 645.

66. For recent survey results, see Luis Noe-Bustamante, Lauren Mora, and Mark Hugo Lopez, "About One-in-Four U.S. Hispanics Have Heard of Latinx, but Just 3% Use It," *Pew Research Center*, August 11, 2020. For recent discussions of the Latinx in the public sphere, see John McWhorter, "Why *Latinx* Can't Catch On," *The Atlantic*, December 23, 2019, https://www.theatlantic.com/ideas/archive/2019/12/why-latinx-cant-catch-on/603943; Ross Douthat, "Liberalism's Latinx Problem," *New York Times*, November 5, 2019, https://www.nytimes.com/2019/11/05/opinion/latinx-warren-democrats.html; Daniel Hernandez, "The Case against 'Latinx,'" *Los Angeles Times*, December 17, 2017, https://www.latimes.com/opinion/op-ed/la-oe-hernandez-the-case-against-latinx-20171217-story.html.

67. Preferences between collective identity labels "African-American" and "Black" also seem to correspond to differences in prior experiences. See Lee Sigelman, Steven A. Tuch, and Jack K. Martin, "What's in a Name? Preference for 'Black' versus 'African-American among Americans of African Descent," *Public Opinion Quarterly* 69 (2005): 429–438.

68. Jamelle Bouie, "Black like Kamala," *New York Times*, August 14, 2020, https://www.nytimes.com/2020/08/14/opinion/kamala-harris-black-identity.html.

69. Dina Okamoto and G. Cristina Mora, "Panethnicity," *Annual Review of Sociology* 40 (2014): 221.

70. Natalie Masuoka, "Together They Become One: Examining the Predictors of Panethnic Group Consciousness among Asian Americans and Latinos," *Social Science Quarterly* 87 (2006): 993–1011.

71. Deborah J. Schildkraut, "Latino Attitudes about Surrogate Representation," *Social Science Quarterly* 97 (2016): 721–722.

72. For example, Natalie Masuoka provides evidence that a Latino "racial" group consciousness, whereby Latinos are understood as a non-white minority group facing discrimination, is associated with increased political participation. See Natalie Masuoka, "Defining the Group: Latino Identity and Political Participation," *American Politics Research* 36 (2008): 33–61,

73. Multiracial identity labels also seem to exhibit context-sensitive toggling with some survey respondents reporting multiracial and monoracial identities in response to

NOTES   245

nearly identical questions in different contexts. See David R. Harris and Jeremiah Joseph Sim, "Who Is Multiracial? Assessing the Complexity of Lived Race," *American Sociological Review* 67 (2002): 614–627. For a review of the broader phenomena of racial fluidity, see Lauren Davenport, "The Fluidity of Racial Classifications," *Annual Review of Political Science* 23 (2020): 221–240.

74. Julie A. Dowling, *Mexican Americans and the Question of Race* (Austin: University of Texas Press, 2014), 98.

75. Dowling, *Mexican Americans and the Question of Race*, 106–107.

76. Derrick Darby, "Du Bois's Defense of Democracy," in *Democratic Failure* NOMOS LXIII, ed. Melissa Schwartzberg and Daniel Viehoff (New York: New York University Press, 2020), 207–246.

77. Karen M. Kaufman, "Cracks in the Rainbow: Group Commonality as a Basis for Latino and African-American Political Coalitions," *Political Research Quarterly* 56 (2003): 199–210.

78. Marcus Anthony Hunter, "W. E. B. Du Bois and Black Heterogeneity: How 'The Philadelphia Negro' Shaped American Sociology," *The American Sociologist* 46 (2015): 219–233.

Chapter 4

1. Margaret Roach, "Why Gardening Offers a 'Psychological Lifeline' in Times of Crisis," *New York Times*, March 16, 2022, https://www.nytimes.com/2022/03/16/realestate/gardening-pyschology.html.

2. Winnie Hu, "Food from Around the World, Homegrown in New York," *New York Times*, July 30. 2017, https://www.nytimes.com/2017/07/30/nyregion/food-from-around-the-world-homegrown-in-new-york.html.

3. Asmaa Elkeurti, "Spotted Lanternflies Are Back. You Should Still Kill Them," *New York Times*, June 14, 2023, https://www.nytimes.com/article/spotted-lanternflies-nyc.html.

4. Eitan D. Hersh, *Politics Is for Power: How to Move beyond Political Hobbyism, Take Action, and Make Real Change* (New York: Simon & Schuster, 2020), chapter 8.

5. Ibid., 68–69.

6. Given language differences, residents split into different groups to study for the citizenship test. Naakh and Klara Vysoky participated in a study group for those planning to take it in Russian, while a neighbor, Wendy Wang, helped other residents prepare to take the test in Chinese. Hersh, *Politics Is for Power*, 68.

7. Shobhita Jain, "Women and People's Ecological Movement: A Case Study of Women's Role in the Chipko Movement in Uttar Pradesh," *Economic and Political Weekly* 19 (1984): 1788–1794.

8. Ibid., 1788.

9. Ibid., 1789–1791.

10. Ibid., 1792.

11. United Nations Human Rights Council, "Report of the Commission of Inquiry on Human Rights in Eritrea," June 5, 2015, https://www.ohchr.org/en/hr-bodies/hrc/co-i-eritrea/report-co-i-eritrea-0.

12. Bay Area News Group, "Bay Area Eritreans Try to Keep the Faith amid Religious Political Schisms," *East Bay Times*, August 6, 2011, https://www.eastbaytimes.com/2011/08/06/bay-area-eritreans-try-to-keep-the-faith-amid-religious-political-schisms/.

13. Because of this, there are two Eritrean Orthodox churches in Cincinnati, Ohio. Kevin Eigelbach, "Eritrean Worship: The Anti-Megachurch," *WCPO Cincinnati*, March 1, 2016, https://www.wcpo.com/news/insider/modern-no-meaningful-entirely-eritrean-orthodox-service-filled-with-ritual-tradition-community.

246 NOTES

14. Bay Area News Group, "Bay Area Eritreans Try to Keep the Faith amid Religious Political Schisms."
15. Terry Nguyen, "Support for Trump Is Tearing Apart Vietnamese American Families," *Vox*, October 30, 2020, https://www.vox.com/first-person/2020/10/30/21540263/vietnamese-american-support-trump-2020.
16. Ibid.
17. There are concerns among Republican organizers that they are losing ground with younger Vietnamese Americans, even in Vietnamese enclaves that used to be strongholds of GOP support. Catherine Kim, "GOP Confronts Big Trouble in Little Saigon," *Politico*, August 24, 2021, https://www.politico.com/news/2021/08/24/republicans-asian-american-voters-506778.
18. Nguyen, "Support for Trump Is Tearing Apart Vietnamese American Families."
19. Ibid.
20. Ibid.
21. Recall from Chapter 1 that we can also be boxed in with respect to our thoughts and feelings as well as our associations. Although this example focuses on being boxed in with respect to our actions, the other two ways also apply to this example.
22. For a brief explanation of blood quantum and how it is calculated, see Kat Chow, "So What Exactly Is 'Blood Quantum'?," *NPR*, February 9, 2018, https://www.npr.org/sections/codeswitch/2018/02/09/583987261/so-what-exactly-is-blood-quantum.
23. In the 1887 Dawes Act, the federal government assigned communally held plots of land to individual Native Americans using blood quantum criteria. Circe Dawn Sturm, *Blood Politics: Race, Culture, and Identity in the Cherokee Nation of Oklahoma* (Berkeley: University of California Press, 2002), 78.
24. Ibid., 86–87.
25. Ibid., 89–90.
26. Ibid., 2–3, 88.
27. Ibid., chapters 2–3.
28. Joey A.X., "Afropunk," *The Culture Crush*, February 20, 2020, https://www.theculturecrush.com/feature/afropunk.
29. Ibid.
30. Quoted in Asad Haider, *Mistaken Identity: Race and Class in the Age of Trump* (New York: Verso Books, 2018), 14. In some cases of coalition-building, it can be useful to both expand group membership and to provide different answers to the question "what is required of us?" for different parts of the coalition. For example, the Zapatista movement based in Chiapas, Mexico, started with an armed uprising in 1994, but after signing a ceasefire after twelve days of fighting, worked to build a large international network of organizations working in solidarity with them on projects to support Indigenous communities and combat neoliberalism, with different roles for differently situated organizations. Scholars have noted their innovative use of online media to reach new constituencies, as well as their use of the diverse network they built to share information without relying on traditional media. This network included Indigenous communities in Chiapas, Mexican organizations based outside of Chiapas, and non-Mexican organizations that could share information and produce media for other audiences. International Zapatista activists may not have faced the same expectations of membership in the network as those working in Chiapas, but they all had different and complementary roles to play in the broader movement. See Thomas Olesen, "The Transnational Zapatista Solidarity Network: An Infrastructure Analysis," *Global Networks* 4 (2004): 89–107.
31. In fact, James Spooner believes that Afropunk has drifted away from its roots with an annual festival with substantial corporate involvement and advertising. A.X., "Afropunk."

NOTES 247

32. Alicia Garza, *The Purpose of Power: How We Come Together When We Fall Apart* (New York: One World, 2020). We present one of her success cases in our text. For a failure case, see her discussion of an unsuccessful affordable housing campaign in Bayview, chapter four.
33. Ibid., 88.
34. Ibid., 89.
35. Ibid., 89.
36. Ibid., 94.
37. Ibid., 91.
38. Ibid., 142–143.
39. Mark R. Warren, *Dry Bones Rattling: Community Building to Revitalize American Democracy* (Princeton, NJ: Princeton University Press, 2001), 103.
40. Ibid., 117.
41. Ibid., 107.
42. Ibid., 108–109.
43. Ibid., 107.
44. Ibid., 111–112.
45. Paul Frymer and Jacob M. Grumbach, "Labor Unions and White Racial Politics," *American Journal of Political Science* 65 (2021): 225–240, 228.
46. Guadalupe San Miguel, Jr., *In the Midst of Radicalism: Mexican-American Moderates during the Chicano Movement 1960–1978* (Norman: University of Oklahoma Press, 2022).
47. This phrase originates from an essay from the feminist blog "Tiger Beatdown." See Flavia Dzodan, "My Feminism Will Be Intersectional or It Will Be Bullshit!," *Tiger Beatdown*, October 10, 2011, http://tigerbeatdown.com/2011/10/10/my-feminism-will-be-intersectional-or-it-will-be-bullshit/.
48. Nikayla Jefferson, "It's Our Party Now," *Sunrise Movement*, November 7, 2020, https://www.sunrisemovement.org/movement-updates/its-our-party-now/.
49. Newt Gingrich, "'Woke' American Military Puts US in Danger. Here's How," *Fox News*, February 21, 2021, https://www.foxnews.com/opinion/woke-american-military-danger-us-newt-gingrich.
50. Kimberle Crenshaw, "Demarginalizing the Intersection of Race and Sex: A Black Feminist Critique of Antidiscrimination Doctrine, Feminist Theory, and Antiracist Politics," *University of Chicago Legal Forum* 140 (1989): 139–167, 141–148.
51. Ibid., 152.
52. Ibid., 149–150.
53. Ibid., 166.
54. In fact, in an early piece, Crenshaw signals an openness to expanding the intersectionality framework to other identities such as sexual orientation, age, and color. See Kimberle Crenshaw, "Mapping the Margins: Intersectionality, Identity Politics, and Violence against Women of Color," *Stanford Law Review* 43 (1991): 1241–1299, 1244–1245.
55. Patricia Hill Collins, "The Difference That Power Makes: Intersectionality and Participatory Democracy," *Investigaciones Feministas* 8 (2017): 19–39, 31–32.
56. Ibid., 35–38.
57. Hajer Al-Faham, Angelique M. Davis, and Rose Ernst, "Intersectionality: From Theory to Practice," *Annual Review of Law and Social Science* 15 (2019): 247–265, 248.
58. Jennifer Nash raises a similar concern: "intersectional theory has obscured the question of whether *all* identities are intersectional or whether only multiply marginalized subjects have an intersectional identity" (italics from original text). Jennifer Nash, "Re-thinking Intersectionality," *Feminist Review* 89 (2008): 1–15, 9.
59. For example, Leslie McCall distinguishes three more precise possibilities for the kind of complexity of identity that intersectionality research calls attention to in

248 NOTES

"The Complexity of Intersectionality," *Signs* 30 (2005): 1771–1800. Those three possibilities are: (1) anticategorical complexity, whereby existing categories are taken to be fictions that "produce inequalities in the process of producing differences" (on p. 1773); (2) intracategorical complexity, whereby intersectionality research calls attention to "people whose identity crosses the boundaries of traditionally constructed groups" to reveal the complexity of their experiences (on p. 1774); (3) intercategorical complexity, whereby intersectionality research uses existing categories to "document relationships of inequality" (on p. 1773).

60. Martina Avanza, "Using a Feminist Paradigm (Intersectionality) to Study Conservative Women: The Case of Pro-Life Activists in Italy," *Politics & Gender* 16 (2020): 552–580, 554.

61. Ibid., 575.

62. Oppression and power relations are certainly relevant to Avanza's analysis, even if they do not exhaust all of the forms of heterogeneity she describes. For example, she notes that mostly white, Catholic, middle-class women activists staffed pregnancy crisis centers that she visited, which served many migrant women. She argues that the staff at these centers practiced a kind of racialized and class-based respectability that contrasted with more radical pro-life groups that were willing to use the term "murder" and use images of cut-up fetuses as part of their protests. Avanza also witnessed disagreement about oppression: she notes that some of the activists saw the Muslim women that came to these pregnancy crisis centers as oppressed by their husbands. Ibid., 570.

63. Latoya Peterson, "Intersectionality Is Not a Label," *Washington Post*, September 21, 2015, https://www.washingtonpost.com/news/in-theory/wp/2015/09/21/how-intersectionality-lost-its-punch/.

64. Ibid.

65. Jane Coaston, "The Intersectionality Wars," *Vox*, May 28, 2019, https://www.vox.com/the-highlight/2019/5/20/18542843/intersectionality-conservatism-law-race-gender-discrimination.

66. For examples of these concerns, see David French, "Intersectionality, the Dangerous Faith," *National Review*, March 6, 2018, https://www.nationalreview.com/2018/03/intersectionality-the-dangerous-faith/; Conor Friedersdorf, "Intersectionality Is Not the Problem," *The Atlantic*, March 8, 2018, https://www.theatlantic.com/politics/archive/2018/03/intersectionality-is-not-the-enemy-of-free-speech/555014/.

67. Al Faham, Davis, and Ernst, "Intersectionality: From Theory to Practice," 259.

68. Jennifer Nash raises a related concern about intersectionality theory, which is that "black women's race and gender are treated as trans-historical constants that mark *all* black women in similar ways" (italics from original text). Nash, "Re-thinking Intersectionality," 7.

69. Haider, *Mistaken Identity*, 32–34.

70. Ibid., 34.

71. Louise Birdsell Bauer, "Professors-in-Training or Precarious Workers? Identity, Coalition Building, and Social Movement Unionism in the 2015 University of Toronto Graduate Employee Strike," *Labor Studies Journal* 42 (2017): 273–294, 281–282.

72. Ibid., 284–285.

Chapter 5

1. Melissa Checker, "'Like Nixon Coming to China': Finding Common Ground in a Multi-Ethnic Coalition for Environmental Justice," *Anthropological Quarterly* 74 (2001): 135–146.

2. We will say more about the significance of these background conditions when we discuss the challenge of scaling up in Chapter 6.

NOTES 249

3. This is not meant to be an exhaustive list of the relevant responsibilities.
4. Elizabeth Cherry, "'Not an Environmentalist': Strategic Centrism, Cultural Stereotypes, and Disidentification," *Sociological Perspectives* 62 (2019): 755–772, 765.
5. Anna Klas, Lucy Zinkiewicz, Jin Zhou, and Edward J. R. Clarke, "'Not All Environmentalists Are Like That . . .': Unpacking the Negative and Positive Beliefs and Perceptions of Environmentalists," *Environmental Communication* 13 (2019): 879–893.
6. Ibid., 883.
7. Ibid., 884.
8. Ibid., 885.
9. Ibid.
10. Ibid., 888.
11. The importance of heterogeneity is well established in the social movement literature. When thinking about the relationship between personal or individual identities and group or collective identities, and how it is rendered more complex by heterogeneity, some researches adopt a "constructionist" perspective. See, for example, David A. Snow and Doug McAdam, "Identity Work Processes in the Context of Social Movements: Clarifying the Identity/Movement Nexus," in *Self, Identity, and Social Movements*, ed. Sheldon Stryker, Timothy J. Owens, and Robert W. White (Minneapolis: University of Minnesota Press, 2000), 41–67. Taking this perspective directs attention to the role of agency in managing identities without glossing over differences. Snow and McAdam put the point this way: "From the vantage point of this perspective, there is considerable indeterminacy between identities and their roots in either personality or social structure. As a result, attention is shifted from the dispositional correlates or structural moorings of identities to their construction and maintenance through joint action, negotiation, and interpretive work" (46).
12. Mark Romeo Hoffarth and Gordon Hodson, "Green on the Outside, Red on the Inside: Perceived Environmentalist Threat as a Factor Explaining Political Polarization of Climate Change," *Journal of Environmental Psychology* 45 (2016): 40–49.
13. Ibid., 40–41.
14. Ibid., 46.
15. Ibid., 47.
16. Ibid.
17. For a good example of putting the exit accountability tool to work, see Jeffery C. Mays and Emma G. Fitzsimmons, "What Does It Mean to Be a Progressive in New York City?," *New York Times*, February 17, 2023, https://www.nytimes.com/2023/02/17/nyregion/progressive-nyc.html.
18. Checker, "'Like Nixon Coming to China': Finding Common Ground in a Multi-Ethnic Coalition for Environmental Justice," 138.
19. Ibid.
20. Ibid., 140.
21. Collaboration within coalitions can be a learning opportunity. For example, organizations share protest tactics when collaborating on joint protest actions. See Dan J. Wang and Sarah A. Soule, "Social Movement Organization Collaboration: Networks of Learning and the Diffusion of Protest Tactics, 1960–1995," *American Journal of Sociology* 117 (2012): 1674–1722.
22. Our project does not require settling scholarly debates about how to define coalitions or alliances. For our purposes, the working definition we introduce here will suffice. We will also use the terms "coalition" and "alliance" interchangeably.

250 NOTES

For an old yet influential account of coalition formation, see William A. Gamson, "A Theory of Coalition Formation," *American Sociological Review* 26 (1961): 373–382.

23. For a discussion of these and other coalition types, see Megan E. Brooker and David S. Meyer, "Coalitions and the Organization of Collective Action," in *The Wiley Blackwell Companion to Social Movements*, 2nd edition, ed. David A Snow, Sarah A. Soule, Hanspeter Kriesi, and Holly J. McCammon (New York: John Wiley & Sons, 2019), 252–268.

24. Ibid.

25. Different groups also differ in whether they prioritize consensus and how they go about securing agreement among group members. These different conceptions of how group decision-making should be practiced are another important source of heterogeneity that should be considered in coalition-building, and which can inhibit coalitions if not addressed. For an example, see Paul Lichterman, "Piecing Together Multicultural Community: Cultural Differences in Community Building among Grass-Roots Environmentalists," *Social Problems* 42 (1995): 513–534.

26. Mario Diani and Ivano Bison, "Organizations, Coalitions, and Movements," *Theory and Society* 33 (2004): 281–308, 285.

27. Ibid.

28. Nella Van Dyke and Bryan Amos, "Social Movement Coalitions: Formation, Longevity, and Success," *Sociology Compass* 11 (2017): 1–17.

29. Ibid., 3. Social scientists distinguish between two kinds of social capital: "bonding" and "bridging" capital. Bonding capital is inward looking and links together ingroup members. Bridging capital, by contrast, is outward looking and links people across social cleavages. We can understand Chloe's engagement with Wyoming ranchers as developing a form of bridging capital, which can be used for communication and collective action to advance projects and undermine tight scripts over time. For more on the bonding versus bridging capital distinction, see Robert D. Putnam, *Bowling Alone: The Collapse and Revival of American Community* (Simon & Schuster: New York, 2000), 22–24.

30. Michelle I. Gawerc, "Diverse Social Movement Coalitions: Prospects and Challenges," *Sociology Compass* 14 (2020): 1–15. There is also evidence to suggest that a diverse group of activists advocating for a single goal are especially persuasive to others by catching their attention. See Erica R. Bailey, Dan Wang, Sarah A. Soule, and Hayagreeva Rao, "How Tilly's WUNC Works: Bystander Evaluations of Social Movement Signals Lead to Mobilization," *American Journal of Sociology* 128: 1206–1262, 1235–1239.

31. Gawerc, "Diverse Social Movement Coalitions."

32. Robert Gifford, "Dragons, Mules, and Honeybees: Barriers, Carriers, and Unwitting Enablers of Climate Change Action," *Bulletin of the Atomic Scientists* 69 (2013): 41–48.

33. Ibid., 45–46.

34. Clare Saunders, "Double-Edged Swords? Collective Identity and Solidarity in the Environmental Movement," *The British Journal of Sociology* 59 (2008): 227–253.

35. Ibid., 228.

36. Neil A. Lewis Jr., Dorainne J. Green, Ajua Duker, and Ivuoma N. Onyeader, "Not Seeing Eye to Eye: Challenges to Building Ethnically and Economically Diverse Environmental Coalitions," *Current Opinion in Behavioral Sciences* 42 (2021): 60–64.

37. Ibid.

38. Hwanseok Song et al., "What Counts as an 'Environmental' Issue? Differences in Issue Conceptualization by Race, Ethnicity, and Socioeconomic Status," *Journal of Environmental Psychology* 68 (2020): 1–6.

NOTES 251

39. Tim Kurz, Annayah M. B. Prosser, Anna Rabinovich, and Saffron O'Neill, "Could Vegans and Lycra Cyclists Be Bad for the Planet? Theorizing the Role of Moralized Minority Practice Identities in Processes of Societal-Level Change," *Journal of Social Issues* 76 (2020): 86–100, 87.
40. Ibid., 88.
41. Ibid., 89.
42. Ibid.
43. Ibid., 92.
44. Ibid., 94.
45. Checker, "'Like Nixon Coming to China': Finding Common Ground in a Multi-Ethnic Coalition for Environmental Justice," 141.
46. Ibid.
47. Corinne G. Tsai and Adam R. Pearson, "Building Diverse Climate Coalitions: The Pitfalls and Promise of Equity- and Identity-Based Messaging," *Translational Issues in Psychological Science* 8 (2022): 518–531.
48. Checker, "'Like Nixon Coming to China': Finding Common Ground in a Multi-Ethnic Coalition for Environmental Justice," 138.
49. Tommie Shelby, "Ideology, Racism, and Critical Social Theory," *The Philosophical Forum* 34 (2003): 153–188.
50. Some philosophers have called attention to the importance of intragroup heterogeneity when analyzing and responding to racism and its ideological support structure, including moving beyond the black-white racial binary in the United States and recognizing differential impacts of discrimination based on skin tone. See Linda Martín Alcoff, "Latinos beyond the Binary," *The Southern Journal of Philosophy* 47 (2009): 112–128.
51. Matthew W. Hughey, "'Black People Don't Love Nature': White Environmentalist Imaginations of Cause, Calling, and Capacity," *Theory and Society* (2022): 1–33.
52. Ibid., 12.
53. Ibid., 25.
54. Bindi Shah, "'Is Yellow Black or White?' Inter-Minority Relations and the Prospects for Cross-Racial Coalitions between Laotians and African Americans in the San Francisco Bay Area," *Ethnicities* 8 (2008): 463–491.
55. Eduardo Bonilla-Silva, "From Bi-racial to Tri-racial: Towards a New System of Racial Stratification in the USA," *Ethnic and Racial Studies* 27 (2004): 931–50.
56. Shah, "'Is Yellow Black or White?' Inter-Minority Relations and the Prospects for Cross-Racial Coalitions between Laotians and African Americans in the San Francisco Bay Area," 471.
57. Hoffarth and Hodson, "Green on the Outside, Red on the Inside: Perceived Environmentalist Threat as a Factor Explaining Political Polarization of Climate Change," 47.
58. Ibid.
59. Robert D. Benford and David A. Snow, "Framing Processes and Social Movements: An Overview and Assessment," *Annual Review of Sociology* 26 (2000): 611–639, 614. In this section, our focus is on sociological research on the use of framing in social movements. However, there is also a large literature on framing effects in political communication and public opinion. For an overview, see Dennis Chong and James N. Druckman, "Framing Theory," *Annual Review of Political Science* 10 (2007): 103–126.
60. Benford and Snow, "Framing Processes and Social Movements," 615–618.
61. Ibid., 628.
62. Ibid., 612. Also see, for an alternative analysis, Doug McAdam, Sidney Tarrow, and Charles Tilly, *Dynamics of Contention* (Cambridge: Cambridge University Press, 2001).

252 NOTES

63. Snow and McAdam, "Identity Work Processes in the Context of Social Movements: Clarifying the Identity/Movement Nexus," 54.
64. Ibid.
65. Checker, "'Like Nixon Coming to China': Finding Common Ground in a Multi-Ethnic Coalition for Environmental Justice," 143.
66. Ibid., 142.
67. Ibid., 143.
68. Ibid., 144.
69. Katherine Knutson, "From Identity to Issue: Policy Agenda and Framing Shifts within Long-Term Coalitions," *Politics, Groups, and Identities* 6 (2018): 281–302.
70. Thomas D. Beamish and Amy J. Luebbers, "Alliance Building across Social Movements: Bridging Difference in a Peace and Justice Coalition," *Social Problems* 56 (2009): 647–676.
71. Mattias Wahlström, Magnus Wennerhag, and Christopher Rootes, "Framing 'The Climate Issue': Patterns of Participation and Prognostic Frames among Climate Summit Protesters," *Global Environmental Politics* 13 (2013): 101–122.
72. Lauren Contorno, "Turtles & Teamsters Revival? Analyzing Labor Unions' Environmental Discourse From the 2014 People's Climate March," *Interface: A Journal for and about Social Movements* 10 (2018): 117–148.
73. Ron Hayduk, Kristen Hackett, and Diana Tamashiro Folla, "Immigrant Engagement in Participatory Budgeting in New York City," *New Political Science* 39 (2017): 76–94, 86–90.
74. Ruth Braunstein, Brad R. Fulton, and Richard L. Wood, "The Role of Bridging Cultural Practices in Racially and Socioeconomically Diverse Civic Organizations," *American Sociological Review* 79 (2014): 705–725, 713–714.
75. Eitan Hersh, *Politics Is for Power* (New York: Scribner, 2020), 3.
76. Ibid., 4.
77. Ibid., 200.
78. Ibid., 90–91.
79. Jeannine E. Relly and Rajdeep Pakanati. "Deepening Democracy through a Social Movement: Networks, Information Rights, and Online and Offline Activism," *International Journal of Communication* 14 (2020): 4760–4780, 4760–4761.
80. Ibid., 4770–4771.
81. Ibid., 4774.
82. Ibid., 4770.

Chapter 6

1. Greta Thunberg, "Transcript: Greta Thunberg's Speech at the U.N. Climate Action Summit," *NPR*, September 23, 2019, https://www.npr.org/2019/09/23/763452863/transcript-greta-thunbergs-speech-at-the-u-n-climate-action-summit#:~:text=%22The%20popular%20idea%20of%20cutting,may%20be%20acceptable%20to%20you.
2. Vijaya Ramachandran, "The World Bank and IMF Are Getting It Wrong on Climate Change," *Foreign Policy*, April 11, 2022, https://foreignpolicy.com/2022/04/11/the-world-bank-and-imf-are-getting-it-wrong-on-climate-change/.
3. Ibid.
4. Ibid.
5. Lazarus Chakwera, "The West Caused the Climate Crisis—It Should Now Pay to Clean Up the Mess," *The Guardian*, October 31, 2021, https://www.theguardian.com/commentisfree/2021/oct/31/west-climate-crisis-cop26-africa-develop-global-heating.

NOTES 253

6. Joost De Moor, "The 'Efficacy Dilemma' of Transnational Climate Activism: The Case of COP21," *Environmental Politics* 27 (2018): 1079–1100.
7. Randy Stoecker, "Community, Movement, Organization: The Problem of Identity Convergence in Collective Action," *Sociological Quarterly* 36 (1995): 111–130, 116.
8. Ibid., 116–117.
9. Ibid., 117.
10. Ibid., 118.
11. Ibid., 118–119.
12. Adam S. Pearson, Jonathon P. Schuldt, Rainer Romero-Canyas, Matthew T. Ballew, and Dylan Larson-Konar, "Diverse Segments of the US Public Underestimate the Environmental Concerns of Minority and Low-Income Americans," *PNAS* 115 (2018): 12429–12434.
13. Ibid., 12431–12432.
14. National Sexual Violence Resource Center, "We Can't End Sexual Violence without Ending Racism," *National Sexual Violence Resource Center*, May 25, 2021, https://www.nsvrc.org/blogs/we-cant-end-sexual-violence-without-ending-racism.
15. Brandon E. Patterson, "Why You Can't Be Pro-Black and Homophobic at the Same Time," *Mother Jones*, July 2, 2015, https://www.motherjones.com/politics/2015/07/black-lives-matter-gay-marriage-lgbt-supreme-court/.
16. Ibid.
17. Amelia Abraham, "Is Single-Issue Campaigning the Best Way to Change the World?" *Vice News*, April 6, 2017, https://www.vice.com/en/article/d7qq97/is-single-issue-campaigning-the-best-way-to-make-change-happen.
18. Ibid.
19. Alicia Garza, *The Purpose of Power: How We Come Together When We Fall Apart* (New York: Penguin Random House, 2020), 235.
20. Ibid., 236.
21. Ibid.
22. Ibid., 237.
23. Marissa Armas, "Latinos Visit Mosques, Pray and More to Show Support for Muslims," *NBC News*, February 3, 2017, https://www.nbcnews.com/news/latino/latinos-visit-mosques-pray-more-show-support-muslims-n716521.
24. The exact parameters of what constitutes a sympathy strike (or action) differ across legal jurisdictions. See Carole Cooper, "Sympathy Strikes," *Industrial Law Journal* 16 (1995): 759–784.
25. Frieda Afary, "Iranian Labor Unions Have Led Inspiring Solidarity Strikes amid the Uprising," *Truthout*, January 19, 2023, https://truthout.org/articles/iranian-labor-unions-have-led-unprecedented-solidarity-strikes-amid-the-uprising/.
26. Ella Mahony, "Labor Must Take Up the Fight for Abortion Rights," *Jacobin*, July 13, 2022, https://jacobin.com/2022/07/organized-labor-unions-abortion-rights.
27. Eleanor Mueller, "Some Unions Lead the Charge on Abortion Access While Others Stay Silent," *Politico*, May 16, 2022, https://subscriber.politicopro.com/article/2022/05/pro-union-pro-choice-organized-labor-goes-to-bat-for-abortion-access-00032466.
28. Ibid. This point was also made in a *Wall Street Journal* op-ed: Michael Saltsman, "Give Pro-Life Union Members a Choice," *Wall Street Journal*, May 8, 2022, https://www.wsj.com/articles/give-pro-life-union-member-abortion-leaders-dobbs-pro-choice-jackson-supreme-court-leak-workers-advocacy-11652026018.
29. Bob Hennelly, "Moment of Truth for Labor? AFL-CIO Still Backing an Anti-Choice Republican in N.J.," *Salon*, July 12, 2022, https://www.salon.com/2022/07/12/moment-of-truth-for-labor-afl-cio-still-backing-an-anti-choice-in-nj_partner/.

254 NOTES

30. Audre Lorde, "Learning from the 60s," *BlackPast*, August 12, 2012, https://www.blackpast.org/african-american-history/1982-audre-lorde-learning-60s/.
31. Lorde gives the example of a student president at Howard University, the most prominent historically black university in the United States, who called for black people to "abandon" the "filth" of gay and lesbian students. She notes that these kinds of statements render the presence of lesbians and gay men invisible among black people and leads to further "fragmentation and weakness" in the black community. Ibid.
32. Cora Lewis, "Who Fights for $15?" *Buzzfeed News*, April 13, 2016, https://www.buzzfeednews.com/article/coralewis/who-fights-for-15.
33. Naomi Scheiber, "Eyeing the Trump Voter, 'Fight for $15' Widens Its Focus," *New York Times*, November 29, 2016, https://www.nytimes.com/2016/11/29/business/economy/fight-for-15-wages-protests.html.
34. Steven Greenhouse, "'The Success Is Inspirational': The Fight for $15 Movement 10 Years On," *The Guardian*, November 23, 2022, https://www.theguardian.com/us-news/2022/nov/23/fight-for-15-movement-10-years-old.
35. Dominic Rushe, "'Hopefully It Makes History': Fight for $15 Closes in on Mighty Win for US Workers," *The Guardian*, February 13, 2021, https://www.theguardian.com/us-news/2021/feb/13/fight-for-15-minimum-wage-workers-labor-rights.
36. Ibid.
37. Ibid.
38. Lewis, "Who Fights for $15?"
39. Who counts as an "unsavory" partner is a matter of perspective. For example, in America's bitterly divided political landscape, partisans may view opposing parties as unsavory partners. Republicans may view Democrats as unsavory partners and vice versa. Our examples should be read with this qualification in mind. The analysis in this section does not turn on reaching any agreement on who does or does not count as an unsavory partner.
40. Garza, *The Purpose of Power*, 234.
41. Bayard Rustin, *Strategies for Freedom: The Changing Patterns of Black Protest* (New York: Columbia University Press, 1976), 59.
42. Clayborne Carson, *In the Struggle: SNCC and the Black Awakening of the 1960s* (Cambridge, MA: Harvard University Press, 1981), 126.
43. Catie Edmondson, "Rise of Far Right Leaves Germany's Conservatives at a Crossroads," *New York Times*, July 26, 2023, https://www.nytimes.com/2023/07/26/world/europe/germany-afd-cdu-far-right.html#:~:text=39-,Rise%20of%20Far%20Right%20Leaves%20Germany's%20Conservatives%20at%20a%20Crossroads,prompted%20an%20acute%20identity%20crisis.
44. James K. Rowe and Myles Carroll, "What the Left Can Learn from Occupy Wall Street," *Studies in Political Economy* 96 (2015): 145–165.
45. The General Assembly would work through concerns aspiring to consensus but could finalize a decision despite firm opposition with 90% of attendees voting in favor. Rowe and Carroll, "What the Left Can Learn from Occupy Wall Street," 153–154.
46. John Ehrenberg, "What Can We Learn from Occupy's Failure?" *Palgrave Communications* 3 (2017): 17062–17066.
47. Ibid., 17064.
48. Maurice Mitchell raises similar concerns about some contemporary forms of activism given tendencies toward "anti-leadership attitudes" and "anti-institutional sentiment." See Maurice Mitchell, "Building Resilient Organizations," *The Forge*, November 29, 2022, https://forgeorganizing.org/article/building-resilient-organizations.

NOTES 255

49. In fact, many activists that took part in OWS did go on to help form new organizations that were structured differently and which articulated more specific projects, such as the Fight for $15, discussed earlier in this chapter, and the Sunrise Movement, which organized to support the Green New Deal. Insofar as the OWS movement spurred future successes, then, it seems that they relied on applying these lessons in new organizational contexts. See Michael Levitin, "Occupy Wall Street Did More than You Think," *The Atlantic*, September 14, 2021, https://www.theatlantic.com/ideas/archive/2021/09/how-occupy-wall-street-reshaped-america/620064/.

50. The structure of political opportunities is one of three key factors that scholars of social movements have emphasized in explanations of the form and outcomes of social movements. See Doug McAdam, John D. McCarthy, and Mayer N. Zald, "Introduction," in *Comparative Perspectives on Social Movements*, ed. Doug Macadam, John D. McCarthy, and Mayer N. Zald (New York: Cambridge University Press, 1996), 1–22, and Sidney Tarrow, "States and Opportunities: The Political Structuring of Social Movements," in *Comparative Perspectives on Social Movements*, ed. Doug Macadam, John D. McCarthy, and Mayer N. Zald (New York: Cambridge University Press, 1996), 41–61.

51. Maraam A Dwidar, "Coalitional Lobbying and Intersectional Representation in American Rulemaking," *American Political Science Review* 116 (2022a): 301–321.

52. Maraam A. Dwidar, "Diverse Lobbying Coalitions and Influence in Notice-and-Comment Rulemaking," *Policy Studies Journal* 50 (2022b): 199–240.

53. Dwidar, "Coalitional Lobbying and Intersectional Representation in American Rulemaking," 312–313.

54. Joanna L. Robinson, "Building a Green Economy: Advancing Climate Justice through Environmental-Labor Green Alliances," *Mobilization* 25(2) (2020): 245–264.

55. Ibid., 253–254.

56. Ibid., 257–258.

57. Ibid., 258–259.

58. Ibid., 258.

59. Ronald Holzhacker, "The Power of Opposition Parliamentary Party Groups in European Scrutiny," *Journal of Legislative Studies* 11 (2005): 428–445.

60. Ibid., 434.

61. Ibid., 434.

62. Ibid., 439–440.

63. Lanny W. Martin and Georg Vanberg, "Policing the Bargain: Coalition Government and Parliamentary Scrutiny," *American Journal of Political Science* 48 (2004): 13–27.

64. Ibid., 16–17.

65. Ibid., 23.

66. Andrew Witherspoon and Sam Levine, "These Maps Show How Republicans Are Blatantly Rigging Elections," *The Guardian*, November 21, 2021, https://www.theguardian.com/us-news/ng-interactive/2021/nov/12/gerrymander-redistricting-map-republicans-democrats-visual. Sue Halpern, "America's Redistricting Process Is Breaking Democracy," *The New Yorker*, May 25, 2022, https://www.newyorker.com/news/the-political-scene/americas-redistricting-process-is-breaking-democracy.

67. Silas House, "A Warning from a Democrat in a Red State," *The Atlantic*, January 3, 2021, https://www.theatlantic.com/ideas/archive/2021/01/warning-democrat-red-state/617501/.

68. It may be that the best we can do is work to change the background conditions, even if this task proves daunting, with the hope that our efforts today lay a foundation

256 NOTES

for future generations to undertake a more impactful change in these conditions. Moreover, whatever work we do now, with the hope of reaping benefits later, will undoubtedly require forming and sustaining various kinds of coalitions to initiate institutional change. But to do this we still need to adopt an ethos of CSA in which we take up our civic responsibilities, utilize CSA processes, and pursue strategies for scaling up to negotiate Rustin's dilemma. In sum, to pursue background change with a long-range view in mind, we still need the guidance for being accountable to group heterogeneity offered in this book.

69. In Germany, there is a hybrid system such that members of parliament can be elected either via plurality voting in a particular legislative district or via proportional representation based on party list voting. For a brief overview, see Rebecca Staudenmeier, "Untangling the German Election Process," *DW*, April 19, 2021, https://www.dw.com/en/german-election-process/a-37805756. In The Netherlands, members of parliament are elected via pure proportional representation, as seats are allocated to parties based on the proportion of votes they received nationwide. For a brief overview, see William Maas, "Dutch Elections Show the Promise and Perils of Proportional Representation," *The Conversation*, June 10, 2021, https://theconversation.com/dutch-elections-show-the-promise-and-perils-of-proportional-representation-157290.

70. Maeve Reston, "Independent Redistricting Panels Aim to Draw Fairer Maps but Still Invite Controversy," *CNN*, December 15, 2021, https://www.cnn.com/2021/12/15/politics/independent-redistricting-commissions-2022-elections/index.html.

71. David Imamura, "The Rise and Fall of Redistricting Commissions: Lessons from the 2020 Redistricting Cycle," *American Bar Association*, October 24, 2022, https://www.americanbar.org/groups/crsj/publications/human_rights_magazine_home/economics-of-voting/the-rise-and-fall-of-redistricting-commissions/.

72. Charles Taylor, Patricia Nanz, and Madeleine Beaubien Taylor, *Reconstructing Democracy: How Citizens Are Building from the Ground Up* (Cambridge, MA: Harvard University Press, 2020), 54–83.

73. Oliver Escobar and Stephen Elstub, "Forms of Mini-Publics," *newDemocracy Foundation*, May 8, 2017, https://www.newdemocracy.com.au/2017/05/08/forms-of-mini-publics/.

74. Mark E. Warren and John Gastil, "Can Deliberative Minipublics Address the Cognitive Challenges of Democratic Citizenship?" *The Journal of Politics* 77 (2015): 562–574.

75. Relatedly, though he does not discuss mini-publics, Fabio Wolkenstein proposes local-level political party deliberation as a means of communicative accountability to intra-party heterogeneity. See Fabio Wolkenstein, "A Deliberative Model of Intra-Party Democracy," *Journal of Political Philosophy* 24 (2016): 297–320.

76. Quoted in Heejin Han and Sang Wuk Ahn, "Youth Mobilization to Stop Global Climate Change: Narratives and Impact," *Sustainability* 12 (2020): 4127.

Conclusion

1. David Leonhardt, "Republicans against Inequality," *New York Times*, June 20, 2023, https://www.nytimes.com/2023/06/20/briefing/republicans-inequality-free-market.html.

Index

For the benefit of digital users, indexed terms that span two pages (e.g., 52–53) may, on occasion, appear on only one of those pages.

9/11 terrorist attacks (2001), 28–29, 36
50:50 Parliament organization, 195–96

African Americans
Afro-Latinos and, 84–86, 93–94, 242
American Descendants of Slavery (ADOS) and, 99–100
black nationalism and, 86, 90, 136–37
black political candidates and, 64
colorism and, 94–96
Democratic Party and, 89–90, 207–8
heterogeneity among, 1–2, 3, 97–98, 99–100, 103
as jazz musicians, 11–12, 18–19, 40, 177
Laotian Americans and, 170–71
LGBTQ community and, 194–95
non-black political candidates and, 63
police abuse of, 92
as punk musicians, 17–18, 119–20
racism against, 194, 201
reparations and, 86, 99–100
tightly scripted identities and, 3, 17–18, 25–26, 42–43
treatment-as and, 95, 101–2
"Afropunk" (Spooner), 120
Alcoff, Linda Martín, 91
Aldridge, Rasheen, 204–5
Allied Communities of Tarrant (ACT), 124–27
Alternative for Germany (AfD), 53, 208–9
Alvarez, Adriana, 203
Amanpour, Christiane, 52
American Descendants of Slavery (ADOS), 99–100

American Federation of Labor-Congress of Industrial Organizations (AFL-CIO), 130–31, 139–41
Appiah, Kwame Anthony
on dynamism of social identity, 96–97
on Ewe identity, 85–86
on labeling and action, 87–88
self-authorship and, 80–81
taxonomy of identity-formation practices of, 79–80, 98–99, 100, 102–3
Arab Americans. *See* MENA Americans
Armstrong, Louis, 12–13
Asian American Justice Center, 212–13
Asian Immigrant Women Advocates (AIWA), 138
Asian Pacific Environmental Network (APEN), 170–71
Asians, 96, 99–100
Avanza, Martina, 136

"backpackers," 16–17
Baker, Ella, 182, 183, 224–25
Baldwin, James, 20–21, 25
Baraka, Amiri, 41–42
bebop, 11, 40–42
Biden, Joe, 22–23, 68–69, 186
biracials, 88, 91
Birmingham neighborhood (Toledo), 189–92
Black Lives Matter (BLM), 37, 84, 115–16
black nationalism, 86, 90, 136–37
Black Panthers, 120–21
Blacks. *See* African Americans
blood quantum criteria, 117–18

258 INDEX

Bolsonaro, Jair, 67–68
Bouie, Jamelle, 99–100
Brazil, 67–68
Brewer, Mary, 214
Brighton neighborhood (Boston), 110–11
Brooklyn (New York City), 147–48, 155–57, 168–69, 174–76, 185–86
Brown, H. Rap, 3
Brown, Michael, 204
Browns Crew, 16, 17–18, 231

CAFE Alliance, 147–48, 156–59, 168, 174–75, 185–86
Carmichael, Stokely, 3, 224–25
Chakwera, Lazarus, 187
Chávez, Hugo, 58–59
Cherokees, 117–18
Chevron refinery explosion (Richmond, CA, 1999), 170
Chipko movement, 112–13
Chiswick Wildlife Group (CWG), 163–64
Christian Conservatives, 27, 43
Clarke, Kenny, 41
Cleaver, Kathleen, 120–21
climate change
   adaptive *versus* mitigating responses to, 187, 220–21
   collective self-authorship and, 154, 164–66
   expressive responding and, 56
   framing of responses to, 155, 160–61
   Global Climate Strike (2019) and, 185
   green jobs and, 154–55
   identity heterogeneity as obstacle to addressing, 163–65
   intersectionality and, 132
   least developed countries (LDCs) and, 186–87, 220–21
   "mules" and "honeybees" in the effort to mitigate, 160, 172–73, 179–80
   plant-based diets and, 165
   psychological barriers to addressing, 160–61, 162
   racialized responses to, 169–70
   right-learning skeptics regarding, 153–55

scaling up responses to, 185–90, 220–22, 223
United Nations Climate Change Conference and, 188
Clinton, Bill, 28–29
collective self-authorship (CSA)
   accountability and, 109, 122–28, 139–41, 154–55, 159–60, 161, 212
   civic responsibilities and, 148–49, 151–52, 154–55, 159–60, 161, 173, 176–77, 178, 180–81, 183–84, 191, 212, 219
   coalition-building and, 108–9, 120–22, 123–24, 129, 140–41, 158–59
   communication and, 98–99, 107–8, 110, 123–24, 125–26, 127–29, 130, 159–60, 161, 176–77, 178–79
   definition of, 81–82
   ethos of, 177
   exit and, 107–8, 110, 125, 127–28, 140–41, 154–55, 159–60, 161, 169–70
   flexibility *versus* restrictiveness in, 115
   framing processes and, 172
   group differences in perspective and, 109, 128–29
   heterogeneity and, 7, 77, 102–4, 115–16, 147–49, 161, 162, 178–80, 183–84, 193, 223
   hobbyism as threat to effective forms of, 182–84, 210, 221
   identity labels and, 107
   identity trouble and, 5, 121–22, 132, 135
   individual self-authorship and, 105–6, 108–9
   intersectionality and, 133, 134–35, 137, 139–40
   jazz and, 177–78
   mutual identification and, 81–82
   online tools and, 182–83
   representation and, 107–8, 110, 126–29, 130–31, 159–60, 161, 211–12, 213
   scaling up and, 188–89, 191
   shared labels and, 81–82
   shared treatment-as and, 81–82
   trust and, 126
   unsavory partners and, 206–9

INDEX 259

"what is required of us?" question and, 109, 117–19, 121–22, 127
"who should be among us?" question and, 109, 117–19, 121–22, 127
colorism, 92–96, 97–98, 101–2
Communications Workers of America, 200–1
Community Alliance for the Environment (CAFE), 147–48, 156–59, 168, 174–75, 185–86
Congressional Black Caucus, 84–85, 91
Congressional Hispanic Caucus, 84
Cotton Club (New York City), 12
COVID-19 pandemic, 36–37, 65–68, 154
Crenshaw, Kimberle, 133–35
criminal justice system, 28–31, 37, 43
Crouch, Stanley, 12, 14, 15

Darby, Derrick, 101–2
Davenport, Lauren D., 88, 91
Davis, Miles, 11, 41
Death (punk band), 17–18, 119
democracy
economic inequality and, 224–25
friends-and-enemies mindset and, 48–49, 50–52, 65–66
identity trouble and, 7–8, 62, 65, 68, 69, 142, 153, 173, 181
intersectionality and, 134
problem-solving and, 237
tightly scripted identities and, 43, 48–49, 56–57, 62–63, 68, 69–70, 71–72
Democrats
African Americans and, 89–90, 207–8
black political candidates and, 64
Clinton Democrats and, 28–29
COVID-19 pandemic and, 66, 67
Democratic National Convention (1964) and, 207–8
Hispanic voters and, 83
misperceptions regarding, 46
Vietnamese Americans and, 116
Denmark, 215–16
descriptive representation, 97, 100
diagnostic framing, 173–75
Dinkins, David, 168
Doane, Pia, 109–10

Dobbs v. Jackson Women's Health Organization, 199–200
Dominicans, 93–94
Dostoevsky, Fyodor, 25
Dowling, Julie, 100–1
Du Bois, W. E. B., 101–2, 103

Ehrenberg, John, 211
Ellison, Ralph, 11–12, 25–26, 78–79
Environmental Direct Action Group (EDAG), 163, 164
environmentalists
framing of responses to climate change and, 172–73
heterogeneity among, 192–93, 220–21
labor unions and, 213–15, 220–21
ranchers and, 149–50, 151–52, 158, 178–79
right-wing views of, 149–51, 154
tightly scripted identity and, 150, 151–52
Eritrean Americans, 113–14, 135
Espaillat, Adriano, 242
Estrada, Efrain, 105–8
European Union (EU), 60–61, 215–16
Ewe dialects, 85–86
expressive responding, 55–56

Faubus, Orval, 42
Ferguson (Missouri) protests (2014), 204
FIDESZ (Hungarian political party), 48, 53
Fight for $15 movement, 202–6
flexible solidarity, 134, 140–41
framing processes, 172
Frank, Barney, 64
friends-and-enemies mindset
collective action and, 49
COVID-19 pandemic and, 66, 67
democracy and, 48–49, 50–52, 65–66
immigration policy and, 52–54
moral grandstanding and, 58
partisan identities and, 44–46, 48–49, 53–54, 71
political polarization and, 44–45
populism and, 61, 63
sports fandom and, 49–50, 52
urban-rural divide and, 61

260 INDEX

Friends of the Earth (FoE), 163–64
fútbol fans, 19, 24

Garvey, Marcus, 86
Garza, Alicia, 123–24, 196–98, 205–6
Germany, 53, 186, 208–9, 215–17, 256
gerrymandering, 217, 218–19
Gillespie, Dizzy, 41
Global Climate Strike (2019), 185
Goldwater, Barry, 28
Gordon, Zoe Hunter, 195–96
group heterogeneity. *See* heterogeneity
gun laws, 28–29, 54–55, 57

Haider, Asad, 138–39
Hamer, Fannie Lou, 208
Harlem (New York City), 12–13, 41, 177
Harris, Kamala, 99–100
Hasidic Jews, 147–48, 155, 156, 168–69, 171
Hawley, Josh, 223–24
Hemingway, Ernest, 25
Hersh, Eitan, 181–82
heterogeneity
  African Americans and, 1–2, 3, 97–98, 99–100, 103
  collective action and, 3, 4–5, 6, 77
  collective self-authorship and, 7, 77, 102–4, 115–16, 147–49, 161, 162, 178–80, 183–84, 193, 223
  descriptive representation and, 97
  environmentalists and, 192–93, 220–21
  epistemic demands and, 98–99
  intersectionality and, 109, 136–37, 142
  Latinos and, 91–92, 97–98
  MENA Americans and, 33–34, 35–36
  populism and, 60
  rural populations and, 61
  scaling up and, 186, 189–90, 199, 209–10
Hill Collins, Patricia, 134, 140–41
hip-hop, 12, 14–17
Hispanics, 83, 92–94, 100–1. *See also* Latinos
Hochschild, Arlie, 50–52
Hodges, Johnny, 40

homophobia, 19–22, 67–68, 116–17, 194–95
House, Silas, 46–47, 49, 79–80, 135–36, 217
Howe, Irving, 25–26
Hughes, Langston, 25
Hungary, 48–49, 53–54, 60–61

identification
  context and, 91, 100–2
  discrimination and, 101
  dynamic nature of, 90
  epistemic demands and, 100
  flexibility in, 88
  motivation from, 90–91
  salience and, 89–90, 242
  self-authorship and, 91
  self-description and, 88–89
  strength of, 90–91
identity optimists. *See* optimists
identity skeptics. *See* skeptics
identity trouble
  accountability chains and, 129–30
  background conditions and, 217–18, 220
  collective self-authorship and, 5, 121–22, 132, 135
  democracy and, 7–8, 62, 65, 68, 69, 142, 153, 173, 181
  friends-and-enemies mindset and, 44–45
  intersectionality and, 133, 135–36
  optimists and, 1–2, 71–72
  political hobbyists and, 181
  skeptics and, 69
  tightly scripted identities and, 71–72, 77, 79–80, 86–87, 103–4, 118–19, 152–53
immigration policy
  friends-and-enemies mindset and, 52–54
  labor unions and, 130–31, 139–40
  Muslim immigration ban and, 198
  populism and, 60–61
Immigration Voice, 212–13
individual self-authorship
  collective identities and, 80–81, 105–6

INDEX   261

collective self-authorship and, 105–6,
  108–9
complexity of, 106
identification and, 91
life plans and, 81, 105, 106–7
Parker and, 78–79
International Monetary Fund (IMF),
  186–87
intersectionality
  anti-discrimination law and, 133–34
  climate change and, 132
  collective self-authorship and, 133,
    134–35, 137, 139–40
  community organizing and, 138
  definition of, 133
  feminism and, 132, 133, 137–38
  flexible solidarity and, 134
  heterogeneity and, 109, 136–37, 142
  identity trouble and, 133, 135–36
  intolerance and, 138
  participatory democracy and, 134
  salience in public discourse of, 133,
    137–38
  scope questions regarding, 135
  tightly scripted identities and, 138–39
In the Heights (film), 93–94
Iraq War (2003–12), 57–58
Italian Pro-Life Movement, 136

Jay-Z, 15–16, 17–18, 78–79
Johnson, Lyndon B., 208
Juice WRLD, 14–15

Kentucky, 46–47, 79–80, 135–36, 217
Kidane, Nunu, 114
King Jr., Martin Luther, 1

labeling
  definition of, 80
  flexibility in, 85–86
  identification and, 87–88
  internalization and, 80
  Latinx identity and, 82–83
  nationality and, 83–84
Laotian Americans, 170–71
Latinos
  Afro-Latinos and, 84–86, 93–94

colorism and, 92–95
Community Alliance for the
  Environment and, 147–48, 155–56,
  168
contextual aspects of identity among,
  100–1
discrimination against, 101, 131–32,
  135
heterogeneity among, 91–92, 97–98
hip-hop music and, 16
Latinx identity and, 75, 82–83, 98–99
partisan politics and, 83
racial identity and, 91–92
subgroup identities and metagroup
  unity among, 100
treatment-as and, 101–2
Trump and, 94
least developed countries (LDCs), 186–
  87, 220–21
LGBTQ community
  African Americans in, 194–95
  elected representatives from, 64
  fútbol and, 19
  hip-hop music and, 14–15
  homophobia and, 19–22, 67–68, 116–
    17, 194–95
  marriage rights and, 194–95
  transgender soldiers and, 22–24,
    42–43
Lil Nas X, 14–15
Lorde, Audre, 201–2

macropolitics. *See* scaling up
Mahony, Emma, 199–200
Mansbridge, Jane, 69–70
March on Washington (1963), 1
McConnell, Mitch, 46–47
MC Rakim, 14
MENA Americans (Americans of Middle
  Eastern or North African descent),
  28–29, 33–39
Merz, Friedrich, 208–9
Mexican American Legal Defense and
  Educational Fund (MALDEF), 131
Middle Eastern and North African
  Americans. *See* MENA Americans
Mingus, Charles, 42

262 INDEX

mini-publics, 219–20
Minton's Playhouse (nightclub in
 Harlem), 13, 41, 177, 180–81
Miranda, Lin-Manuel, 93–94
Mississippi Freedom Democratic Party
 (MFDP), 208
Monk, Thelonious, 41
Morales, Polo, 198
moral grandstanding, 57–58
motivational framing, 173–74
Movimiento Estudiantil de Aztlán
 (MEChA), 131
Muslim identity, 87–88

National Sexual Violence Resource
 Center's (NSVRC), 194
Nation of Islam, 196–98, 206
Native Americans, 117–18
negative partisanship, 45–47
Netherlands, 60–61, 216–17
"Never Trumpers," 76–77
New York City
 Harlem section in, 12–13, 41, 177
 Williamsburg/Greenpoint
  neighborhood in, 147–48, 156,
  168–69, 174–76
Ney, Bob, 57–58
Nguyen, Tram, 115–16
Nixon, Richard, 28
non-compete agreements, 223–24

Obadele, Imari Abubakari, 86
Obama, Barack, 34, 55–56
Obergefell v. Hodges, 194–95
Occupy Wall Street (OWS) movement,
 210–12, 255
optimists
 colorism and, 101–2
 COVID-19 pandemic and, 68
 democracy and, 152
 descriptive representation and, 97
 heterogeneity and, 1–2, 97–98, 102–3
 identity-based political connections
  and, 64
 identity trouble and, 1–2, 71–72
 political reasoning and, 63
 qualified optimism and, 1–2, 97–98, 152

Orbán, Viktor, 60–61
O'Steen, David, 200–1
Ostfeld, Mara, 94

Parker, Charlie ("Bird")
 bebop as means of forging new
  identity for, 40
 identity questions confronted by, 11,
  12–13, 18–19, 177
 Minton's Playhouse nightclub and, 13,
  41, 177
 self-authorship and, 78–79, 180–81
partisan identities
 friends-and-enemies mindset and,
  44–46, 48–49, 53–54, 71
 in Hungary, 48
 moral grandstanding and, 57–58
 negative partisanship and, 45–47
 social sorting and, 45
 as source of political information,
  63–64
 as tightly scripted identities, 46–47,
  48, 217
Patterson, Brandon, 194–95
Peaceful Gardeners, 107–8, 126–27
People's Party, 59–60
Peterson, Latoya, 137–38
The Philadelphia Negro (Du Bois), 103
political hobbyists, 181–84, 210, 221
populism
 definition of, 59–60
 friends-and-enemies mindset and,
  61, 63
 immigration policy and, 60–61
 People's Party and, 59–60
 tightly scripted identity and, 60, 61,
  69–70
prisons, 28–31, 37
prognostic framing, 173–74, 176
Proposition 23 (California), 213–14
punk music, 17–19, 119–20
Putin, Vladimir, 83–84

racial identity
 biracials and, 88, 91
 collective action and, 3
 colorism and, 92–93

INDEX 263

illusory elements of, 169
Latinos and, 91–92
MENA Americans and, 33–34
white identity and, 33–39, 76
Ramachandran, Vijaya, 186–87
Ramos, Paola, 16, 75, 82–83, 231
ranchers, 149, 158, 178–79
Randolph, A. Philip, 2–3
rap music, 12, 14–17
Reagan, Ronald, 28
reparations, 86, 99–100
Republicans
climate change and, 154–55
COVID-19 pandemic and, 66, 67
Hispanic voters and, 83
in Kentucky, 47
misperceptions regarding, 46
"Never Trumpers" and, 76–77
"Republicans in Name Only" (RINOs)
and, 76–77
Tea Party and, 50, 52
tightly scripted identities and, 76–77
"Trump Republicans" and, 76–77, 83
Right to Information movement (India),
182–83
Robinson, Joanna, 213–14
Roe v. Wade, 199–200
Roosevelt, Franklin D., 2–3
Roosevelt Island Garden, 109–10
Russia, 83–84
Rustin, Bayard
biographical background of, 2–3
on black identity, 3
on coalition-building, 4–5
Democratic National Convention
(1964) and, 208
economic justice goals and, 4, 5–6,
224–25
on Jewish identity, 1
"Rustin's dilemma" and, 4, 5, 6–7, 32,
48–49, 103–4, 140, 223
South Africa's apartheid regime and, 5–6

scaling up
abortion rights and, 199–201
autonomous local decision-making
and, 213–14

background conditions and, 215, 221
bonds of solidarity approach and,
198–99, 201–2, 205–6, 221
challenges associated with, 189
climate change responses and, 185–90,
220–22, 223
collective self-authorship and, 188–89,
191
Democratic National Convention
(1964) and, 207–8
Fight for $ 15 movement and, 202–6
formal recognition of representatives
and, 210–13
framing of issues and, 190–91
heterogeneity and, 186, 189–90, 199,
209–10
identity as a resource in, 190–92
linked-struggle approach and, 194–95,
199–201, 204–6, 221
Occupy Wall Street movement and,
210–12
opposition political parties and, 215–16
single-issue approaches and, 195–98,
201–2, 204–6, 221
strategies for, 193–99
unsavory partners as challenge in, 205
self-authorship. See collective self-
authorship (CSA); individual
self-authorship
September 11 terrorist attacks (2001),
28–29, 36
Service Employees International Union
(SEIU), 200, 202–3
Shawnees, 117–18
skeptics
collective action and, 62–63
democracy and, 1–2, 62, 63, 152
identity trouble and, 69
political reasoning and, 62
unity appeals and, 69, 71–72
slacktivism, 181
soccer. See fútbol fans
social sorting, 45
Spain, 60–61
Spooner, James, 119–20
Stuart-Smith, Sue, 105–6
Sweden, 60–61

264 INDEX

Tatum, Art, 40
Teamsters, 200–1
Tea Party, 50, 52
Thunberg, Greta, 185, 187, 221–22
tightly scripted identities
African Americans and, 3, 17–18, 25–26, 42–43
Black jazz musicians and, 11–13, 15, 18–19, 40
Christian conservatives and, 27
collective action and, 3, 32, 42–43, 49, 52, 62–63, 64, 70, 79–80, 119, 148
COVID-19 pandemic and, 66–68
democracy and, 43, 48–49, 56–57, 62–63, 68, 69–70, 71–72
expressive responding and, 55–56
freedom of thought and freedom of association restricted by, 38–39, 52, 71, 79–80
fútbol fans, 19
hip-hop musicians and, 15–19
homophobia and, 19–24
identity-policing and, 26, 151–52
identity trouble and, 71–72, 77, 79–80, 86–87, 103–4, 118–19, 152–53
intersectionality and, 138–39
military service and, 22–24
partisan identities and, 46–47, 48, 217
political elites' mobilization of, 66–67
populism and, 60, 61, 69–70
punk musicians and, 17–19
unity appeals across identities and, 69–71
whiteness in US Census Bureau's classification scheme and, 33–39
Toledo (Ohio), 189–92
Torres, Ritchie, 84–85, 91–93
Torres, Victor, 155–56
transgender people, 22–24, 42–43, 82–83, 195
treatment-as, 95–96, 101–2
Trump, Donald
Hispanic voters and, 83

inauguration (2017) of, 55–56
Latinos and, CROSS
Muslim immigration ban and, 198
"Never Trumpers" and, 76–77
transgender military service ban enacted by, 22–23
"Trump Republicans" and, 76–77, 83

Ukraine War (2022), 83–84
United Autoworkers, 200–1
United Nations Climate Change Conference (UNCCC), 188
United We Stand Community Garden, 107
unity appeals, 68
University of Toronto graduate student strike (2015), 141–42

vegans, 165–67
Venezuela, 58–59
Veterans Health Administration, 23–24
Vietnamese Americans, 115–17
Vyosky, Klara, 110–11
Vyosky, Naakh, 110–11, 136

Wadkins, Katherine, 17–18
Walker, Alice, 92–93
Warren, Elizabeth, 223–24
Warren, Mark R., 124–25
Weisman, Neil, 109–10
white identity, 33–39, 76
Williamsburg/Greenpoint neighborhood (New York City), 147–48, 156, 168–69, 174–76
Winfrey, Oprah, 15
Women's March, 195–96
World Bank, 186–87
Wright, Richard, 25–26

Yadon, Nicole, 94
Young, Lester, 12–13

Zapatista movement, 246